Mustang Ace

FORTUNES OF WAR

Mustang Ace

THE STORY OF DON S. GENTILE

BY MARK M. SPAGNUOLO

CERBERUS

First Published in 1986

PUBLISHED IN THE UNITED KINGDOM BY;

Cerberus Publishing Limited
Penn House
Leigh Woods
Bristol BS8 3PF
Tel: ++44 117 974 7175
Fax: ++44 117 974 0890
e-mail: cerberusbooks@aol.com

British Library Cataloguing in Publication Data.
A catalogue record for this book is available from the British Library.

ISBN 1 84145 021 9

Printed and bound in Great Britain by Biddles Ltd, *www.biddles.co.uk*

To Patsy Gentile,
who loved his son and never wavered
in his love and support,
but who never quite understood
Don's quest to be a combat pilot

Author's Note

In writing this biography of Don Gentile I have tried to tell the truth, and because of my exhaustive research I feel that I know the man like no one else. My thirty-odd years in the health field have trained me to be an excellent clinical observer of people and have helped me in my attempt to put myself 'inside Gentile's head'. Therefore, I feel this work reflects than man as he truly was. He was shy, devoutly religious, loving, caring, sensitive man who performed his military duties with skill and courage, all the while suppressing the nagging fear of death that haunted him when he was alone in the cockpit of his single-seated fighter.

If after reading this book you feel as I do, that Don Gentile was done a disservice when he was passed over for the Medal of Honor, I would seriously appreciate hearing from you. I realise that it is now over fifty years (coming up to sixty) since Don Gentile performed these heroic deeds but a posthumous award of the Medal of Honor would go some way to right this wrong.

M.M.S.

Contents

Preface

I first heard of Captain Don S. Gentile in 1944 when I read 'One Man Air Force,' a magazine article written by Ira Wolfert. Gentile's military exploits made an indelible impression on me. On January 30, 1951, after studying for my finals at Central Michigan University, I had my first opportunity in several weeks to read a newspaper and was saddened to learn of his death.

It was not until 1981 that I read anything further about this great combat pilot. Don Gentile was listed among some forty-seven Italian-Americans who had received the Medal Of Honor from their adopted country. I had not heard that he had received the award, so I decided to do a little research at Michigan State University Library. I discovered Gentile was, in fact, nominated for the Medal Of Honor but his name was removed before it could be reviewed by the authorities. My research also made me aware that there had been little written about him other than the Wolfert article and some newspaper clippings. When I mentioned this to my son, he said, 'Why don't you write his biography, Dad?'

This was a typical response from Tony, who thinks I can do anything, and I didn't take the thought seriously until some time later. One day I mentioned the idea to a patient, Dr Douglas A. Noverr, Professor of English at Michigan State University, C.M.U. graduate, and author of several books. He urged me to write this book. I also discussed it with my wife, Sarah, who gave it her blessing, even though she was about to become a literary widow for the four years, three months, and twenty-one days that I pursued Don Gentile's 'battlefields' over thousand of miles, five miles above Europe. Their encouragement and my ignorance of the job ahead made me believe I could author such a work.

The mystery and challenge increased when I was told by military and governmental authorities the following:

1. The records of the 8th Air Force Fighter Command had been destroyed in a fire in St Louis, Missouri.

2. Prior to the fire, someone had taken the records of the 336th Squadron.

3. In order to obtain records from England's Royal Air Force, it would be necessary to travel to England and spend several months studying their military archives.

These obstacles were compounded by the fact that I was not a pilot, but I had spent six years and obtained two degrees under the stewardship of the good Jesuit Fathers. I think their persistence with me finally bore fruit, for I did overcome.

Although this book contains a great deal of biographical data concerning Don Gentile and his role in the 8th Air Force's assault on the Axis, it is more than that. Its real purpose is threefold: to illustrate the 'big picture' surrounding military command decisions and to attempt to explain the reasoning behind our efforts to gain air supremacy over the enemy; to identify and address the controversies, falsehoods, and misinformation that have persisted about Gentile these forty-odd years, and, lastly, to enable you, the reader, to feel as though you are actually witnessing the events as they unfold and understand what this sensitive, warm, and caring young man went through to achieve the acclaim he received.

As I started my research I heard many unfavourable comments about Gentile: he had been arrested; he was a spoiled rich kid; his combat kills were arranged and falsified by himself and his wingman, John Godfrey. I had such a negative impression of him from these early comments that I almost did not accept the challenge of writing the book. But I made a promise to myself to research and answer all the comments and to tell the story the way it was, regardless of how it made Gentile look. I felt the reader deserved an honest account, and so I spent hundreds of hours poring over military mission reports, encounter and after-action reports, unit records, government documents, interviews with pilots, family, friends, and critics. No one demanded how the story should be written.

I hope the result communicates the real nature of Don Gentile and his deeds.

Sherlock Holmes, when preparing to research a case, would assess the time it would take to solve it by the amount of tobacco he would smoke: 'Watson, I believe this might be a six-pipe problem.'

Being a non-smoker I used a similar criterion and can attest that this is an 8,210-cup-of-coffee book. May you, dear reader, find the biography more palatable than Sarah's coffee.

Finally, I would like to address the question, 'Where do we get such men?' During the centuries since Columbus discovered America, Italy founded no colonies because it was not a unified nation until the 1860s. Before then, Italy was a patchwork of kingdoms dominated by European nations.

Italians wishing to come to the United States frequently served foreign countries. Columbus served Spain. Giovanni Caboto, known as John Cabot, served England in his discovery of the northern stretches of the Western

Hemisphere. Amerigo Vespucci, voyaging for Spain, determined the new land was a separate continent and not Asia. Historians named the new land America in his honor. Giovanni ad Verrazano, in the service of France, was the first European to sail into New York harbour.

Missionaries such as Father Salvaterra and Father Chino explored, colonised, and evangelised the West. Enrico Tonti, an Italian soldier of fortune, served as second-in-command to the French explorer Robert La Salle, helped claim the Mississippi for France, and formed the first European settlement in Arkansas. His brother Alfonso founded the city of Detroit and for twelve years served as its governor.

Mark M. Spagnuolo, D.D.S.

Acknowledgements

I wish to express my gratitude to the many people who have put up with my persistent requests for information. I am particularly indebted to Darrell L. Frolke of Bradford, Ohio, a Chief Mechanic with the 344th Squadron, who gave me seven books about the Eagle Squadron and the 4th Fighter Group which helped me get a feel for the subject. To Vern Haugland, a flyer and author of many books, including two about the Eagle Squadron, who told me how to start the project by getting Gentile's flight log. At the Air Force Museum, to Mrs Vivian White, Kathy Cassidy, and to Research Director Charles Wormman, who went out of his way to be very helpful. To Sergeant Myers, Edward T. Russell, and especially to Harry Fletcher, an expert on Karlsruhe (German records), and the many other military and civilian research personnel at the Albert Simpson Historical Research Centre, Maxwell AFB, Alabama; the Air Force Inspection and Safety Centre, Norton AFB, California. To Frank J. Grenon of the P-51 Fighter Association; Colonel Stone of the Selfridge Military Air Museum, Mt. Clemens, Michigan; the Michigan Air Guard Historical Association. To William N. Hess, author of many books about fighter aircraft and editor of the American Fighter Ace Association; Hans Ring, head of the German Fighter Pilots Association. To the Verband-Ehemaliger, Militarchiv, Federal Republic of Germany, and the Waste Record Centre, Berlin, Federal Republic of Germany. To the officers of the USAF Book and Magazine Section, the Aeronautical Chart and Information Centre, and other USAF agencies who gave valuable assistance. To George Chalou of the National Archives and Record Service of the General Services Administration in Washington, D.C. To Father Ambrose Finnegan and Brother Jeffrey of the Shrine of Our Lady of Consolation at Carey, Ohio; Pat Best and Mr White of the Flesh Public Library, Piqua, Ohio; Marilyn Helman of the Piqua Daily Call; Leroy Nitschke, Historian for the 4th Fighter Group Association; Robert O'Brien of Dayton, Ohio, who prepared my photographs; Suzette Mahr of Words & Deeds who so patiently did a fine editing job on the manuscript.

In England, to the Imperial War Museum for various files and pictures. To the British officers and men of the light armour unit which now occupies Debden, the 4th Fighter Group's English base, who spent time with my wife and I and gave us a guided tour of the facility.

To the Troy Chamber of Commerce and the Piqua Chamber of Commerce.

To the Gentile family: Pat Gentile, Cincinnati, Ohio, who gathered various military and family records; Major Joe Gentile, a fighter pilot like his father and now stationed in Spain, who allowed me to study his father's cinefilms from the gun cameras of various aircraft, and his flight log; Isabella Gentile Beitman, Yuba City, California, who provided extensive material, and her husband Jess, who edited the military portion of the manuscript.

From the very beginning I received dozens of hours of understanding aid in the form of taped interviews from Patsy Gentile and his lovely daughter, Edith Gentile Barbato, now of Dayton, Ohio, and her husband Tony.

Also very helpful were telephone interviews with Colonels Steve Pisanos and Jess Taylor, and Don Baird, reporter for the Columbus Dispatch newspaper. Don gave me his personal notes from interviews with 'Cowboy' Megura, Steve Pisanos, and other airmen, conducted when he wrote an extensive Memorial Day article in Capitol Magazine, the Sunday supplement of the Columbus Dispatch.

I do sincerely appreciate the moral support and understanding from my family, particularly my wife and younger daughter, Natalie, who had to sit patiently and listen, several hundred times over the years, to my excited dissertations each time I unearthed a new discovery from the records.

Lastly, to my mother, Rose Spagnuolo, who missed our nightly conversation but was understanding and never complained.

Prologue

From the time Pasquale Gentile was very young, he pestered his family to allow him to go to the United States. His persistence finally paid off when his father said in desperation, 'Buy the boy a ticket and let him go! We're not getting any work done, always arguing about this!'

His mother purchased a ticket, gave him a few dollars, and tearfully said goodbye. Thus Pasquale left his farming family and their small village in southern Italy.

He arrived in the United States on April 30, 1907: fourteen years old, in a strange new country, without any relatives or friends, unable to speak the language, with but a few cents to his name.

He found work breaking rocks in a stone quarry near Dayton, Ohio, for $1.60 a day. He went from there to Cleveland to work, constructing water lines across the city as part of a trench-digging crew.

One day there was a cave-in, killing one man and burying Pasquale up to his armpits. As they pulled him out of the dirt, he thought he was very lucky this time - but maybe not the next.

He travelled on to Pulaski, West Virginia, to work twelve hours a day, seven days a week, on a dam project for $1.90 a day. When the project was completed, he worked in the coal mines, but left after another cave-in almost took his life.

Gentile disembarked from the train at Columbus, Ohio, and walked along the railroad tracks for several miles. He was hungry and worried about where he would get his next job, when he heard faint voices speaking in Italian.

He followed the voices until he came upon some workmen laying a gas pipeline along the railroad right-of-way. The workmen, mostly Italians, told him they were not hiring any new help.

He sat, dejected, the rest of the day, watching the men work. Late that afternoon, a horse and buggy driven by an elderly, white-haired gentleman pulled up in front of him.

The man, in Italian, said, 'Boy, why are you not working?'

'They told me you didn't need any more help,' replied Pasquale.

'Well, they told you wrong. If you want a job, tell the foreman the superintendent wants him to give you a pick and shovel and to get started digging at the far end of the trench.'

The superintendent brushed his thanks aside, got back into the buggy, and rode away. Pasquale remained with the company for twenty-eight years and rose to foreman. At the end of Prohibition, he fulfilled a lifelong dream. He opened the Genova Bar and Grill in Piqua, Ohio, and operated it while continuing to hold his job as foreman.

On the first of April, 1918, the Royal Air Force came into being as the first separate fighter air service in the world.

Pasquale married an Italian girl, Josephina, and on December 6, 1920, they were blessed with the birth of their only son, Dominic Salvatore Gentile, at 1402 Garnsey Street, Piqua, Ohio.

Dominic was his parents' pride and joy, the focus of all their hope and affection. He was a handsome little boy, with dark brown eyes and black curls. From the beginning, he was a happy, high-spirited infant, and his parents never missed an opportunity to show him off.

One morning Josephina came into Don's bedroom and noticed his skin was pink but his lips were a cherry red color. His respiration was very shallow and erratic. The family doctor discovered the baby was suffering from carbon monoxide poisoning caused by gas escaping from the bedroom's space heater.

After consultation with other physicians and specialists, all agreed their son would never recover. The case was hopeless and little Dominic was destined to die.

The revelation that their son was dying struck the Gentiles with a savage force. From that moment, they lived in the particular sunless world reserved for parents of dying children. For them, there was no greater torture than watching helplessly as their beloved son fought desperately to breathe.

Hour after hour they prayed, hoping to win God's mercy by the fervent passion of their prayers. They refused to believe that God had deserted them. They felt that if God had rejected their prayers, then they must find someone who was closer to God, someone He could not refuse, to intercede on their behalf.

Someone told them about the Shrine of Our Lady of Consolation, 100 miles away in Carey, Ohio. The shrine is dedicated to Mary, Mother of God, the Consoler of the Afflicted.

In desperation they set out in the darkness of an early February morning. They bundled the infant and drove the one hundred miles down snowy, rutted roads to Carey, Ohio. As they drove farther and farther away from Piqua, an icy wind blew snow flurries across the highway and the sky grew lighter.

The white sky began to turn pink and the pinkness spread itself like a vast tent, picking out the small clouds against the sky and leaving a blazing trail of scarlet and crimson in its wake. The sky became saturated with the sun's redness. And so the sun rose, thrusting forth its generous radiance and pouring crimson light over the vast countryside, sparing nothing, flooding every inch of the horizon.

Pasquale and Josephina were simple, God-fearing folk who interpreted this breathtaking celestial spectacle as an omen that God was looking down with approval on their pilgrimage to the shrine.

At last they reached Carey. Although he had never been there before, Patsy Gentile seemed to know where he was going, as if some mysterious force was guiding him to the shrine. Finally they reached the main church of the shrine, with its romanesque brick exterior and massive bell tower.

They entered the church and kneeled before the shrine of Our Lady of Consolation. They felt her presence as they pleaded that their son be spared. They poured out their sorrow and vowed that each year on this day they would return and make a pilgrimage.

After returning to Piqua, Josephina scarcely left her son's side. She hardly slept and had not even the strength to cry. She kept repeating, 'Please, Lord, have mercy upon my son. Let him live.'

Hour after hour, day after day, she sat by the bed where the half-conscious infant lay huddled on his side. His face was bloodless, his body contorted, his eyes rolled back in his head. Josephina never undressed or went to bed. When she had to sleep, she lay back in a stuffed chair next to his bed and dozed. During this terrible ordeal, her beautiful black hair became tinged with grey.

Patsy Gentile was tremendously supportive of his wife with his love and understanding during this torment. No man was ever more gentle or more compassionate than he.

The everyday life of the rest of the world seemed almost superfluous. Patsy kept his grief to himself, although fear and panic gripped his heart. He never let Josephina know how thin his hope was or how hard he was trying to control the waves of anxiety and frustration that kept rolling over him.

One morning Josephina came down to the drawing room, thin and pale, but wearing a slight smile. The doctors had noticed a slight improvement. Day after day, little Don continued to improve, until he again became a normal, healthy boy. The doctors could not account for his recovery, but Josephina knew what had happened. Their pilgrimage to the shrine had brought the intervention of God, and truly, a miracle had taken place.

Thereafter, the Gentiles made an annual pilgrimage to the shrine. Throughout Don's life his mother surrounded him with her tender love and spoke often of the 'miracle.' She felt he was a special person, receiving God's merciful blessing of life.

Josephina had a great moral influence over Don. It was she who instilled in him the strong Christian faith which sustained him throughout his life.

In 1914, Hermann Goering was a promising infantry officer. He developed severe arthritis from extensive front line trench duty. His condition was so severe he could hardly walk, and he had to be hospitalised. It was determined he could never return to the trenches. He transferred into the air service, and by the war's end had become one of Germany's most famous flyers. He succeeded von Richthofen as commander of the legendary 'Flying Circus.'

In 1922, Goering met Hitler, and was so mesmerised he joined the Nazi Party and became a loyal devotee. Goering's possession of the Pour le Merite (the Blue Max), his rank of ex-captain, and the aura which surrounded a distinguished fighter pilot, made him desirable and useful to Hitler and his party. Portly, five feet nine inches tall, Goering was dynamic - a personality - a mixture of benevolence and warmth, super human self-control and willpower, cunning and self-assurance. This blue-eyed, enthusiastically persuasive and arrogant man had a disarming air of superiority and made those he contacted fall prey to his charm.

Hitler appreciated the importance of Goering and never forgot his loyalty, and when the Nazi Party gained control of Germany, he made him second-in-command.

PART ONE

A PILOT IN THE MAKING

1925-1935

There was never a time when aeroplanes were not a part of Don Gentile's life and his desire to be a pilot. When he was five years old, he had his first rendezvous with destiny.

He and his mother were on their way to downtown Piqua when suddenly a form too huge and fast to be a bird skimmed the rooftops of the city. Don was fascinated and stood transfixed. His small eyes followed searchingly into the sky long after the aeroplane had disappeared.

As he continued to cling to his mother's skirts, he asked, 'What was that, Mama?'

'That, darling, was a dangerous new-fangled gadget called an aeroplane.'

'I would like to be up there with it.'

'If God wanted us to fly He would have given us wings.'

That moment was the sunrise of young Don's future. Aeroplanes became his entire life, the very air he breathed.

That same year the Gentiles were blessed with a beautiful daughter, Edith. They all lived in Josephine's mother's house on Garnsey Street.

Grandmother owned a grocery store and Josephina would take Don and Edith with her when she went there to work. Don would play throughout the day with the canned and boxed merchandise; the entire store was his playpen. His favourite activity was taking the caps off the bottles, but when his father would return from work his mother-in-law would present him with a bill for that day's damage.

This continued for several months, until Patsy got fed up and went out and bought a lot on South Street, where he erected a ten-room house. It was here that Don built a wooden platform in the swaying branches of an apple tree. He spent hours in this domain, navigating his imaginary aeroplanes through the heavens, unobserved and undisturbed through the ever changing cloud patterns of the sky.

He and his little sister, Edith, would sit all day looking through all sorts of books on flying with pictures of various aeroplanes. As he got older the books became more sophisticated, showing the planes' instrument panels and how each instrument functioned.

Their parents bought them a little bicycle which they had to share. Don would pedal with Edith sitting on the seat, holding tight to her brother's waist. Since they were only permitted to ride in their own driveway, they would go up and down it all day long. Don would make sounds and pretend he was navigating a Sopwith Camel[1] across the skies of France for the Lafayette Escadrille[2] of World War I fame.

When Don was eight years old, he entered Favourite Hill Elementary School. He attended school there until the fourth grade.

In the second grade an older boy would call him a 'guinea' and beat him up. Every night Don would go home with his face bruised and his clothes torn. When asked, he would say he fell off his bicycle or fell down on his way home. Finally his father realised he had been fighting and proceeded to teach him the art of self defence.

'Don, you got two fists - use them and hit him back. It's going to hurt but you hurt him too.'

The next day Don fought back the way his father had taught him. That evening the other boy's father came to the Gentiles' house and said, 'That little guinea son of yours beat up my son.' He continued to call Patsy all sorts of names and told him he was on his way to the police station to swear out a warrant for Patsy's arrest.

Patsy replied, 'Let me help you get there sooner,' and with that he picked up the man and threw him out the door into a mud puddle. From then on Don never again tolerated being called any derogatory ethnic names.

One day Don came home late from school with a block of wood under his arm. When he came into the kitchen Patsy said, 'What are you going to do with that wood?'

'I am going to make a kite,' replied Don.

'Make a kite out of a block of wood?'

'Yeah, I am going to make a kite out of this block of wood.'

'You can buy a kite already made, you won't have to mess around with that wood.'

'I want to make one myself, I want one different than the other kids got.'

Don went into the basement, set the wood down and came up to dinner. After dinner his father said, 'You're kind of funny, you walk in here with that block of wood - trying to make a kite out of wood. Do you know what you are doing?'

'Yeah, I am going to make a plane out of it.'

'Make a kite first that flies good...'

'No, no, no, I am going to make a plane out of it - a model plane,' interrupted Don.

'You better go to school and study reading and writing in place of wasting your time trying to make a plane out of wood.'

Don began to laugh and they did not discuss the matter any further.

A few days later Patsy had a difficult time getting his single edge razor to cut his whiskers. He took a new blade out of the packet and tried again with a similar result. Every blade in the package was the same.

Gentile looked intently at his mostly unshaven face in the mirror. As he focused on it he became more and more disgusted and frustrated. He strode over to the neighbourhood drug store and confronted the owner.

'What kind of razor blades do you buy when you buy them?' he said, openly irritated. 'This thing don't cut any more than a steak knife would cut.'

'I don't know anything about it,' said the owner. 'I never shave with a single edge.'

'Well this you have here now won't cut my whiskers,' replied Patsy, as he threw the packet of blades on the counter. The druggist graciously exchanged the razor blades for a new package.

Outside, the air was cold and damp against Patsy's face. When he got home he went to the basement to stoke the furnace. There he found Don whittling on a block of wood with his razor blades.

'That's why my razor blades don't cut; you been cutting wood with them!' exclaimed Patsy in surprise.

'I used some of them but I didn't hurt them,' said Don innocently. 'My knife can't cut the wood smooth enough.'

'You had better not do that any more. I have to use them to shave, not to cut wood.'

They went upstairs and sat at the kitchen table. Patsy looked at his son with a quizzical expression. 'What are you trying to do anyway? What are you doing - you go to school to learn to read and write or you go to school to kill time? What kind of stuff you got in your mind you wanta do?' he asked sympathetically.

'Daddy, when I get through with everything I want to fly, that's what I want to do. I want to fly - that's always on my mind. I want to be up in the air.'

'Oh, you are just like the other kids - you want to do everything and you are going to end up doing nothing! You better listen to me. Go to school and learn writing and reading. That's what's necessary, not bothering making kites or model planes out of a block of wood...all that kind of stuff. I don't know what you are talking about or what you are trying to do.'

In 1933, Ernst Udet, a World War I German Ace, was impressed with the performance of the American-made Curtis-Wright BFC-2 Hawk while attending the Cleveland Air Races. He convinced his old comrade Goering to buy two for $11,500 each. This plane became the famous 'Sturzkampfflugzleug,' commonly referred to as the Stuka Dive Bomber.

Several months later Don began to pester his father to take him down to Troy, Ohio, some twenty miles from Piqua, to see the Waco aeroplanes constructed by the Weaver Airplane Company. The Waco emerged, phoenix-like, from the corpse of the World War I Curtis Jenny[3] aeroplane.

It did not pay for anyone to manufacture new aeroplanes as long as you could buy a surplus Jenny for five or six hundred dollars. But by the mid-twenties the Jennies were wearing out and slowly a market began to develop for new and better aeroplanes.

This was the golden age of aviation. Those sleek Waco biplanes with their steel-tube welded fuselage were made in a number of different models. It almost seemed as though no two aeroplanes the company produced were exactly the same type. Their fifteen different models remained in production as long as there was a demand from even one customer. This was not a great feat since most were custom-made, some with the individual pilot's own styling.

Don spent hours studying these stout-hearted, resolute birds with their fabric-covered wings, wooden propellers, and open cockpits. He listened attentively to the strange airtalk of the pilots, peeking into the aeroplanes' cockpits and examining the many magic knobs and buttons.

How he loved to watch them, particularly the Waco Nine with its distinctive OX5 engine4. He looked on eagerly as the oily 390-pound engine with its exposed radiator and valve gear clattered into a roar. The sight thrilled him. On Saturdays and Sundays, throughout his adolescent years, Don and his father would stand for hours, watching the construction of these fine planes.

A few years later Patsy was working out of town and unexpectedly came home a day early. As he drove the company car down the street toward his house, he noticed his son and some other boys climbing a ladder to the roof of the garage.

He watched as Don ran down the crest of the roof with a big umbrella, the kind farmers use for shade on their tractors. As Don gathered momentum the ground looked mighty far away, but the promise of flight was greater than his fear of falling. He left the roof and suddenly and magically the umbrella popped open, blossoming into a great canopy that swung him gently to the ground. His father hurriedly parked the car and went running over to where Don had landed.

'What are you trying to do, break your fool neck?'

'Daddy, when I get through with school and start flying I may have to jump out of an aeroplane sometime. Then I will have to know how to do it.'

'You are going to kill yourself. You had better quit that kind of stuff!'

Patsy went into the house and told his wife what Don was doing. She said, 'I know he has been doing that. I feel terrible about it but he will not listen to me.'

'Well, I can make him quit. I'll take the umbrella away from him and break it up,' replied Patsy.

'I don't know if that would do any good, he might get another one someplace.'

They both watched anxiously out the kitchen window as their son continued his perilous game. But not knowing quite what to do, they did nothing.

In 1932, the Gentiles moved to 539 South Wayne Street and Don transferred to St Boniface Elementary School. It was not until he entered this Catholic school that Don learned what faith really meant. Before St Boniface he was considered one of the roughest kids in town. He was a leader of a gang of youngsters who called themselves the 'Hill Top Kids.' Like most boys of ten or twelve, they liked to show off and wanted the townspeople to think that they were a lot tougher than they really were.

In typical boy-fashion, he was always into some kind of trouble, shooting out street lights with his slingshot, knocking down people as he raced along the sidewalks of Piqua, flying the model planes he built through a neighbour's freshly-washed window, getting into fights when other kids taunted him about his desire to be a flyer.

But his inspiring years at St Boniface made him a completely different person, a more mature and understanding one. It was here that he met and came under the spell of a tiny, sweet, rosy-cheeked nun, Sister Teresa, who reinforced and strengthened his faith. She was kind, patient, and understanding and always saw the good in a person.

Sister Teresa never scolded Don or raised her voice while correcting him when, headstrong, he had done something wrong. At first he resented her intrusion, but gradually her kindness and love caused him to confide his innermost secrets. Oh, how he loved her and her saintly ways. She gave him the faith to believe in himself and the belief that if he prayed and lived the Christian life God would answer his prayers and shape his dreams into reality. She was a tremendous influence in the development of the good that was in him.

Four years later, when Don was ready to graduate and leave St Boniface, Sister Teresa called him to her. She congratulated him, particularly on maintaining a B-plus average, and presented him with a small silver statuette of the Infant Jesus as a graduation gift. 'Keep this with you at all times Don,' she said, 'and God will be kind to you.'

He never forgot her parting words and years later they proved prophetic.

Don loved to spend endless hours reading about such aces as Baron Manfred Von Richthofen, Billie Bishop, and Eddie Rickenbacker. He would fantasize and see himself as the handsome, blue-uniformed young man in the Sopwith Camel.

In his daydream, his hand lightly grips the rubberhanded stick, as his keen eyes expectantly search the vast reaches of the sky. Then, he attacks five enemy planes. It is a suicide move for a lone eagle to take on such a formidable armada. With the swoop of a hawk, he dives, while the Lewis gun blazes a message of death. The dismayed Germans, warned by the bullets etching a line of charred holes in their wings, attempt to run, to slide under the protective cover of a cloud. Too late - our hero Gentile clamps a steady finger on the trigger grip, continuing his deadly tattoo. Each of the five enemy planes spins to a fatal crash. Bleeding profusely, our young hero Gentile flies back to the Escadrille field. He thinks nothing more of it as they dress his wounds. He only smiles, and says it was an interesting adventure.

From the beginning of powered flight, the biplane was considered the ultimate weapon. It had twice the amount of wing, braced together in a rigid, lightweight, box and made from wire, wood, and fabric. These biplanes were more manoeuvrable; they could dive, loop, and turn in a very small circle. It was later found that doubling the wing created an interference drag which decreased the lift of the plane. Many fighter pilots still believed the monoplanes would always be at the at the mercy of the biplanes. The Spanish Civil War proved the higher-speed monoplane could fly circles around the slower biplanes and easily destroy them.

Another limitation to the wood-and-fabric biplane was the positioning of the guns; the engine was the only part of the plane with enough bracing to support them. The all-metal monoplane had wings strong enough to hold up to eight guns, rather than the two of the biplane.

The monoplane's better aerodynamics and ability to carry more and heavier armaments still did not gain total acceptance, because it was thought, erroneously, that lightness was the secret to successful flight. It was later proved you could build an aeroplane of almost any size and weight if you had an engine of at least one horsepower to every pound of weight.

During Don's youth in the thirties, there was a frantic effort by engineers the world over to increase engine horsepower. Engine efficiency and lift force were increased by improved fuel quality and octane. Finally, special alloy metals were developed which were stronger and lighter. The aeroplane was streamlined with enclosed cockpits and retractable landing gear. All these improvements allowed this stronger, lighter, more powerful monoplane to reach greater altitudes and speed, and to withstand the structural stresses of tight turns and steep dives. British and German engineers worked frantically to construct an aeroplane which would outperform the other's.

1936-1938

During his adolescence Don would talk nightly about flying. How far it was from Piqua to Pittsburgh or New York City. How much fuel would be needed to make the trip. How fast different planes would fly. And on and on.

'Why are you wasting all your time saying stuff like that?' Patsy Gentile would ask in a persecuted tone. 'Why don't you go and have your supper, relax, then study the lesson in the book the teacher gave you so you know the material for her examination. That's what's necessary for you rather than trying to tell me about flying across the country. How do you know anything about flying?'

'Well, someday I will,' said Don. 'That's what I want to do when I grow up, to fly.'

Don's fantasies and hobbies had him begging his parents for flying lessons.

'Don, you know you can't!'

'Please, can I learn to fly?'

'I said no, and that's the end of it!'

The Gentiles were a typically close-knit Italian-American family, and Don's parents were overprotective, particularly so since his childhood brush with death. They could not comprehend why anyone would want to fly, and when it came to their own flesh and blood, they became frightened. They were like the hen that had hatched an egg and watched it metamorphose into a strange bird.

'Dad, I want to learn to fly.'

'How are you going to take flying lessons?'

'I can go to Vandalia Airport. There is a captain who gives lessons for fifteen dollars a half-hour.

'Fifteen dollars for one half an hour? Do you have the fifteen dollars?'

'I don't have the fifteen dollars. I thought...well, maybe you would give it to me...maybe I could work for you...do something in your bar.'

'All right! All right! If you want to work and earn fifteen dollars for your lessons, I will give you the money but you will have to work Friday and Saturday nights. You can pick up all the empty glasses and bottles on the tables, but don't remove any with drinks in them because you are not old enough. If you do that, I will give you the money on Sunday morning.'

Although Don was very bashful and afraid of people when he started work in 1936 at sixteen years of age, he eventually could talk right along with the customers and kid them back as he picked up the empties.

One night two burly strangers walked into the bar. They sat down and ordered Cokes. During the evening they frequently pulled notebooks from their jackets and, with no attempt at concealment, jotted down notes. One, a vigorous man despite his girth and the white hair that showed from under his hat, got up from the table and walked over to the pay telephone and made a call. Several minutes later two city policemen came in and walked over to their table. They motioned to Patsy to join them. The white-haired man asked angrily, 'You know what you are doing wrong here?'

'I try to run a nice place. Why, am I doing something wrong?' replied Patsy humbly.

'Do you know what you are doing wrong?' the white-haired stranger, whose face had now become beefy red with rage, repeated harshly.

'No, I don't, but I would be glad to hear about it. If you tell me what I have done wrong I would be glad to correct it and make it right, because I don't want to do anything wrong.'

'We received a complaint at the state capital that you are employing a minor. You have to hire employees who are over twenty-one years old and you have that boy over there who isn't even eighteen years old.'

'You are right he's not yet eighteen, but here is the way I got it in my mind. That boy, he is my son and he wants to take lessons every Sunday. He wants to go to Vandalia and learn to fly. They want fifteen dollars for every lesson and I told him if I have to give him fifteen dollars to learn to fly I'll put him to work and make him earn it.

'I have him picking up the empty bottles and glasses. He does not deliver full glasses with the drinks in them to the customers. If he does this I give him fifteen dollars on Sunday morning for his lessons. You know, that was not the real reason I wanted to do that - to help him pay for the lessons. I have more help than I really need and I can get along without his help. But this is the way I see it.

'Young boys today are like a bunch of sheep. When they see greener clover on the other side of the fence, they want to stick their head through the wire and take a bite. One day they say, let's go over and take a bite and all those boys go through those holes in the fence and some of them get their necks scratched by the barbed wire. I say he can learn in my place and get away from those rough boys that try to teach the other boys how to hurt the feelings of other people.

'So that is why I try to keep this boy under my supervision: trying to raise this boy to be good to the public; good to the law; good to himself without hurting the feelings of no one; not because I try to use him here instead of hiring someone else, because I have more help than I need. So now you tell me I am wrong - so I tell this boy not to come back. But what happens when he gets together with these rough boys, I don't know. But I do know it has to be all right if he is under my supervision.'

Disconcerted, the white-haired state official groped for a reply. After regaining his composure he said, 'We will have to re-evaluate this situation. You keep your son working for you and we will get back with a decision from the state.'

That was the last word Patsy heard from them and Don continued to pay for his lessons by working for his father in the bar.

Civil War broke out in Spanish Morocco and spread to Spain proper. The Russians sent equipment and men to aid the 'Loyalists.' The leader of the insurgents, General Francisco Franco, called on the Fascist nations of Italy and Germany for assistance against the Communists. They both sent aid, with Germany sending a small experimental air force. One of the services performed by the air force was moving 10,000 fully equipped Moorish troops from Tetuan, Spanish Morocco, to Seville, Spain. The planes were the Junker 52s, civilian Lufthansa Airlines' workhorses, which were easily converted to bomber transport by taking out their seats and changing the lower smoking rooms into bomb bays.

The Luftwaffe learned a great deal from their support of Franco. The Junker 52 proved to be ill-suited for bombing, with marginal accuracy. The Heinkel He 51 biplane fighter was ineffective and was replaced by the Messerschmitt 109 B-2. This ended the era of the biplane as an effective fighter because of its inferiority to the Russian-built monoplane F-16.

The Messerschmitt was a radical new fighter. Its advanced aerodynamics made it the most manoeuvrable combat plane in the air.

The World War I 'V' flying formation was abandoned in favour of a two- plane unit of pilot and wingman, allowing the pilots more time to look for the enemy in the sky instead of concentrating on their position in the 'V.' The limited availability of radio, air-to-air or air-to-ground, was a grave error.

The JU 87 Stuka Dive Bomber, with its hawk-like appearance and the shrieking sirens attached to its landing gear, gained a reputation far beyond reality. It terrorised the populace and destroyed bridges, roads, and entire cities. The success of the Stuka and medium bombers caused the German Air Ministry to shift away from long-distance bombers. This was a fatal decision which proved to be their undoing in the Battle of Britain.

Don felt a fulfilment and a sense of ecstasy as he began his pilot instruction. Captain Brown, his mentor, was a former World War I pilot who wore a leather jacket, whipcord breeches, leather helmet, goggles, and a white silk scarf. He was a hard taskmaster, impatient with mistakes, but with a reputation for expertise in handling planes and students under any conditions. One day Don's father decided to go with him when he took his lesson.

'Why do you want to come along, Dad?'

'I want to see what kind of plane you fly and how you take off and land.'

'Why?'

'I give you fifteen dollars every Sunday, so haven't I got a right to look at you to see how you are doing? The way it is I don't even know if you will ever fly.'

After they landed the plane, Don began talking with another student while the captain walked back to the hanger where Patsy was standing. The captain looked up and saw his eyes on him, questioning.

'Captain Brown.'

'Yes, sir.'

'I am Don's father and I would like to ask you a question if you don't mind?'

'Whatever you want to ask, go ahead, and I'll try to answer if I can.'

'I have only one boy in the family, and it looks like that's all I can have. I don't expect to get any more boys because the other side went out of condition and I don't believe I can get any more. I have heard lots of boys talking about their occupation - bragging about doing this or that, then I find out they don't do anything. They are throwing their time and money away and that's about it. Do you think Don can make something out of himself, or is he just killing time like the boys we were just talking about?'

'Well, Mr Gentile, I want to answer your question this way. I have a lot of students taking lessons and your boy is the best student I have ever had. You tell him once and he never forgets. He rarely makes the same mistake twice. He has had only nine lessons and next Sunday he will solo. He has a natural instinct as a pilot. If he continues the way he is doing he will make an excellent pilot. If I were you I would not be afraid to trust his instincts, because I think he is cut out for the flying business.'

'Thank you very much, Captain. If that's the way you feel about it, I will go ahead with the extra expense and I hope he makes it. Thank you again for what you tell me. I take your word and I think I can let it go that way.'

'Dad,' said Don as they climbed into their car for the ride home, 'what were you and the captain talking about?'

'Do I ever ask you what your mother gave you for breakfast this morning? I am not going to tell you what the captain talked to me about either. That's it! Let's go home.'

Next Sunday Don soloed - a pilot at age seventeen, in 1937. He came home and danced all through the house. 'Oh, what a thrill, what a fantastic thrill!' Don said in his high-pitched voice. In a few minutes he sat down, turned to his father, and said uncertainly, 'I can't go to Vandalia to fly anymore. I have to go to Greenville to fly a different ship.'

'What do you mean, you got to fly a ship in Greenville?'

'They have a bigger, newer plane over there and I am going to take a few lessons,' replied Don. 'It also is going to take a little more money.'

'What am I going to do - raise your wages?'

'No, no, Dad, you don't have to raise my wages. I will work the same as we have been but I have to go to Greenville and find out what I will have to do...I never been there before. I'll let you know what it's all about. Well, I had better get to bed because I am going there early tomorrow morning.'

Patsy frowned, his thoughts instantly turning to a perplexing problem he could never resolve. He mused aloud, 'Who does he take after? Not the Gentile side...there was someone on his mother's side...there was a story about an uncle. Now he wants to sail around in a big shiny ship in Greenville. I don't know what I am going to do with that boy!'

Don walked into the kitchen and sat down at the table and said, 'Dad, I went to Greenville today and seen the plane they want me to fly. It's the biggest thing I've seen and, boy, I can't wait to get to fly it. It's the nicest plane I have ever seen.'

'How much is it going to cost to fly that plane?' asked Patsy, ever conscious of cost in those depression times.

'They told me fifteen dollars but it would not be quite a half an hour.'

'How long a time for fifteen dollars?'

'It would be about fifteen minutes.'

'Can you do as good in fifteen minutes as one-half an hour?'

'I don't see why it would not be just as good.' replied Don.

The first time he flew this new aeroplane its engine began to miss after being airborne for only ten minutes. He was scared and rattled when he noticed the gas gauge instrument was registering empty.

Don was midway between the Greenville airport and Covington, too far to land at either field, so he frantically searched the countryside for a safe place to land. Suddenly his engine quit, so he had to make a quick decision: He would land in a cornfield. He shoved the control stick and dove down towards the field. Don gradually pulled out of the dive and settled into the rows of cornstalks and decelerated violently to a standstill, with the aircraft erect.

He got out of the cockpit and surveyed the damage. Don was lucky; he was all right. But the plane had suffered minor damage, and he had destroyed three rows of corn almost the entire length of the cornfield.

A farmer came running over from his tractor at the far end of the field.

'Hey!' yelled the farmer, his voice quivering with indignation. 'What the hell are you doing in my cornfield? You destroyed my corn; you are not going to get away with that. You pay me for my corn!'

'I can't pay you today, I don't have any money with me. I got the aeroplane in Greenville, it ran out of gas. It's their fault, they should be the ones to pay.'

The farmer's wife called Patsy at his bar, warning him, 'Your son is in trouble over here.' She told him where the farm was and urged him to come as soon as possible. Patsy called the police station and asked to speak to Tony, the night watchman.

'Tony, you mind doing me a favour?' asked Patsy.

'Sure, if I can do any good, I would be glad to.'

'My boy got into trouble in a cornfield just west of Covington - I have the farmer's name and address. My son wants to get out but the farmer is mad and won't let him leave. I think if I take you along, maybe there won't be any trouble. If I get there and he gives me a hard time like he did my boy...Well, I don't know. I don't want to raise hell with the fellow. I don't want to get into a fight with the farmer on his own land. It's one o'clock and you don't come on duty until midnight...would you...would you do that for me?'

'Sure, I'll be right down. Do you have any way to get to the farm?'

'Yes, I have a car. I'll pick you up.'

When they arrived Don was standing next to the plane, while the farmer waved his arms and yelled ethnic obscenities.

'I heard what happened over the telephone and came over as soon as I could from Piqua. I brought the law with me.'

'What's the law got to do with my farm?'

'I don't think he wants to buy a farm or anything like that. I just brought him for company, that's what I brought him for. Now if you would be an understanding kind of guy, you would know my son had to make a force landing and this was the only available field he had to save his life and not get killed. He had no choice but to land in your cornfield. Now how much corn do you think he damaged?'

'Well, I don't know.'

'You raise corn and naturally you figure on selling it when it gets ripe. If you come anywhere close for me to take care of it I will be glad to do that. That would be great. I could make you satisfied...not because I want to give this boy credit, that he had a right to land here, but because I hate to see any young fellow get killed whether he is my boy or even your boy. It was safer to land in the cornfield than a ditch or the woods, just because he ran out of gas. You figure out what I owe you for the damage to the cornfield.'

The farmer's wife walked down to the cornfield and said, 'Felix, the boy had no choice but to land in the cornfield. It saved his life. The corn is only worth ninety cents a bushel. How many bushels did he destroy? Ten bushels? If his father gives you ten dollars for ten bushels of corn you lost, what would you lose?'

'You telling me what I have to do with my corn?'

'I'll tell you what I will do,' replied Mr Gentile. 'If you give this young boy a chance to get out of here I will drive him to the airport in Greenville. They will come and get the plane. It's their fault because they did not give him enough gas. They should pay you for the corn damaged. If they don't pay you the ten dollars, give or take a dollar or more, it doesn't make any difference - you send me the bill and I will mail you a check. This is the law here that is hearing what I am saying and he will see to it that you get your money. Is that agreeable?'

'Felix do that for me...don't be mean with the boy. You saved his life, that means more than any ten dollars worth of corn,' replied the farmer's wife.

'You want to run this damn farm, then you run it,' said the farmer as he stomped back toward the house.

An hour later two men from the airport came and told them about the emergency gas tank and that it was not turned on. Tony, the night watchman, said, 'Did you tell the boy about this tank and how to turn it on?'

'No, we didn't tell him about it. We thought he knew about it.'

'Well, he hasn't been flying in this plane before and did not know about it. He thought the plane's main tank was completely full and it wasn't. On account of that you people will have to pay the farmer for the corn.'

Mr Gentile told the farmer's wife, 'I don't want any trouble. I want to settle everything nice and calmly. The boy got down without getting hurt and the corn will grow again. If you don't receive the money from the airport, you send me the bill. I will give you my name and address. If there is any problem, send the bill and I will get a check out immediately.'

'I'll tell Felix what you said.'

One of the men from Greenville asked, 'How are we going to get it out of here?'

'If you pick it up and turn it around, I think I can fly it out of the cornfield,' replied Don. 'I might destroy a few more cornstalks but I'll try not to.'

'You think you can get out that way? Let's pace it off,' answered the man.

Don paced the distance from the plane to the fence on the far end of the field. He thought he had fifty feet to spare. He would have to fly on a terribly bumpy field, overcoming the friction created by the partially bent cornstalks and the lack of visibility, with an imposing fence at the end of his 'runway.'

To complicate things further, the wind shifted. It was just a slight breath of wind, but it was blowing the wrong way. It added another element of danger to an already perilous situation.

Don fingered the tiny silver statuette of the Infant Jesus, the symbol of God's protection which Sister Teresa had assured him so many years before would keep him safe.

He climbed into the cockpit, adjusted his leather flying helmet and pulled down his goggles.

'Start her up.'

The engine sprang into life with its song of power. He waited until the engine reached the correct pitch, then he trundled awkwardly over the irregular surface of the field, slowly accelerating and gaining speed. The knowledge that within the next few minutes this engine would decide his fate sharpened all his faculties.

At the halfway mark, he tried to lift the plane but it would not leave the ground. He knew now he was committed; he would have to fly her out. He continued to roar down the field, picking up more and more speed as he lurched along. At last the plane bounced into the air and Don nursed it slowly aloft.

He was rapidly reaching the end of the cornfield and approaching the fence. Don continued to climb, gaining speed as he went, and cleared the fence by one foot. He circled the cornfield and became aware of eyes watching on either side of the field, the eyes of men who were concerned he had made the wrong decision and was going to crash. As he waved to them, they looked at each other and, with a great release of emotion, shouted in unison.

While taking his lessons in Greenville, Don met a man who was willing to sell a homemade single-seat, open-cockpit aeroplane for $300. When he got home he began to pester Patsy for the aeroplane. His father was vehemently opposed to the purchase.

'You got three hundred dollars?' questioned Patsy.

'I don't know, Dad. I have a little money in the bank.'

'How did you get the money?'

'Well, you gave me some now and then to go out on dates. When you gave me five dollars to take a girl out, I put three or four dollars in the bank and splurged the rest on the girl. I now have almost three hundred dollars.'

'Now listen you are not going to buy no plane for three hundred dollars!' his father replied angrily. 'That's impossible...you can't even buy a plane without a motor for that amount. You had better keep your money in the bank if you have three hundred dollars and not give it away, because he can't sell you no plane for three hundred.'

Don went down to the bank, drew out his money and bought the plane. Someone called Don's mother and said, 'Your son just bought himself a death trap to fly in.' Josephina went screaming to Patsy and begged him to go down to the Greenville airport to cancel the sale.

When Patsy saw the deplorable shape of the plane, he knew he had to cancel the sale. The plane appeared to be put together with all the wrong parts. It looked like it would fall over if a slight breeze came along, let alone fly. He asked to see the manager of the airport.

'Is that thing the plane purchased by the boy from Piqua?' asked Patsy.

'Yeah, that's the one he bought,' replied the manager. 'It cost a little more than three hundred dollars and he has thirty days to come up with the rest. When he does I will give him the plane.'

'How can you sell that plane to a minor? The boy would be taking a chance trying to fly a thing like that. Why, that thing looks like it is ready to fall down. You can't sell that plane to anybody. The wind is going to take it away from you if you leave it outside. That supposed plane is a wreck.'

'Oh, it is a good plane. It needs a little work, but it will fly.'

'Now listen, before you sell that plane to that boy you had better think it over twice, because you are not going to sell that plane to that boy. I am the father of that boy and that's why I came down here. You can't sell that plane to a minor. I know, because my lawyer told me you couldn't. We want our money back.'

'Oh, I don't know about getting your money back. If you don't want to buy the plane you lose the three hundred dollars.'

Patsy went home and asked the night watchman, Tony, to meet him at his bar that evening. After the policeman heard the whole story he said, 'I don't think he can sell your son an aeroplane because Don is not yet twenty-one years old and therefore doesn't have a license to fly. He may have soloed, but he cannot buy and fly an aeroplane without a license. I'll do a little investigation and get back with you tomorrow night here at the bar.'

The next night Patsy asked the policeman, 'Did you find anything out from what we were talking about last night?'

'Yes, I talked to the city attorney, John Dagonhart, and he says you cannot sell a plane to a minor or someone who does not have a flying license.'

'What about the three hundred dollars?'

'Well, I don't know about the money. I don't know what you are going to do about that.'

'Would you do me a favour and run over to Greenville with me before you go on duty tomorrow? The reason I want you along is I might get in an argument, and with you there you can tell me to behave and I will. But if you don't come along and I get into a row, I don't know if I will do right or wrong. You know three hundred dollars is a lot of money to a working guy.'

'I'll come along with you, Mr Gentile. Sure, I would be glad to do it.'

The next day they went over to Greenville and confronted the field manager. He rose wearily to his feet, perturbed, and began to pace the floor. 'I don't have the money, the man who owns the plane has it,' he said. 'You will have to get it from him and the only way that can be done is by suing him - if he still has it and if you can find him. I am not going to put up three hundred dollars of my money because some kid made a mistake. The plane doesn't belong to me; it's in storage here. This guy owes the field rent and has not paid it. Since he hasn't paid the storage fees, I don't think you will get your money either.'

As they drove back to Piqua, Patsy concluded the money was lost. If he hired a lawyer to sue, it would cost more than $300 to obtain a judgement in court. And if the man did not have the money he would have wasted even more money, time, and energy for nothing.

When he saw Don again he said, 'Okay, you've learned a lesson. You have gotten three hundred dollars worth of experience now. Are you satisfied? Saving dollar by dollar to get three hundred from me and your mother to put into the bank so you can buy a plane, and now you threw it away. No money. No plane. Losing three hundred dollars, that should teach you a good lesson. I am glad you lost it because that way you know how bad it is when you work hard to earn money and then throw it away. That's a good lesson and I am glad.'

Don sheepishly put his head down, then went outside. He felt terrible -numb and a little nauseated. His mind tried to cope with the enormity of what he had done.

He tried to reconcile his desire to own his own plane with his desire not to hurt his parents. He finally concluded he would continue his pursuit of buying a plane but he would not do it without his father's knowledge.

The world looked its bleakest at this time, and he began to despair of ever getting into aviation. Then he recalled the words of Sister Teresa, and he started to pray fervently, every night and every morning. He found a solace in prayer which nothing else but his fierce determination to fly afforded him. It seemed to him that only through prayer could this overwhelming wish to become a flyer be achieved.

Then Don realised that the silver statuette of the Infant Jesus, the symbol of God's protection which Sister Teresa had assured him so many years before would keep him safe, intervened in his behalf.

He would most assuredly have been killed if he had flown that homemade death trap. He was convinced that the Lord, in His mysterious way, had saved his life again. But this ill-fated purchase did not stop him from bringing up the subject again and again, every chance he got. At night he would say, 'Dad, I see in the paper where a guy is advertising a good aeroplane for only a thousand dollars.'

'How do you know it's a good plane,' fired back his father, 'just because they got an advertisement in the paper? You don't see the plane, you see the advertisement and the price. How do you know the plane is worth that much?'

'Well, they say so in the ad.'

'They advertise and can put anything in the paper. You can print anything, as long as you are willing to pay for it. The news is what is the truth, not necessarily the advertisements.

'Listen to me, what I am telling you is for your benefit, listen to what I want to tell you. I never had too much of this school education. When I came over here at fourteen years of age I was without language, without money, without anything.

Just a pair of slacks, a pair of old shoes, one shirt, and one pair of underwear. I had to find myself a place to stay, had to eat, make a living, I couldn't go to school. I had to work hard for what little I made. Now I am going to raise you and your sister like kids are suppose to be raised. Your mother has worked hard to keep you kids going like the other kids on the streets, with a good pair of shoes and a suit of clothes. Do you know what that means? You had better make up your mind before you believe an advertisement in the newspaper for one thousand dollars for an aeroplane in Indiana. You don't know if it's saleable.'

The next night Don came home with another advertisement. Every night he would show his father a new ad in the paper. It got so his father could not enjoy sitting down for supper at the kitchen table. Patsy would get excited and upset every time Don either mentioned flying or a new ad in the newspaper.

One day after some extensive oral gymnastics over the purchase of a plane, Don got up and went out to play. Patsy turned around at the kitchen table and said to his wife, 'Josephina, what's wrong with your son?'

'I don't know what's wrong. That's all he has on his mind - flying...flying. He wants to fly.'

Don kept bringing up the subject again and again, another time and another time, always the same story - he wanted a plane. Day and night - a plane - he wanted a plane. He kept this up for more than a year. His mother would hear him once in a while, but his father heard about it all the time.

One day Don came home from football practice in a state of excitement. 'Dad,' he said, 'now I have found the plane I really like.'

'What plane you like? You got a plane wrapped up in that newspaper?'

'There is an advertisement that in Baltimore, Maryland, they have a plane...a good plane...you can't beat it. It's a cool motor, six cylinders, and they want to sell it for only one thousand four hundred and fifty dollars. If you want to do me a favour and loan me the money, I'll go to Baltimore, buy the plane, and fly it back home.'

'What's wrong with you anyway? You can't fly a plane across the country just because you made a solo down at Vandalia. You need more education than that in order to fly a plane across the country. Don't listen to what the other kids are telling you. I tell you what I will do. If you do what I tell you I will stick to my word. You sit down at the table and get a tablet and write a letter just like I tell you to write.'

Don jumped up, got a tablet and pen and said, 'I am waiting.'

Patsy dictated:

Dear Sir:

I got the Columbus newspaper and saw your advertisement for this plane you have for sale and I was very interested to look at it and read about it. I want to be a pilot and fly as soon as I can get ready to fly because I already have got my solo flying and I think I can fly. My father has got the $1,450 and he will not let me have it to come to Baltimore and get your plane and fly across the country to land here at Piqua airport. He wants me to tell you that if you would be willing to sell this plane and that you are telling the truth about what condition this plane is in and it is good like you say.

You fly over here and land on the east end of Piqua, Ohio. We have a small airport that you can land. Please send a letter, telegram or call letting me know what hour and day you will arrive and I will be there with my dad waiting to look the plane over. If everything is really the way you say in the advertisement, my dad will pay you the $1,450 cash, besides buying you a railroad ticket to take you back to Baltimore. Don't forget to let me know ahead of time just what time you expect to be in Piqua airport and the day and I and my dad will be there.

Truly yours,

Don Gentile

Don read back the letter to his father and said he wanted to change a few words. Patsy said, 'No, you don't change one word. Put it in an envelope just like it is. You no change anything. I am not going to get the dictionary and make up words for the letter. I made it up in my head...that's all it is and that's all it is going to be.'

Several days passed without an answer from Baltimore. Don kept hounding his father to let him go to Baltimore to get the plane. His constant nagging was driving Patsy up the walls, until one day he told his wife, 'One of these days you are not going to have a table in here. I am going to hit this table with my hand and knock all the plates up on the ceiling. I am getting sick and tired. Its all I hear every night...flying...flying...flying. I can't take it any longer.'

The following weekend while Patsy was working in his tavern, Don came running in as fast as he could. He was so excited he could not speak, and his eyes flashed wildly. When he regained his composure he said, 'He is going to be here tomorrow night at 5:30. Oh boy, I am going to have a plane tomorrow night.'

Don't get that in your head, you are going to have a plane tomorrow night. Maybe when we inspect the plane and it's as advertised you may have a plane tomorrow night. But if it is not as represented you no have a plane - understand?'

The next night Don was so excited he did very little work in the bar. He would work a while, go out the back door and disappear for a few hours, then come back and report that had not yet arrived. He kept this up for most of the evening, until finally he walked in with the young man who owned the plane.

'I am glad to meet you, sir,' said Patsy. 'Glad you made it. The boy was afraid you would not come.'

'I should have gotten here earlier but it is the first time I ever flew in this part of the country. I got lost, and I could not find the Piqua airport. I had to do quite a bit of circling until I found it.

'Let's go to the airport and look this plane over,' said Patsy. 'Would you be willing to do that?'

'That's okay with me.'

They looked the plane over and it appeared to be in good condition. 'If you don't mind, it's still light yet, I would like you and the boy to get into the plane and fly around, and show him all the details about the plane. When you think he knows all the details about your aeroplane, let him take it up alone. If it proves everything is fine, I will take you to my tavern and pay you. After that we will go to train station and I will buy you the ticket back to Baltimore. Is that satisfactory?'

'I would be glad to do that,' replied the young man.

Everything turned out to be as described, so eventually they went back to the tavern and Patsy counted out $1,450 in fifty-dollar bills. He took the young man to Pennsylvania Station in Piqua, but he could not make a connection until the next day. They were told there was a later train out of Dayton, some thirty miles away. Patsy drove him to Dayton, bought him his dinner, and waited until the train came. He handed him the ticket, shook his hand, and wished him good luck.

Don loved the single-seated Aero Sports biplane. He accumulated more than 300 hours 'beating up'[1] Piqua with the aeroplane. This buzzing habit earned him the nickname 'Bullet' Gentile.

Don was not one to follow the book to the letter. He respected it, but he did not always fly by it. Performing aerobatics at low altitude was strictly forbidden, and he knew it, yet he could not resist the urge.

He would buzz Betty Levering's house and blow in her curtains, make the geraniums in Marge Dill's front yard lose their petals, and buzz the church steeples.

The local police would chase Don in their cars, trying to identify his aircraft. They tried time and time again to get his plane number, but Don would so manoeuvre his aircraft, it would be impossible to read it. The police would complain to his father about his low, crazy stunt flying, but since they could not positively identify his plane, they could not cite him for breaking the law.

'What is Don's aircraft number?'

'I didn't know the aeroplane had a number,' replied Patsy innocently. 'Where is the number? I don't know anything about it.' Even if Patsy knew the number, he would not have given it to them.

Once, Don butted in and flew with a formation of planes from Wright-Patterson Air Force Base, and was grounded for thirty days by the Civil

Aeronautics Board.

In the town of Piqua, which flanks the Great Miami River, a canal was built in 1837 which linked the Ohio River at Cincinnati, to Lake Erie, at Toledo. Across this majestic river on North Main Street was the Main Street Bridge. The narrow old structure, with its close-set stone arches, became the source of a long-brewing quarrel between Don Gentile and his classmates.

'If you think you are such a hotshot pilot, let's see you fly under that bridge. You can't do it Don, you're chicken if you don't.'

The bridge frightened Don, but it also held a fascination. He had to fly under it. His sister Edith said, 'Don, that's stupid. You will get yourself killed. Please don't do it.' Yet Don knew he would fly under it. He had to, for his own satisfaction. It became an all-consuming desire, fuelled by his classmates doubts that he could. He knew Edith was right...it was foolhardy, but the challenge was there and he knew he could do it.

Don got a rope and a tape measure and determined the height of the bridge, and then he measured the height of his aircraft from its wheels to the top of its upper wing. His calculations showed he had less than three feet total clearance. Three feet! This meant the optimum flying height would be eighteen inches between his wheels and the water, and a similar amount between the upper wing and the lower portion of the bridge. Wow! This was tighter than he had originally thought; a real tight squeeze. He would be flying at about 100 miles per hour, and if he came in too low he would hit the water and flip over. If he was too high he would hit the bridge.

Either way, he would probably get killed, but if he flew with mathematical precision he could...yes, he could and would make it. For a brief, frightened moment, he was tempted to throw in the towel, and yet he had trusted in the Lord before and He had never let him down.

Gentile took off very early in the morning so there would be few witnesses to his bridge attempt. Gossamer threads of cloud veiled the sky in delicate silver. There was a strong wind blowing, and as he came down a few feet above the river he noticed he had quite a bit of drift. He was approaching the span from the west and it looked depressingly narrow. Don considered pulling up, but he forced himself to hold his course.

As he neared the bridge he could see his sister with a small cluster of his 'witnesses.' Edith looked frightened, so to bolster her courage, he smiled and waved. Unbeknownst to Don and the group, on the opposite side of the bridge a local character was engaged in his usual morning ritual of fishing while imbibing the nectar of the gods.

To hold the aeroplane steady, Don had both hands on the stick and his elbows braced tightly against the sides of the cockpit. For a moment he thought he was

Don in his single-seated Aero Sports biplane.

going to hit with his starboard wing, but then he was passing clear under the bridge. To speed his passage out the other side he pushed the throttle. The engine roared, and its exhaust created a giant wave which completely engulfed the unsuspecting fisherman.

In surprise and fear the man fell into the river, losing his fishing pole. The last the onlookers saw of him he was running away from the river, yelling that he had been attacked from the deep by a scaly creature some 300 feet long. His later reports of the sea monster became more descriptive and its length increased to 750 feet.

When he eventually found out what had really happened, he went to Mr Gentile's bar and said, 'Hey, you owe me a fishing pole!'

'Fishing pole? I owe you a fishing pole? What the hell is this about a fishing pole? I don't owe you anything.'

'Your boy went under the Main Street Bridge.'

This was the first Don's father had heard about his adventure.

'Your boy went under the bridge, and when he raised his plane up the exhaust hit the water and covered me with it. It scared the hell out of me, and I fell in the river and lost my fishing gear. Now you owe me the price of my fishing equipment.'

'I didn't tell you to go fishing at that bridge!'

'Well, you pay for it!'

'You should have attached the fishing pole around your neck so when your pole goes away from you, you would go with it.'

Later that night he asked Don about the incident.

'Did you go under the bridge?' Don did not reply. 'I ask you Don...did you go under that bridge?'

'Who told you?' Don asked.

'Dammit, it's all over town.'

'Well... Yeah, I went under the bridge.'

'What the heck is the matter with you! You want to kill yourself?'

'Oh, I knew I would not kill myself. Some of my classmates were ribbing me about being afraid to go under the bridge, so I got mad and showed them I could do it.'

'What would you have done if you would have hit the top of the bridge? Where are your brains?'

'Well, that could have happened, but I thought I could get by without hitting the top or bottom and I did it.'

Patsy tried to stay mad but he started to laugh.

His wife said, 'You bought him that aeroplane, it's your fault.'

'Yes, I bought him the plane, and it cost me. Remember before I bought that plane how many nights we chewed the rag about it, and I didn't want to buy it. You told me, if it will make him happy, buy him the plane. He just wants to fly around town. Yeah, that's the way it started but look what he went and done.'

Don conducted himself in the same manner when driving a car. He would twist, turn, and race his father's car all over the Ohio roads, sometimes at breakneck speeds of more than 100 miles per hour, and frequently pursued unsuccessfully by the local constables.

He had a reputation of being a pretty crazy, reckless kid. He knew he was breaking the law, but he could not help himself - speed and the exultation of a race gave him indescribable euphoria. He liked the competition of pitting himself against death: driving fast, playing daredevil, and beating the greatest competitor.

One day Don took a date to one of the favourite soda bars in the neighbouring city of Troy. While they were sitting laughing and enjoying a milk shake, two local boys entered and walked over to their table.

"Hey baby,' said one of the boys. 'Why don't you go for a ride with us American-types instead of wasting your time with this greasy dago foreigner?'

'No, I came with Don and I am going to leave with him after we finish. Now will you kindly leave us alone so we can enjoy our shakes!' snapped the girl.

'You stupid broad, to go with a foreign greaseball like that!'

As Gentile stood up, he was conscious of heads turning their way, of faces looking up from the other booths, and of all eyes concentrating on him.

'Look, I was born and raised in Piqua and go to high school there, so I am as much an American as you,' said Don mildly. 'Why don't you both leave and go bother someone else. We are minding our own business and would appreciate you doing the same, okay?'

'You think you are better than us, don't you...you...you damn dago. I have a mind to take you outside and clean your clock good,' the boy replied, his face dark with rage.

'I don't want to cause any trouble in here. I just came to have an enjoyable drink and mind my own business. But if you want trouble, you wait until we leave to call me that and you'll see what will happen.'

'Let's go now, wop.' The boy strode to the door, followed eagerly by his grinning friend. They walked over by the car meters, near the curb. Before Don was ready, the belligerent one swung with such a force that, had it connected, it would have practically knocked Don's head off at the shoulders. But Don ducked and came up with a right cross to the jaw, causing his adversary to hit the ground hard. Gentile turned and said to the other boy, 'You want some of the same?'

His friend said, with a faint sick smile, 'Nope.'

The owner came screaming out of his store, shouting, 'I don't want any trouble in front of my store, go somewhere else!'

'I am sorry this had to happen, but he started it,' Don said. 'I don't have to put up with him calling me names. I'm sorry, but it's over now. We're going.'

Don drove off and headed for an ice cream parlour on the square in Piqua. As they were sitting and talking, his date noticed Don stiffen and a look of scepticism appear in his eyes. She turned and saw the two young men they had trouble with in Troy enter the parlour. They walked over to where they were seated and began calling them both obscene names.

'Didn't you have enough, you want me to give you more?' Don said as he stood up.

'That was a lucky punch. You come outside, I'll clean your clock good. You yellow or something?'

They went outside, arguing for some time before they began to fight. When Don again knocked out the bigger one, the other boy ran to his car and drove madly towards West Water Street. Don jumped into his father's car and followed in hot pursuit.

When the boy reached his home, he jumped the fence and started in the front door. Don grabbed him before he could enter. They were wrestling when the door flung open, and the boy's father came rushing towards young Gentile, swinging a broom handle. He began savagely beating Don over the back until his weapon was a splintered mass.

Several days had passed when, as Don was leaving the football practice field at the high school, a process server handed him a subpoena stating the boy's father was suing him for trespassing and assault.

Patsy wanted to hire a lawyer, but Don refused. He thought he couldn't possibly get into trouble if he told the truth. The other boys had started the fight, calling him obscene names in front of everyone. What else could he do but defend his honor and that of his girl friend. He was a proud American, no better but as good as anyone else. His parents had humble births in Italy, but they too were good Americans. Don said, 'How can I lose if I just tell the truth? God knows, I was provoked.'

Don had his day in court, his first and last brush with the law. He told his story and then the city attorney stated their case. As Don listened, his usual enthusiasm and idealism gave way to a cynical disbelief at the revelation of the seriousness of his 'crime against the state.' After the summation by both sides the judge said, ' I don't know why this case had to come to my court. It appears that this was a simple kids' fight, and in my day it ended there.'

'Your honor, this involves assault,' interrupted the city attorney, 'and the law states...'

'Counsellor, I am well versed in the position of the law in this matter! Would the defendant rise and face the court. Young man, this case would not have been tried in a court of law, but since you were on the boy's father's property, that makes it another matter. The law is quite clear on this point. The sentence is ten days in jail and a fine of twenty-five dollars, plus court costs.' His voice became apologetic when he added, 'Now I will drop the ten days if you pay the fine and court costs.'

Don said nothing as his father paid the $29 fine. When they left the court, they walked down the hall towards the stairs. As they approached the top of the stairway, they heard the murmur of hushed voices and saw a crowd of spectators standing around the boy's father.

Furious, he turned on Don and his father and said, 'Why don't you greaseballs go back where you come from, you...you damned dirty dago bastards.' Don's father winced and then stiffened. A hot intensity showed in his eyes, but he kept staring straight ahead and walked through the parting crowd.

As they drove home, Don, his face white and contorted, spoke for the first time. 'Daddy, I feel bad. I am sorry. I didn't think it would go this far, you know, court and all. I didn't want you to pay the fine. I'll pay you back.'

'How are you going to pay me? Where are you going to get the money? You are not working no place.'

'Someday I will get some money and pay you.'

'Don, I want you to listen to me. Get away from that bad stuff, when someone calls you a foreigner or bad names. You know you were born and raised in Piqua. They say that to get you mad. Just walk away, then you don't get into no trouble. I could have gotten into a scrap over there in the courthouse with the boy's father but I walked away - that's the smart thing to do...Don, remember what I tell you.'

'I know what you mean, Daddy, but it is really hard to sit there and take it. I'll try hard.' As they drove back home they passed the ice cream parlour and as he glanced towards it, he saw boys and girls, arm and arm, laughing and disappearing into the parlour. He thought, why can't I be one of them, why can't I be accepted? Who do they think they are? I am as good as they are. I was born and raised here...like them.

All the frustration and resentment swirled through his head and he made a fervent vow. 'I'll show them. I'll make them proud of me. I'll someday be a big ace, a hero, and this town and my country will be proud of me. Just wait and see.' He closed his eyes and prayed, and with his prayer came an inner peace. So ended the year 1938.

During Don Gentile's childhood, a storm was brewing in Europe, which in adulthood would engulf him in World War II. The Versailles Treaty imposed a hard peace on Germany, but did not create the setting for war, only the justification. The catalyst for the next war, set in motion two days before the signing of the treaty, was a secret protective pact between the new German Republic and its General Staff. The Republic needed protection against the virulent Bolshevism, and the army needed help in being sheltered from the Allies. The terms of the treaty dissolved the General Staff, its War College, and reduced the army to a mere 100,000 men. The world rejoiced with the destruction of the German implements of war.

General Hans von Seeckt, the chief architect behind the military resurgence of Germany, looked upon World War I as one of many battles Germany would lose, but thought ultimately she would be victorious. He began building an elite, modern mobile army. How could this be accomplished under the very noses of the Allies? He formed a joint German-Russian group in the summer of 1922 known as GEFU, which produced aircraft, guns, artillery shells, and other military armaments in Russia. At the same time, schools were established which trained Germans in modern warfare. Those killed in training accidents were returned to their families in Germany in crates marked 'Machinery.'

Seeckt, in less than three years, built a modern new German military structure, but had to step down because of some trivial indiscretions which caused a small flurry in the world press. In October, 1926, he diverted his support to Hitler, because he saw him as the most capable leader to survive the cesspool of political factional parties in the economically depressed Germany. Their aims were the same - to become powerful and form a mighty Reich.

In 1926, when Seeckt was forced to resign, the German Air Service consisted of two fighters and two bomber squadrons. By 1931, this had changed to four fighter, three bomber, and eight observation squadrons, with several hundred future airmen. On January 30, 1933, Hitler became Chancellor of Germany, with a military nucleus to form a mighty war machine.

1939-1941

War in Europe began after years of screaming threats and menacing troop movements, and a desperate grapple for peace at almost any price. It began at a time when most Europeans had resigned themselves to its coming and some Americans, including Don Gentile, knew that eventually the United States would be involved. Don wanted to enlist in the Army Air Corps, and this was to become the biggest headache his father Patsy had yet encountered.

'First you want to solo, that's all you wanted to do,' recited Patsy. 'Later you wanted to own a plane. Now you want to get into the Air Corps. What else will be next?'

Every night Don would go to church and light candles at the altar, seeking from God the strength to pursue his lifelong dream: to become a great flyer - an ace - and return home a hero. He had such a fierce determination to succeed that he often daydreamed about his triumphant return as a hero.

He could see the parade down Main Street, see the bands and the baton-twirling majorettes, feel the handshakes, hear the cheers and the laudatory speeches. 'That crazy Gentile kid - he made it big, he's an ace, a hero. They are going to name a park after him.'

His fantasies were so vivid, in his mind's eye it was as if they had really happened. The line between reality and wishful thinking blurred and confused. He was the ace - the man who helped save his country from the evils of Fascism.

His sister, Edith, later recalled that Don first started talking about the air force when he was in the ninth grade. He was preparing his parents for his graduation. 'As the years passed, Dad was more emphatic about college, but Don was just as emphatic about the air force,' she remembered.

'Every night at the dinner table it was the same story. They would go round and round until Mom would have to break it up. That went on for four years. By the time Don was a senior, the situation got so bad I'd hate to go to the dinner table, but it was a must. Dad had always insisted we eat the main meal together. In the morning going to school Don would say to me, 'Edie, I have to enlist in the air force, I just have to fly. If Dad makes me go to college first, it's like he's putting me in a pen.' He said he could always go to college later.'

When Don was in his junior year of high school, he started writing to the U.S. Army Air Force. Their answer: 'You must have two years of college.' He wrote to the Navy and got the same answer. He finally wrote to the Marines, with the same result. They all required two years of college. Patsy was happy, but Don didn't give up.

Don told his parents he would be drafted and placed in the infantry and would have less chance to survive than if he were fighting from an aeroplane.

'No matter how much you know about an aeroplane, whether you can fly one or think you can, you still have to have two years of college, that's the law in this country,' informed Patsy. 'You don't have two years of college, only high school. Now if I were you, I would go to college, wait two years and then join the Air Corps.'

'No Dad, I am not going to wait two years to fly a plane. Two years from now I don't know what will happen. I'd be drafted. I'd never be allowed to finish college. I want to be there when the fighting starts.'

For months he tried to figure out a way to get into the air force - any air force - without the required two years of college. His hope turned to despair and his despair to renewed prayer, and his prayer to another miracle.

During a restless sleep one night Don dreamed he was falling, falling slowly into a dark pit. The pit began to elongate into a tunnel. At the other end of the tunnel he saw a dim light; the light quickly brightened until it reached an unearthly brilliance. Yet, even though this light was of an indescribable brilliance, it did not hurt his eyes or dazzle him.

Despite the light's unusual manifestation, Don felt it was a being. He felt rather than heard a voice, not a man's voice, but a hearing beyond the physical sense. Over and over again the voice said, 'You shall fly, Don. Enlist in a foreign air force, enlist in a foreign air force.'

Don awoke in a cold sweat. During the long hours until the darkness changed to dawn, he racked his brain, trying to get to the meaning of the vision. He was positive God had sent him a message, but what did it mean?

He began to pray, asking for the guidance to comprehend. And then he noticed the crumpled newspaper at the foot of his bed, the paper where only a few hours ago he had read the sports page. He could not take his eyes off the newspaper, it was if he was mesmerised. Slowly he began to focus on an article in the lower right hand corner of the front page. The headline read, 'U.S. Pilots Help Chinese.' Suddenly the meaning of the vision became clear - this was the foreign air force.

He put in a long distance call to the Chinese Embassy in Washington, D. C., but once again, he faced frustration and defeat. The Chinese were only interested in pilots who were former U.S. Army flyers. Don was discouraged. His hopes had been reborn only to be dashed on the rocks of despair. But by no means was he ready to give up.

Several days later, at Wright Field, he struck up an acquaintance with a Canadian flying officer, and during the course of their conversation Don told him of his troubles.

'I believe I can help you,' the officer said. 'A special committee is here in the States signing up pilots for the RAF Already some of your American daredevil cousins, members of the Eagle Squadron - that's what their outfit's called - are knocking the 'h' out of the Huns.'

Great Britain, its back to the wall, was less concerned about scholastic standing than with obtaining experienced pilots who had a desire to fly, and the Royal Canadian Air Force was one end of the pipeline which fed the desperately needed pilots across the Atlantic and into the Royal Air Force squadrons.

The Royal Canadian Air Force formed recruiting committees in Ottawa and New York under the command of Air Vice-Marshal Billy Bishop. Bishop was. Canada's leading World War I ace, with a record of seventy-two enemy planes destroyed. He induced his American wartime flying colleague, Clayton Knight of Rochester, New York, to head up the American recruiting force. Knight was a famous aviation illustrator.

The day after England declared war on Germany, Bishop called Knight and asked him if he would help select American pilots who might want to volunteer for duty with the Royal Canadian Air Force. He pointed out most Canadian pilots were already in the conflict, and the flight training schools were suffering from a lack of student recruits. The Clayton Knight Committee ultimately supplied ten percent of the R.C.A.F. enrolment and ninety-two percent of the American volunteers in the R.A.F.

The men who contacted the Clayton Knight Committee had various reasons for not being in the United States Air Corps. There were those who lacked the requisite college training, such as Gentile, or could not pass the physical examinations. The U.S. insisted upon 20-20 vision, while the British would accept flyers with 20-40 vision correctable with goggle lenses.

A good many of the committee's finest pilots were American cadets, washed out for lack of flying ability. The Canadian rules governing age limit and marital status were also more liberal. A pilot, to be eligible, needed at least 250 hours of 20-S flying experience, a Civil Aeronautic license, a high school diploma, and two character recommendations. Men under twenty-one could join up with their parents' or guardians' consent.

At first, the Clayton Knight Committee was a cloak-and-dagger affair, because they did not want to compromise U.S. neutrality. Some prospective R.A.F. recruits were caught by the F.B.I. trying to enter Canada to enlist and were forced to return to the U.S.

Hearing about the committee, Don began a renewed effort for parental approval to join the Royal Air Force. He told them he wanted to become an ace and return to a secure peacetime job after making a name for himself. They said, 'No, no, no!' and Don said, 'Yes, yes, yes.' The Piqua war was on again in full force with neither side giving any quarter.

Young Gentile, without his parents' consent, wrote the Royal Canadian Air

539 S. Wayne Street
Piqua, Ohio
May 28, 1941

Clayton Knight Committee
Statler Hotel
Cleveland, Ohio

Gentlemen:

I am sending you some of the Documents that are necessary to complete my requirements. Inclosed you will find a "copy" of my birth certificate, four photographs of myself, an my parents consent.

The rest of the requirements will be sent to you as soon as possible.

Mr. Dine the high school principal will send you proof of my high school education, and also one of the letters of recommendation. The other letters of recommendation will be sent by _____ of State _____.

A photostat copy of my last page of my log book and current license and rating is being made now. I will send you those a soon as I will receive them.

Yours truly,
Don Gentile

Don's May 28, 1941 letter to the Clayton Knight Committee

Force for information on enlisting. They sent him a large packet of official documents to complete. On May 28, 1941, he sent the letter on page 51 to the committee.

As the letter reflects, Don did not meet all the requirements for acceptance. He did not have the 500 hours of total flying, or the 250 hours of 2-S time. In fact, he had less than forty hours of total flying with no 2-S time. His flight time was only in small aircraft with sixty-five horsepower engines, while the bigger 2-S planes used 250 horsepower. How could he satisfy this requirement? There was no way he could accumulate that amount of flying time, even if he could afford it. What could he do...?

He knew it would be wrong but every fibre of his being urged him on. 'This is your last chance, don't be a fool - who will know? Be a success - come back a hero - show them.'

His jaw tightened and his nostrils flared. He got up and went to his bedroom, locked the door, and began padding his Flight Log Book. That night he prayed to the Lord to forgive him and to bring him success in this desperate desire.

The local authorities did not want to assume the responsibility for completing the forms without his parents' consent. They were afraid they would be blamed if he did not return from the war.

That night Don discussed the situation with his young sister, Edith. 'Don, you will never get Mom to sign those papers.'

His face broke into a smile as he said, 'Oh, I'll win her over. It's Dad, he is the hard one to break.'

The next day Don hugged and kissed his mother and told her how happy he would be if she would only sign the papers. Don had a way with his mother. If she was angry, he'd flash that smile, put his arms around her, tease a little, and say, 'your little boy.' His mother could not resist his charms and would eventually give in to him.

Her hard exterior melting, she smiled and said, 'Oh, all right, Don.' Without Patsy's knowledge, he got his mother to sign her permission for Don to join the Royal Air Force. Later he received a letter stating he must also have his father sign.

'I said, no, I won't,' Patsy stated gruffly.

'What do you mean, you won't?' replied Don.

'I mean just what I said.'

'You had better sign or else.'

All night long Patsy rolled, tossed, and turned in a fitful sleep. He kept mulling over and over, in his semiconscious state, the words 'or else.' Those words bothered him. He struggled for the source of the meaning, what did he mean by them, what fool thing would he do?

For a long time he stared at the ceiling as though paralysed. Suddenly everything came to him all at once. Don would run away and enlist in the Canadian or British Army. 'That,' reflected Patsy, 'must be what he intends to do if I will not consent to his enlistment.' Patsy felt weak, almost physically ill. His reaction to this revelation left him trembling. He wavered for several minutes, than came to a decision.

The next morning at breakfast he told Don, 'Look me right in the face, don't look at my feet, look right into my eyes. This is the truth. You might be able to fly an aeroplane - I don't know anything about that - but remember that besides flying you need more education. I only went through the third grade in the old country. Over there I had to walk barefoot through snow to learn what I had to learn. If I did not have that kind of education I could not be holding my job all these years with this big corporation.

'I have been working all my life and I know you need an education. I tell you what I will do and this is coming from my heart. I will stick to my word. I like you and like to see you get someplace. You have to appreciate what I am telling you, too. You haven't quite finished high school, and you know you haven't done well because you have this flying thing in your mind. You get your high school diploma and the next day, or anytime you want, I will fly, write, or go to Canada with you and sign the papers in front of those Canadian officers. Let's have no more discussion about it. between now and then. Don't come in tomorrow and say, Daddy sign. Forget it until you bring me your diploma.'

The next few months Don studied very hard and graduated. His final semester he earned almost all As.

In August, 1941, Gentile received a notice from the Knight Committee to appear at the R.C.A.F. recruiting office in Windsor, Canada. He and his father drove to Canada to sign the preliminary papers.

They started early in the morning with Don driving, most of the time at breakneck speeds, passing trucks and cars, turning, weaving, and twisting down narrow two-lane highways. During this long drive, Patsy was very quiet and hardly spoke; he just sat there, looking like an unhappy boy.

When they arrived at the recruiting office, they met three officers wearing Canadian uniforms.

The older officer said, 'Oh, you are Mr Gentile from Ohio?'

Don replied, 'Yes, sir,' and he was smiling. His father was trying to smile but could not, because he was hurting too much.

'We have some papers here for you,' continued the older officer. He went to his desk, pulled out some papers, and sat down. 'You will have to pass your physical examination first, then your dad can sign these papers.'

Don went into another room for the physical. The officers continued talking among themselves, while Patsy sat alone on a bench in a corner of the room. He sat there with his arms folded across his chest, looking down at his feet. He was very sad. Everything was gone inside him. He could not think. He prayed he was doing the right thing for the boy.

His thoughts were interrupted by the doctor, who came out of the examining room, put his hand on Patsy's shoulder, and said, 'Mr Gentile, you have a good, sound boy. There is nothing wrong with that boy's body.'

The elder Gentile replied, 'Why, thank you, Doctor. I appreciate hearing that.'

The older officer picked up some forms from the desk and placed them in front of Patsy. 'Now Mr Gentile you have to sign, giving us permission to induct your son into the air force.'

'Sure I do that - that's why I came here;' answered Don's father. 'But before I sign I would like to ask you one question. What does this really mean? This is the only son I have and I done everything to raise him up to this age. I don't want to give him up without knowing what's it all about. Can you give me an idea what he is going into? What's this air force?'

'Sure I will, Mr Gentile. He has to go from here to Fort Hayes in Cleveland, Ohio, for a flying test tomorrow.'

'We are going to go today,' interrupted Don.

'Wait, Don, let's hear the rest,' cautioned his father.

'From Hayes he will be given a two-week leave home. He will then fly out of Dayton to Glendale, California, for six months of advanced flight training. If he qualifies and gets his wings, next he will be sent to Ottawa, Canada, where he will go through an intensive training for two weeks. And then he will sail overseas to England.'

'How long overseas?' asked Patsy.

'That would be very hard for me to answer,' replied the officer. 'Once he goes through all this training and travels overseas into the hands of the British government, we won't have anything to say. If this war lasts twenty years, he is liable to be there for twenty years.'

Mr Gentile turned and looked at his son and said, 'Well, Don, did you hear what this officer is saying? Do you still want me to sign?'

'Daddy, that is why I came here and that is what I expect you to do for me.'

'All right. Good luck to you. I will sign.'

They were all seated at a table, Don and the two officers on one side, and Mr Gentile on the other. When Patsy said he would sign, Don jumped up, leaned over the table, and kissed his father above his right eyebrow. 'Don't worry, Dad, you got a son as long as I live. I will never forget what you and Mom did for me.' Then Don said, 'All right, we have to go to Cleveland.' They shook hands all around, walked out of the office, and got into their car. It was a little after dinner time and Patsy said, 'Let's go home now, Don.'

'No, Daddy, I am going to Cleveland.'

'Are you crazy? How are you going to get there before it gets dark?'

'Oh, it won't be dark. I'll make it in daylight.'

'We could take another day. I could get the day off from my company.'

'No, we will go today. You can't take another day off.'

Don raced along the highways at excessive speeds. Patsy thought, 'Where are the State Highway Patrols today? They must all be asleep. When you want a policeman you can never find one.' The tension began building up until he finally said, 'Where in the hell are the police that they don't catch you and lock you up?'

'Aw, Daddy, I know what I am doing. I am not hurting anyone.'

Just as the sun was setting, they arrived at Fort Hayes. They went into the administration building and talked to the Officer of the Day.

When Don informed him why they were there, he responded, 'Well, I don't think you have enough daylight. Why don't you return tomorrow?'

'Please do me a favour. I can't come back tomorrow because my dad brought me and he can't take another day off to bring me back tomorrow. Would you do me a great favour and give me the test tonight? I would really appreciate it.'

The flyer went over to another officer and discussed this for a few minutes, then said, 'Come on, champion, let's go.'

They walked down to a Curtis P-40, and Don looked it all over, checking the wings, tail, and everything inside. He said, 'I never seen anything like this before. It is going to be a hard thing to figure out.'

Mr Gentile said, 'Now listen Don, if you don't know what you are doing and are doing it to show off, then you gonna drown yourself in Lake Erie and I'll die right here with you. I am not going home, and your mother will have no son or no husband because I will never go home by myself. If you are not sure don't get in.'

Don looked the plane over again and said, 'I am going to make it.'

The officer came over and said to Don, 'Are you ready, champion?'

'Yes,' replied Don. They got into the plane and Don flew around for about ten minutes. After they landed, the man said, 'Now, Don, you take it up yourself.' Don took off, did a few rolls and dives, and made a bumpy landing.

The officer said, 'Go up and try again.' It was getting very dark but Don went up, circled the field, and made a perfect three-point landing. He jumped out of the plane and the officer put his arm around his shoulders, saying, 'Well, champ, I have to tell you this. You will make a good pilot. In this flying business you have to be careful and watch out for mountain peaks and high structures. If you do those two things you will make a good pilot. Good luck. Stop in the office and I will give you a form to take along with you.'

They left the base and stopped at a gas station in Mansfield, Ohio. Don said,

'Dad, I am so tried I can hardly stay awake. I have been driving all day, so would you mind driving the rest of the way home?'

'Sure, I would be glad to drive the rest of the way if you are not in a hurry to get home, because I am not going to drive crazy like you do!' Don jumped into the back seat and instantly fell fast asleep. He did not wake up until they arrived home.

When Don saw his mother he threw his arms around her and kept repeating, 'You got a pilot - you got a pilot in the family.' He left the house and went downtown to see his friends, and tell them about his being accepted as a pilot cadet in the R.A.F.

Two weeks later he received a telegram from Cleveland advising him of the day and time he was to leave Dayton for Glendale, California. On August 17, 1941, his father put him on a TWA aeroplane to Polaris Field, Glendale, California. He completed the six months training in three months, at the top of the class. He received his wings and was commissioned a Pilot Officer[1] in the R.A.F. on November 11, 1941.

He called that day from California and told his parents, 'Mom and Dad, I can't kiss both of you over the telephone but I wish I could. I am so happy. I can't thank you enough for what both of you have done for me. I got my wings and out of all the cadets only three of us qualified as pilots and I was the first one. I am not bragging, it's the truth, I got my wings!'

'Good luck to you,' replied his father. 'When are you coming home?'

'I should be home next week, Dad. See you then.'

The day he came home on a forty-eight hour leave, everyone went to meet him, all his relatives and close friends. It was a great reunion. His mother had a huge four-course Italian meal waiting for them. Don was very happy, and he would tease his mother, trying to prepare her for his departure to England in a few days.

That night Piqua was playing football against their arch rival, Troy. Don wore his blue R.A.F. officer's uniform and went with his father to Troy to see the game. When they arrived, team members and spectators, particularly the girls, crowded around him.

He was the centre of attention the entire evening. The game announcer let the fans know that one of their own was on his way to combat in England. The whole stadium stood up and cheered. Throughout the evening, his father sat with his arms folded, smiling and saying nothing. He was very proud of his son but very fearful for his survival.

The day before Don's departure for England, he and Edith said their tearful goodbyes. They had been very close; he was not only her brother, but a kind and understanding good friend as well. They promised to write every day and Edith promised to keep him posted on what was happening at home. He asked her to take care of their mother and to reassure her each day that he was fine and that there was nothing to worry about. He also asked Edith to remind her that he was a special person and that the Blessed Mother would protect him and return him to her.

Hearing about the committee, Don began a renewed effort for parental approval to join the Royal Air Force. He told them he wanted to become an ace. They had not thought beyond his training period. Now the full significance of his going overseas to England, a combat zone, stunned them. His mother was overcome with grief when she heard he must leave her in a few hours and journey alone into a European holocaust of God knew what dangers.

At breakfast on the day of his departure Josephina sobbed almost continually. Beseeching him to stay home, she gazed at him tenderly and protectively, whispering, 'My boy, my little boy.' The farewell at the Pennsylvania train station with the family, relatives, and friends was a touching, emotional scenario.

When his father got ready to say goodbye, he took him aside and said, 'Son, you're on your own now. If you're ever in trouble, just write me and I'll help you. Whatever it is and wherever you are, I'll help.'

They embraced and Don said, 'Thanks Dad, I'll remember that.' Don often thought about his father's offer of help during combat over Europe. It had a sustaining influence on him when he got into a tight spot, but whenever he wrote home he always told them that everything was just fine.

When Don went to say goodbye to his aunt, she began to pound with both fists on his chest saying, 'You can't go. I won't let you go, you don't know what you're doing, how could you do this to your mother.' But Don just kissed her, saying, 'Don't worry, I'll be all right.'

When it was time to kiss his mother goodbye, she wrapped her arms protectively around him and wept, wept until everyone else was crying, too. As she talked to him softly in Italian between her tears, tiny drops smaller than the pearls on a lady's ring began to form all the way across her upper lip. Her colour turned waxen and her eyes looked as dead as agates. The skin tightened along her cheekbones until her face assumed the appearance of a skull. Then, suddenly, she fainted.

When she recovered, she would not get off the train. Tearfully, she clung to whatever she could grasp to prevent the train from taking him away from her.

Soon the conductor said, 'Lady, we can't hold this train any longer. We are already fifteen minutes behind schedule now.' He turned to Don saying, 'Son, can't you see what this is doing to your mother? Why don't you stay home?'

Edith, watching her grieving mother, couldn't understand how Don could go away like this. She cried, 'Don, you're a louse to put Mama through this!'

With an aching heart Don pulled away from his suffering mother's grasping

Pilot Officer Don Gentile of the British R.A.F. (Royal Air Force).

arms and threw himself into the train seat and began sobbing uncontrollably. His father got his mother off the train, but as it started to move, she broke away and with outstretched arms she began running along the tracks, crying in Italian, 'Don don't leave me...please Don...my baby don't go - please Don come back.'

'Mama please...please...please don't, Mama...'

The train headed northward to Ottawa, Canada, and the landscape blurred and distorted as Don viewed it through moist, sorrowful eyes. His reflection in the window mirrored the distracted and troubled look on his face. He talked to this image, saying, 'I feel like a louse, but I know what I am doing. I know what I have to do.'

As the train thundered through the night, taking Don away from his loved ones, it was propelling him toward his destiny. He had a mission and he had to fulfil it. He had a firm, absolute conviction that his fate was in the hands of God. Whatever happened to him, Don was willing to bow to His will. He was conscious of never having had any aspiration other than to be a flyer, an ace, and bring honor and respect to his family while serving his beloved country.

When he arrived in Canada he sent home a telegram, but then two weeks went by without any other word from their son. His family did not know if he was still in Ottawa or where he was. They tried on several occasions to obtain information about Don from the Canadian government, but they were rebuffed. This was military information which they were not privileged to share.

One night they received a call from Halifax, Nova Scotia. It was Don! He had just arrived there. Patsy was speaking to him when Josephina started begging to talk to her son. He gave her the telephone and in her excitement she started talking in Italian. All at once the telephone went dead. The telephone company had closed the line to Halifax when they heard the voice speaking Italian. Patsy tried to contact someone to reconnect the call, but they could not call back without knowing the source of his call.

'Pasquale!' The word came like a bullet from Mrs Gentile. 'You have to go to Canada and find out what is wrong with our son. Oh, go - please go. I have a terrible feeling he is not all right. Please go right away.'

The next day Patsy stopped by his bar to get an employee to drive his car back from the Valdalia Airport, where he would catch a flight to Halifax, Nova Scotia. While he was talking to a patron he unconsciously picked up the day's mail without looking at it and put it in his pocket.

When he arrived in Nova Scotia, he was wearing a summer suit with a straw hat because Ohio was experiencing an unusual warm Indian summer. As he stepped off the plane Patsy was gripped by the intensity of the cold. He began to shiver uncontrollably and saw that the grounds of the airfield were covered with several inches of snow. The wheels of the aeroplane had sloshed through the snow and now were axle deep in water. A stiff breeze caught his straw hat and sent it flying across the airfield. As he watched it sail out of sight, Patsy decided that was the last he would see of his hat.

At the Army headquarters no one knew his son or where he had gone. One of the officers thought he might have returned to Ottawa. Patsy went back to the airfield and took the first available flight to Ottawa. On landing he went straight to the hotel where his son was supposed to be billeted. Again he could not find Don.

The desk clerk suggested he try the R.C.A.F. airfield, some fifteen miles out of town. Late in the afternoon, as fluffy snow sifted down on the airdrome from overcast skies, Patsy rode up to the main gate in a taxicab. He got out of the cab and approached the Sergeant of the Guard, who was conferring with two other guards outfitted with rifles and fixed bayonets.

Patsy was denied access to the base, and the sergeant ordered him and his taxi to leave the area. Patsy told the cab driver not to leave because it would be too far for him to walk back to town. The orders to leave became more menacing, and Patsy was fearful he might get shot. He kept trying to explain he had come a long way, and pleaded with the guard for some information about his son. The argument continued for several minutes, until the sergeant ordered the two soldiers to guard Patsy while he made a telephone call.

Through the window of the sentry post Patsy could see the sergeant was engaged in a heated conversation, gesturing and looking up from time to time to watch Patsy. Several minutes after he hung up a motorcycle with a sidecar came to the gate. Patsy was ordered to get in the sidecar and was taken to a large brick administration building inside the base.

He was ushered into a small office staffed by three French officers, busy writing reports. One of the officers looked up and asked, 'What can I do for you?' Patsy explained the reason for his journey to Canada.

'I am sorry, but we are not supposed to give out such information. I would like to tell you where he is, but there is a law during wartime that prohibits us from giving out military news. However, I will do something for you because you have come so far, although I am not supposed to do this either. I will give you his address in England, and you can send him a letter and ask him whatever you want. I am really sorry but that is the best I can do for you.'

Patsy thanked the officer, telling how much he appreciated even that information. The motorcycle driver took him to the main gate, but from there he had to walk several miles in the cold freezing weather to the end of the field where the guards had ordered the taxi to wait.

When Patsy arrived at Union Station in Ottawa and worked out the train schedule for his return to Ohio, he decided to send his wife a telegram. He wrote the telegram in Italian, telling her what he had learned and the time of his arrival home.

He handed the message to a Western Union clerk, who disappeared into the back of the office. A few minutes later, without warning, Patsy was jerked backwards by a tall, powerfully built man. With a single muscular wrist, he held Patsy's heavy, sagging body by a handful of jacket.

Belligerently, the large policeman demanded, 'Who are you? Why are you here?' He fired questions at Patsy faster than Patsy could answer. 'Why do you write in this language? Why don't you write in English?'

Patsy replied innocently, 'I didn't do anything wrong. Why do you jerk me like that for?'

'What does this telegram say?'

'This telegram is telling my wife what time I will get home if I ever get there.'

'Why don't you write it in English?'

'Sir, my wife can't write or read English. There is nothing wrong in that telegram. I am just telling her what time I will arrive in Piqua.'

Pointing to a chair in the lobby the tall man said, 'You sit down here while I get an interpreter. We'll find out what's in that telegram.' The interpreter talked at great length to Patsy in Italian, but Mr Gentile could hardly understand him.

Patsy turned and looked up to the policeman and said, 'Sir, I don't know anything about interpreters, but this guy can't talk any more of the Italian language than I can talk Japanese. I can barely understand him. What kind of an interpreter did you hire anyhow?'

The tall policeman stared down at Patsy and replied, 'You will have to send your telegram in English. We won't allow you to send it in Italian.

'If I can't send a telegram in Italian, I won't send one at all. I'll just let it go. When I get there I get there,' responded Patsy.

For a long time the officers debated about what to do with him while they studied Patsy's intense expression. The tall policeman finally said, 'All right, you can go, but without sending that telegram. Do you understand?'

'Yes sir, I understand.' Patsy walked out of the telegraph office and boarded the train for Windsor.

When he arrived at Windsor customs, two policemen, one speaking English and one French, were questioning those trying to enter the United States. When Patsy's turn came, they asked for his passport. He did not have one. 'What do you mean you don't have one?' asked one of the policemen.

'Well, no one told me I would need a passport when I flew out of Valdalia, Ohio. I could have gotten a passport but they just sold me the ticket to Canada and I got on the plane. Now you say I have to have a passport, but no one told me before.'

'Are you an American citizen?'

'Yes, I am.'

'Do you have any papers to prove it?'

Patsy opened his coat and took out some papers along with four unopened letters. The two policemen looked at each other quizzically and one of them said, as he reached out to take the papers, 'What have we here?' He riffled through the papers until he came upon a letter from a soldier stationed at Fort Knox. He opened it and began reading: 'Dear Mr Gentile, I am now a soldier at Fort Knox, Kentucky. I am sick and tired of this life in the service but just as soon as I get out could I have my old job back....'

The police officer demanded, 'Who is this soldier? Why does he hate the service? What kind of a job do you have for him? Come on, come clean.'

'I have a little bar back at Piqua, Ohio, and he used to work for me. I don't know anything about whether he likes the service or not. So about that I could not tell you. If he does come back maybe I would give him his job back.'

'Now listen,' the policeman warned, 'we could put you in jail until you tell us the truth.'

'Every word I said is the truth. If you put me in jail and feed me bread and water and not let me sleep, I think I could stand that pretty good. But the next day I would contact the American Consul to get me back into the United States.'

'A man without a passport is a spy!' The policeman had intended only to scare some of the condescension out of Gentile. But Patsy's anxiety now made him realise the possibilities of the situation. He could teach Patsy and others like him a lesson. A man without a passport could in fact be a possible spy.

He noted the sweat on Patsy's forehead and threatened, 'If you come back to Canada again without a passport, we will shoot you as a spy. We are going to let you pass into the United States, but never come back without a passport or you know what we will do to you. You understand that?'

'Yes, I understand. I will know better next time,' Patsy said humbly.

For the first of many times over the next few years a deep sadness penetrated the Gentile household. The family was loving and close, and not knowing Don's whereabouts was agony. The coming of the first Christmas without him was as devastating as a bomb on a silent night.

In the next few lonely weeks, Don experienced extreme homesickness and a longing to be with his loved ones. He fought to overcome these inner feelings, not because he thought they were bad, but because he disliked what he felt they represented - a weakness of his willpower and a distraction from his mission to become an ace fighter pilot.

On a cold, grey day in December, 1941, the little tanker Leticia docked in Liverpool, England, with Don Gentile and thirty-seven other recruits for the Eagle Squadron. There his loneliness was assuaged by the grateful British, who were thankful for the aid in this hour of need.

The England where Don arrived was suffering from all the traumas of a country under siege. After several years of war, conditions were poor. There was a severe shortage of food; canned goods were almost non-existent, and the wheat content of bread was drastically reduced. The allowance for soap was only four three-ounce bars per month. Coal was so scarce that the ration was barely enough to heat one room, even during the winter months. The alcohol content of beer was so reduced it was almost impossible to get drunk.

Don was sent to No. 9 Service Flying Training School (SETS) at R.A.F. Hullavington. Soon after arrival, he learned that his knowledge of flying didn't add up to much. He knew how to fly, but he had a great deal to learn about flying fighters and the why of flying.

The training aircraft was the Miles Master, a low wing monoplane which could reach speeds of 225 miles per hour, and had a higher ceiling than anything Don had flown previously. Its 700 horsepower Rolls Royce engine, with a three-blade adjustable pitch propeller, made it really hot. It was constructed of plywood sheeting which would wrinkle from the moisture when it rained. The inexperienced pilots worried that the sheeting would come unglued in flight, but the wrinkles had no affect on the plane's flying ability. The more apprehensive flyers would wait for the sun's warmth to dry out the wing surfaces, and as the midday sun reached its maximum heat the wrinkles in the plywood skin would slowly smooth out.

Don loved to fly this powerful aeroplane, and he soon mastered all the intricacies of aerobatics, formation flying, and night and instrument flying. His instructor, Pilot Officer Kelshall, thought he was ready to solo after only three and three-quarters hours of dual training time.

Flight Lieutenant McCarthey, the training Flight Commander, gave Don his final check-ride. Afterwards he climbed out of the front seat, taking his parachute with him, and said,' Go do your stuff, tiger!'

Don was very confident; his love of flying consumed him. He couldn't wait to take off on this grey, leaden day, even though the overcast hung low over the airfield.

Pointing the aircraft into the wind, he went roaring down the runway and into the air, climbing through the cloud formations into the dazzling beauty of the sun-drenched cloud-tops. For about a half an hour he performed aerobatics and cross-country flying until an old familiar urge came over him. He flew low and did some hedgehopping across the English countryside, buzzing anything that moved. It had a drug-like effect on him; the closer he got to the ground the greater the thrill.

For several days after Don's solo, the base received complaints from local farmers who claimed their chickens were not laying eggs and that their cows' milk was sour. Fortunately for Don, the large number of training aircraft in the area made it impossible to place the blame on any one pilot, and after a time the farmers quit complaining and the animals returned to normal.

Formation flying was the most popular and exciting part of the training. At one time, all nations flew a 'V' formation, but Germany's combat experience in the Spanish Civil War brought out its disadvantages. The number one rule of all air combat is to sight the enemy first, in order to attain a superior position for the attack. But with the 'V', the pilots were busier concentrating on keeping their position in formation than looking for the enemy. It was replaced by the Rotte,[2] a two-plane unit of great flexibility. The British called the two-plane unit an element, an aircraft and a wingman; a flight was a unit of four; a unit of sixteen was a squadron; three squadrons or forty-eight aircraft made up a group. Each squadron had its own radio call sign.

A squadron would fly formation in four finger sections of four aircraft. The sections were given the names of colours and flew the following configuration:

	White		
Red	I	Yellow	Green
I	II	I	I
II	III	II	II
III	IV	III	III
IV		IV	IV

The squadron leader was designated White I and had his own radio call letter. This arrangement allowed pilots to easily identify each other with a minimum of radio communication.

At the start of formation training, the student pilots flew perilously close to each another one minute and the next minute were several blocks away. By the end of the training they were flying a very tight formation through all the simulated combat techniques, which would allow them to attack the enemy's fighter bombers from various positions - head on, from the beam, dead astern, directly below, and below and astern.

The most difficult and dangerous training, particularly in near-daily overcast conditions in England, was night flying. The wartime blackouts intensified its difficulties, so one could easily lose orientation and sense of balance. Night flying over England required diligence in watching out for high structures and barrage balloons, some of which extended several thousand feet into the atmosphere.

Wandering into highly industrialised areas without proper authorisation could bring you under suspicion of being an enemy, and the long slender fingers of the anti-aircraft searchlights would blind you and prevent you from diving, climbing, or sideslipping away from them. They would follow your every move until their flak destroyed you.

Landing in the total darkness made Don nervous, but he calmed himself when he was frightened by talking to himself. The airfield flare pots would only dimly light the field, and they could not be seen at 1,000 feet altitude. It was especially hazardous when the flares and the aircraft navigation lights were extinguished because enemy aircraft were suspected of being in the vicinity. During these training exercises the pitch-black sky was filled with frightened students groping their way in the darkness. Don flew with his rosary wrapped around the control stick, and he would break out in a cold sweat whenever he flew unseeing through someone's slipstream.

One night after an armament lecture they heard an aircraft flying above them, first circling the field low and then slowly fading away. The sound was repeated several times, until from high above they heard the thin wailing scream of an aeroplane spinning down. One of the instructors took out his pipe, studying it intently while he scraped the bowl and cleaned out the old tobacco. He blew in its stem to make sure it was not blocked. Taking a pouch from his pocket, he sprinkled some tobacco into the pipe, packed it in solidly with his fingers, and then put it in his mouth. Just as he lit it they heard a crash. As the others stared dazedly at each other, the instructor, puffing his pipe, studied them with the concentration he normally reserved for his lectures. For a moment the students forgot the shock and focused their attention on the instructor, whose steady scrutiny had begun to make itself felt through the silence. The instructor looked at them intently for several seconds more before speaking. 'I believe that was one of your boys on a night flight. Poor chap, he spun in and bought it.'

Don later learned that seven of the student pilots who were completing this night test flight had been killed.

Early 1942

Gentile completed the two months training at No. 9 SFTS and on February 27, 1942, was posted to No. 57 Operational Training Unit (OTU) based at Eshott Air Force Base near Morpeth, England. Here he was to learn how to fly the Spitfire.

When Don first saw the Spits his face lit up. For days he walked around wearing a fixed grin, for what he had wished for all of his life could now become a reality. Once he mastered this combat plane he would be posted to a fighter squadron, and soon he would get the five kills needed to become an ace.

The chief designer of the Spitfire was Reginald Mitchell. In 1933, he had undergone lung surgery and had taken a Continental holiday to convalesce. When he returned, still a very sick man, he was convinced Germany was bent on war. He refused all medical advice to rest and instead devoted what remained of his life to developing the Spitfire, believing it could influence the outcome of the war. In 1937 Reginald Mitchell died at age 42 before he saw his beloved Spit come off the production line.

During the training lectures, Don learned about every inch of the plane. The fuselage was built with the aft section extending upward to form the tail fin. The wings were made of box-like girders that fitted inside each other, giving the craft the resilience of a leaf-spring. This revolutionary elliptically designed wing had immense strength and room for eight machine guns. The wheels retracted into the wing without bumps or bulges, unlike the German Messerschmitt 109, whose 20mm cannons in each wing created large bulges and somewhat decreased the efficiency of the aeroplane.

The Spitfire had gone through many modifications, and now the Spitfire MK Vb had a maximum speed of 369 miles per hour at 19,500 feet. It could climb 4,750 feet per minute and had a service ceiling of 36,200 feet. The armament became a mixture of two 20mm cannons and four .303 inch machine guns, comparable to the German fighters. The Spitfire had tracer bullets to warn the pilots when they were almost out of ammunition, while the Germans had an indicator which showed the level of their ammunition supply. The Messerschmitt 109 had the tightest turning circle, only 750 feet compared to the Spitfire's 880 feet, and this was an important factor in air fighting. The Spitfire could take more stress on its frame and seldom broke up in the air, while the Messerschmitt wing and, particularly, its tail were structurally weaker.

Don was an excellent pilot. He could do anything with an aeroplane in the form of aerobatics. He had complete confidence in himself, but soon he was transformed into a deflated neophyte. He realised flying an aeroplane is only part of fighting with one.

He had to learn to constantly turn his head as far as he could, for over five hours without stopping, to keep from being bounced by the enemy. He had to fly on oxygen at 30,000 feet in sixty-degrees-below-zero temperatures for hours; the necessary helmet, goggles, and oxygen mask gave him a feeling of restriction. He would have to fly with his windshield frosted with ice and instruments frozen; with his guns jammed or out of ammunition.

He had to learn that shooting from a plane was a different kind of shooting. Flying an aeroplane is only important as a means of getting armament into the air; a plane is only a platform of guns which the aircraft must get into position to shoot. His ability as a pilot would mean nothing unless he was a good shot and could destroy an enemy taking evasive action by twisting and turning in flight. Don had to learn that when his guns fired, the recoil would cause a momentary drop in the airspeed of almost forty miles per hour. He learned that in firing your guns you must hold your aeroplane steady while twisting, diving, or turning with the enemy.

To practice 'dogfighting', two aircraft would pair off and endeavour in every way possible to shoot the other down. Occasionally an instructor would fly the other plane, and he would attempt to get on Don's tail. Don would hurtle his plane through the sky, and after several minutes of searching a quick glance in the instructor's mirror would reveal Don sitting on his tail. The instructor would try to shake him but to no avail.

Occasionally Don would come out second best; it was then that he learned the uselessness of all aerobatics in actual combat. The two most effective means for complete evasion were a half roll and a controlled spin. If you have been hit, the controlled spin will make the enemy believe you are out of control and about to crash. In a dogfight the beam attack is probably the most difficult but most effective way to destroy the enemy.

The optimum distance for firing your guns is 250 yards. A pilot must teach himself restraint, suppressing the impulse to fire the minute the enemy is sighted, even though his weapons can destroy at half a mile. The chance of making an effective strike at that kind of distance would be remote and result in minimum damage.

The Spitfire's two cannons can only fire for six seconds, the four machine guns for sixteen seconds. Therefore a pilot must deliver short bursts to the enemy, rather than blast away and prematurely empty his guns. Gentile learned that most aces hold their fire until they are within 100 to 200 yards, where a short burst becomes more effective. But they had to be careful in getting too close, because the flying debris from a disintegrating plane can cause serious damage to one's own aircraft.

The classroom door opened one day to admit a short stocky officer. He walked to the podium:

My name is Peters. I am the OTU Intelligence Officer. If I might take a little of your time, I would like to give you a profile of the bloody enemy. The individual German pilot is well trained and experienced in all aspects of air warfare.

At the beginning of the war the Germans selected their flyers from unmarried men between seventeen and twenty-four years of age. They had to possess exceptional physical, mental, and moral attributes, all of which were tested in unique ways. The candidates were asked to write an essay on the German culture, war, and love, while a loudspeaker blared hysterical, nerve-racking laughter. Later each was tied to a revolving wheel and asked to do mathematical problems while counting the wheel's revolutions and responding to various signals by means of hand-held controls. When this was completed they were subjected to electric shocks while tied to the wheel, and the reactions were recorded by a movie camera.

Next, the aspirants were led into a beautiful room furnished with various chairs. Some of the chairs were comfortable, soft and luxuriously padded; others were hard, wooden, straight-backed and very uncomfortable. On tables around the room were books, magazines, and pornographic literature. Through a one-way window the candidates were observed. If they settled into a comfortable chair and read the pornographic literature, they were immediately washed out. On another occasion, they were marched to a cliff fifty feet above a lake and ordered to jump, and if they showed the least hesitation, they were dismissed from the Luftwaffe.

After these preliminaries, flight training began. The Versailles Treaty prevented the Germans from having an air force, but since the treaty did not prevent glider training, some 80,000 gliders were operating in 'clubs' throughout Germany. Gliders were the purest form of flight. You really have to know how to fly to handle a glider, particularly through thermals (rising air currents) to climb. The holders of all the altitude records before World War II were Germans.

He paused and then continued:

The Versailles Treaty had another loophole, which did not prevent the construction of a civilian airline. The Germans formed the world's first commercial airline. They produced fleets of war planes disguised as civilian aircraft. Thousands of pilots were trained under the guise of civilian airlines, pilots who later became the air force which was first operational in the Spanish Civil War. The flyers were rotated every six months to provide combat experience for as many crews as possible.

A pilot graduated after a minimum of 200 hours of flight time and rigorous military training. The Luftwaffe pilots became the world's best trained, most fanatical, dedicated, and seasoned fighting machine. They are led by leaders who have fought continually since Spain, Poland, France, or the Battle of Britain campaign. They employ excellent tactics, fly well-tested machines, and the chaps have an obsessive conviction they are invincible.

Some are superb in aerial gunnery and can shoot accurately at 600 yards. These shooters are the only aircraft allowed to fire, while the rest of the squadron provides cover, guarding and firing only when absolutely necessary. The shooter can now completely concentrate on the selection of his victim, reckon the angle of his flight, distance, and speed. This has led to high kill scores for some individual pilots, but leaves the guards more vulnerable, with less experience and ability to defend themselves. Our enemy does not like to meet us on equal terms; he must have the advantage before he will fight. He has the habit of attacking out of the sun with the advantage of height.

The individual Jerry is, as aforementioned, well-trained and an excellent shot and pilot. His leaders are superb; they have been trained and raised along rigid, structured lines, and, as long as combat fits into their predetermined and familiar mould, they fight superbly. But combat is notorious for unexpected eventualities, and this is where they get into trouble. There are exceptions to the rule, but most Germans lack an instinct for unexpected attack; they cannot do the unpredictable and catch their opponent off guard.

Germany entered the war with an overwhelming air supremacy. They had more and better aeroplanes than any other nation on earth. The star performer was the Me 109, whose worth was proven during the Spanish Civil War. It was as fast as the Spitfire; it could out turn it. The Germans take full advantage of their more powerful engines. The Luftwaffe fighter tactics call for a dive from superior height - a diving pass on and through the more manoeuvrable foe. Now the enemy has another fighter superior to the 109, the FW 190. It is clearly superior to anything we have at this time.

The Luftwaffe on the Western Front is composed of two crack wings, the JG-26 and the JG-2. The JG-26 is an elite group which is also known as 'The Abbeville Kids', 'The Yellow Nose Boys' or 'The St Omer Boys'. The noses of their aircraft are painted yellow, and these pilots are some of the most successful and skilled aces in the history of aerial warfare. Most wear the Knight's Cross, one of Germany's top decorations. In fact, the Knight's Cross is so prevalent it's as if it was their squadron badge. To remain in the outfit, each man has to shoot down a certain number of planes and keep on shooting them down. Some of the formidable aces spawned by the unit include Adolf Galland, with 104 victories, Egon Mayer with 102 victories, Whilhelm

Galland with fifty-five victories, and Werner Moelders with 115, including fourteen in Spain.

Peters finished by relating the purpose of the OTU.

We will teach you how to fight an air battle. That is your business and you must know it well. But this knowledge is worthless unless you act decisively, instinctively, and fast. We will teach you all the ramifications of the Spitfire and its armament. When the course is completed, you will be able to go find the beggars and clobber them out of the sky.

The OTU program initiated mutual support tactics as practised and proven in combat by the R.A.F. The insistence on perfection resulted in an aggressive, well-tempered fighting squadron, finely tuned to the anticipated conditions of actual combat. The pilots were encouraged to engage one another in simulated individual combat as well as flight combat.

During this time Don learned radio-telephone communication and perfected and gained additional skills in flying. The training course was tough, to say the least; however, Don did well and enjoyed every minute of it. Aerial and ground gunnery were other new skills he had to master. But he welcomed the challenges as a reminder of the purpose of his training, and recognised each as an important factor in his becoming an ace on June 9, 1942, Don completed the No. 57 OTU course. He was assessed above average as a pilot, average in gunnery. He rushed to the unit bulletin board to see where he had been posted. All the pilots but two received combat assignments. Don's heart sank as he read his posting as an instructor at one of the flight training schools. He was stunned, but at first the blow did not register too deeply. He turned and groped his way through the crowd, then wondered if he had somehow misread the posting. He returned to look at the board again. He had not misread it. All his hopes and aspirations had been geared to being a combat pilot and achieving acehood. Now he became obsessed, convinced that some terrible mistake had been made. Angry and frustrated over this obvious error, he returned to his quarters to contemplate his course of action. He prayed for divine guidance.

Next Don went to the office of Wing Commander J. Farmen to personally plead his case for a combat squadron. Patiently the commander listened to Don's earnest pleadings. The C.O. had heard similar arguments before but as he raised his eyes to the young pilot officer's, he thought he had never seen anyone look so desperately miserable over an assignment. 'I am sorry, Pilot Officer Gentile,' he said quite fatherly. 'We both know we need more good instructors to get the R.A.F. wings up to full strength with well trained fighter pilots. You have shown a strong proficiency for flying, and our staff feels you have a great potential as an instructor.'

'Sir, I joined the R.A.F. to fly in a fighter squadron, not to be an instructor. I appreciate your confidence in me as an instructor, but I am afraid I'd be a complete fizzle at the job itself. I'd like to get out of the assignment.' Don's voice was low, and he sounded close to tears.

Farmen leaned back in his chair and looked the boy over for a moment. 'Pilot Officer,' he started, sadly. He fiddled with his pen, screwing and unscrewing the cap. His face changed and began to harden. He then gave Don a long stare and said, 'Pilot Officer, we assign positions in the best interest of the air force, not the individual. Your request is denied. Good day.'

Seemingly resigned, Gentile began teaching his students some of the important things he had learned in his training to become a fighter pilot. He taught them everything he possibly could, and worked them and himself hard, but he still could not suppress his longing for combat. He was getting so restless he would have almost volunteered for the Luftwaffe, if necessary, to get away from the training school.

His joining the R.A.F. to become a combat fighter pilot was based not on bravado but on a very sincere desire to become a someone - an ace - to make a name for himself across the skies of Europe and go home a somebody - to get a good civilian job - to make something of himself. This was his mission in the beginning, was now and would always be. This desire was all consuming, always on his mind, day and night. The only way he could relax and get away from it all was to go up in a fighter and do aerobatics.

One Sunday morning, while flying his Spitfire to let off steam, Don saw a stadium with a dog race in progress. As he circled he became fascinated by the activity. He, had never seen greyhounds run but had read about the sport.

At the start of the race, eight greyhounds were placed in individual stalls in a starting box. A mechanical rabbit was started around the quarter-mile oval sand track. Most of the dogs began to rock back and forth, waiting for the lid to open and free them. When the lure was opposite the starting box, a red-coated man on a white horse gave a blast on his silver horn, the doors of the stalls opened, and the dogs were out and running.

Each greyhound seemed to have his own preferred pattern of running. Some were sticking to the rail, some running ten feet out, others circling so wide they seemed to skim off the outside fence. There was one beautiful creature that would hug the rail on the straight-away but would go wide on the turns. As one dog tried to pass, the leader turned his head and fought him off as best he could in his racing muzzle. By the time the dogs rounded the last turn, the fans were all standing and cheering.

A thought struck Don. With hardly a pause, he pressed the stick to the right;

a touch of the right rudder and he had completed a wing over and was heading at grass-top level towards the stadium. Up one side and down the other, he roared at grass-clipping level. The spectators in the stadium panicked and ran in all directions. The greyhounds scattered all over the park, some yowling, some jumping the fences, but all sprinting faster than the mechanical rabbit.

The man on the white horse defiantly stared, shook his fist, and gave a blast on his silver horn. Then he jumped from his mount and ran like a scared rabbit seeking shelter. Don chuckled as he circled high above the stadium; he had a panoramic view of the entire field. He continued to circle until all had found shelter except the mechanical lure. It continued undaunted, zipping around the track.

Don had heard that as punishment for disobedience or wrongdoing, pilots were often sent forward to combat units. The desire to become an ace was so important to him, he had decided to risk being court - martialed by deliberately getting himself into trouble.

When Don returned to base and landed, he was not surprised to be ordered to report immediately to the office of the base commander. The adjutant led him into the commander's office, and as Don approached the desk he saluted smartly and stood braced at attention. Ignoring Don's salute, the C.O. dismissed the adjutant with a motion of his head and continued examining the records before him. Gentile unobtrusively lowered his right hand to his side. While he waited his eyes wandered around the room, finally pausing at the clock on the wall behind the C.O. Three more minutes had passed. Sweat began to bead his forehead.

When at last the C.O. glanced up and nailed Don with a furious look, Don knew he was in trouble - deep trouble - and wished he had not buzzed the dog track.

'Stand at attention, Pilot Officer,' thundered the C.O. Don snapped to and remained at attention.

'Gentile,' he said, speaking slowly. 'Your file shows you have excellent qualifications as a pilot. On paper you also appear to have the making of a highly skilled instructor. But this morning you have demonstrated to all, beyond a shadow of doubt, you do not have the proper temperament to be an instructor.' The C.O. began to pace the floor, his eyes still riveted on Don's. Don turned pale and drops of sweat rolled down his temples. He began to wonder if his grand plan was such a good idea after all.

At last, after what seemed an eternity, the C.O. pressed a buzzer on his desk and the adjutant reappeared. 'Place Pilot Officer Gentile under arrest and in confinement until we dispose of this bloody matter.'

Don was locked in a ten-foot square wooden cage which was used for solitary confinement in disciplinary cases. The facility was located in the west corner of the main hanger, quite visible to all at the base. Its walls and ceiling were constructed of spaced wooden slats. The cell contained a cot, a sink, a water closet, and a table and chair.

He sat for hours in the chair, his back straight, his ankles crossed precisely under the desk, and his hands folded on the very centre of the desk top, as if symmetry might make him less conspicuous, while the students and base personnel filing through gave him long, expressionless stares. He was not allowed to speak to anyone or to receive visitors, except the guard who brought him his three meals each day.

The emotional strain from the uncertainty of his position finally was too much for him. The fear that he had travelled so far only to have his hopes and aspirations reach such an ignominious end was more than he could stand. In a flash, he kicked in the door of his cell and strode boldly, unannounced, into the c.o.'s office and spoke his ultimatum.

'Sir, I am an American citizen. I ask that you either court-martial me and send me to the Eagle Squadron, or put me on the next boat for home.'

The C.O. sprang to his feet and yelled for the adjutant. There was a bang of a chair overturning, and the adjutant opened the door. 'Convene the board for a court-martial at once, and escort this prisoner back to his confinement! By God, we will court-martial you! Get him out of here!'

When Don took the stand at his court-martial, he was conscious of the faces of the three judge-officers looking up at him, of their eyes concentrating on him. Curious eyes, unfriendly eyes. Don felt terribly alone. He had sat at the defendant's table throughout the proceedings with silent composure. Now he stood facing the court, and it was his turn to respond to these serious charges. He earnestly and unhesitatingly told them the truth of why he buzzed the dog track. It was a gamble, but as the story unfolded, the judges listened intently. In the end, it was his fervent sincerity which won them over as he argued to be sent to a combat unit, preferably the Eagle Squadron.

The court saw the strain in Gentile's face dissolve into elation for the first time when the results were announced. 'Post Pilot Officer Gentile to a combat unit immediately. That is all, Gentile.'

Don saluted, about-faced and left. As the door closed behind him he felt physically ill. He stood in the outer office for a few moments in order to regain his composure. He slowly became aware of the personnel there, all studying his agitation. He was sure they had heard the proceedings in the other room. Embarrassed, he glanced around the room, and as his eyes met the others, they turned back to their office work. All but one. He was a sergeant whom Don had previously befriended and confided in his desire for a combat posting. Smiling, the sergeant said, 'Congratulations, sir. Good show.' The others stopped working and stared, bewildered, not comprehending the why of what he had said.

Don hurried back to his quarters to pack. Filled with jubilation, he saluted every object in sight, repeating each time, 'Thank you, sir. Jolly good show.' As he approached the building, he affectionately padded the breast pocket where he always carried the one-inch statuette given to him by Sister Teresa.

Gentile's new assignment was the 133rd Squadron of the Eagle Squadron at Beggin Hill. The Eagle Squadron was composed of the 71st, 121st, and 133rd Squadrons of Great Britain's Royal Air Force in World War II. The formation of this all-American elite fighter group was the brainchild of two men, Charles Sweeney, a very successful businessman living in England, and his uncle, Colonel Charles Sweeney, a famous soldier of fortune from Salt Lake City, Utah.

No. 133 Eagle Squadron, R.A.F., gathered at the Beggin Hill Airfield, Kent, England, June 10,1942.

Rear row (left to right): Leonard T. Ryerson, George H. Middleton, Richard N. Beatty, Ervin L. Miller, Dick D. Gudmundsen, Donald Lambert, Don S. Gentile, J.M. Emerson (Intelligence officer), F.J.S. Chapman, M.D., D.G. Stavely-Dick, Grant Eichar, Chesley Robertson. Front row (left to right): Gilbert Omenus, Edwin D. Taylor, Bovurn C. King, Squadron Leader Eric Hugh Thomas, Donald Blakeslee, George B. Sperry, Eric Doorly, K.K. Kimbro, Willom H. Baker

They envisioned this all-American unit in the R.A.F. much as the Lafayette Escadrille, where Americans had served in the French air force during World War 1. The 243 volunteers came from all parts of America and ranged in age from fourteen to thirty-eight. They were the first Americans to wage war against Hitler. During the two years the unit was active in combat, almost one-third of them were killed fighting 'someone else's war,' while their contemporaries back home were content to hang around the corner drug store and girl-watch.

Part Two
Eagle Squadron

June 22, 1942 - September 16, 1942

On June 22, 1942 Gentile went on his first combat mission to Boulogue, France. The post loudspeaker called all pilots to the briefing room, a small masonry structure much like a classroom. Wooden benches faced a platform with various maps arranged above it; the side walls were hung with silhouettes and photographs of the enemy aeroplanes. At the back of the room was a movie projector used for showing the cinefilms from the gun cameras. As the pilots entered the room, a noncom tacked coloured ribbons to the map. The ribbons extended from the base to Boulogue.

After all the pilots were seated, someone at the back of the room called out, 'Attention!' The pilots rose as the wing commander and the squadron leader walked down the aisle carrying maps and typed instructions from Fighter Command. Once they reached the platform, everyone sat down again.

The briefing began with the information the pilots would need for the Boulogue operation. The approach to the target was laid out, but because the enemy constantly changes the location of their antiaircraft guns, balloon barrages, and fighter aircraft, they are allowed some flexibility.

The wing commander now calls for a time tick (the calibration of the pilots' watches). 'When I say okay, it will be exactly 12:14.' The pilots synchronise their watches. 'The 71st Squadron will take off at 14:14, the 121st at 14:20, and the 133rd at 14:27. Good luck and good hunting.' As he leaves, everyone rises to attention. The commander is followed by the weather officer, who describes the atmospheric conditions as a hot fine day with a fair breeze. He reminds them to dress properly because the temperature at 22,000 feet is fifty degrees below zero.

The planning is over now. A tense immobility and quietude settles over the room, and the room fills with tobacco smoke. A smiling Gentile glances around, then becomes solemn when he observes that some of the pilots are quiet. They stare at the cigarettes they hold, watching the twisting smoke dance lazily up towards them. They play with them in their fingers, turning them every which way, studying them but not really seeing them at all.

Don sits quiet and expressionless, but inside he is quaking. His heart is gripped by terror. Oh, how he wants to go home - to sit on his mother's lap.

They board the lorries, and on their way to the squadron's dispersal shack they pass the Spitfires, widely spaced around the field to prevent them from being destroyed in a single attack. For added protection, each aircraft is standing in a blast shelter consisting of three solid block walls.

Gentile can hear the crew chiefs warming the engines. The pilots enter the shack and head for their lockers to don boots, Mae Wests, and flying clothes. They put on their parachutes and leap into their planes. There is a slight ground haze, but the sky is clear. They taxi their planes into position on the runway for takeoff.

They are nervous now as they wait, like the relay runner waiting to take over the baton. Later, when their time to carry the action comes, they will be calm. But now they are tense and nervous as the long lines of idling planes wait. At 14:27 the 133rd is given the order to take off. Don pushes the throttle forward and trundles awkwardly across the flight line, swinging his Spitfire from side to side. This manoeuvre is necessary because the long high nose of the Spit makes forward vision impossible. As he moves along he leaves behind a small cloud of blue smoke. His speed gradually increases until his tail is up as he passes the control tower. Airborne, he feels sweat rolling down his forehead in cold rivulets. He begins praying and talking to himself. 'Okay, squirt, take it easy. You will be all right.' He is flying as the wingman to Flight Lt. Colby King. Colby, a bald, heavy-set, former Lockheed test pilot in his thirties, is one of the most experienced pilots in the squadron.

'Don, combat flying does not mean you have to be a redhot pilot,' Colby reminds him. 'Seventy-five percent of combat is in the eyes. An inexperienced pilot's greatest battle weakness is the inability to see. Even the most experienced pilots only see seven or eight percent of what goes on in aerial warfare. Everything happens so fast that the brain cannot register it fast enough. A diving plane at 600 miles an hour goes by so fast it is gone before the eye can see it and register it on the brain. If your eyes, reflexes, and co-ordination are good, then you will have little to worry about.'

Colby asked, 'Don, have you heard of Sailor Malan?'

'No, I don't believe I have. Who is he?'

'He is a South African who served in the Merchant Navy before enlisting in the R.A.F. in 1935. He was nicknamed Sailor as a reminder of his nautical days. He was a survivor of the Battle of Britain and authored the R.A.F.'s ten rules for air fighting:

1. Never fly straight and level for more than thirty seconds in a combat area.
2. Always keep a sharp lookout for enemy fighters. Keep your finger out and your head on a swivel. Watch for the enemy in the sun.
3. Height gives you the initiative. Don't waste it.
4. Always turn and face the attacking enemy.
5. Make your decision promptly. It is better to act quickly even though your tactics are not the best.
6. When diving to attack, always leave a portion of your formation above to act as top cover.
7. Wait until you see the whites of your enemy's eyes. Fire short bursts of one or two seconds, and only when your gun sight is definitely on the target.
8. While shooting, think of nothing else. Brace the whole of your body, have both hands on the control stick, concentrate on your gun sight and the target.
9. Go in quickly, punch hard, and get out.
10. Initiative, aggression, air discipline, and teamwork are words that mean something in air fighting.

'Don, I think you should learn these ten rules. They will come in handy.'

'I certainly will.'

'Now stick to me, kid, until you learn and gain your confidence; I'll take care of you if you keep on my wing.' As they climbed into the sky, Don pulled the wheels up, adjusted the pitch control back, and set the throttle for a climbing speed of 200 miles per hour. He closed the hood and started feeling claustrophobic.

He was flying in the safest spot - in the centre of the pack and surrounded by protective planes. He stayed glued to the wing of King through all the dives, twists, and turns. The only thing he saw was King's wing, but when he got back to base, he found out that some of his squadron as well as the enemy had been shot down.

Don was disgusted with himself and not very proud of his performance. Never in his life had he been so ashamed. He sat on the edge of the bed, cupped his head in his shaking hands, and quietly talked to God. He prayed hard for God to give him strength to endure this ordeal with courage - to help him to complete his lifelong mission. After a while he began to feel a strange internal peace, and slowly he began to regain his self-confidence.

Don flew a series of missions as King's wingman. He did exactly as Colby had told him, sticking so close that only a few yards separated their two aircraft. He felt he had little to worry about with Colby flying interference for him. He had so much confidence in Colby's getting him through safely that he never stopped to consider what he would do if he suddenly found himself without him. He was to find out on his eighth mission.

On July 31, 1942, the 133rd Squadron, flying with the 72nd and 65th Squadrons of the Royal Canadian Air Force, acted as return close escort and bottom squadron to twelve Boston bombers[1] detailed to bomb Abbeville Aerodrome. Sclageter JG-26, the Abbeville Kids, was stationed there; they had nine squadrons of fighters based at various airfields in the Abbeville area.

The R.A.F. felt the bomber was the ultimate instrument of air power, and the fighter, when used to assist the bombers, was merely a means to an end. There were two methods by which fighters could protect the bombers. In the first, squadrons of fighters, some sixty to one hundred miles away and usually out of sight of the bombers, could sweep ahead of and behind the bomber force. These fighters had complete freedom to pursue the enemy and were called bomber support by the fighter squadrons.

The second method, bomber escort, was done within sight of the bombers. The close-escort fighters are nearest to the bombers, never allowed to leave and pursue the enemy, while the escort-cover squadrons protect the close-escort fighters and the bombers, some being allowed to chase the enemy. When there was a likelihood of severe opposition, they would use high-cover and top-cover squadrons for protection, with some of them permitted hot pursuit.

The 133rd Squadron disappeared into the mists of the approaching day. Don roared over the treetops of England with the rest of the squadron, hell-bent and enemy-bound. After they gained altitude and formed up with the rest of the group, he relaxed somewhat. Since the Battle of Britain, with the German's excessive aircraft and pilot losses, the enemy was staying near to their home airfields. The R.A.F. was forced to carry the battle to the enemy, daring him to rise and fight. At the beginning, he did, but as his losses mounted, he knew he could not sustain them; he ignored the British planes by sitting on the ground and watching them fly around, using up their fuel.

It was decided by Bomber Command a Ramrod[2] would force the enemy to action. If he remained on the ground, the bombers would demolish his airfield. If he engaged in combat with the bombers, he would have to face the destructive force of the Spitfire fighters.

German commanders faced a dilemma when they had to decide how to respond to these minor raids. The Luftwaffe had little chance of winning a prolonged battle with the growing Allied fighter forces, but it was bad for the morale of the German pilots and a source of encouragement to the French civilian population if every such raid was ignored. If the Germans did choose to engage, however, they knew they were falling in with Allied wishes and fighting partly on their enemy's terms.

Don enjoyed a particular thrill as they flew low over the silvery English Channel, the water coldly beautiful. Midway across the Channel, he began twisting his head from side to side, keeping a watchful eye for any enemy. Visibility was unlimited and the sky seemed an infinity of blue; what a beautiful hot July morning. It was breathtaking.

Today Don was flying a Spitfire Vb, serial number BM 530; he preferred it to the older IIs they had flown in training because it had improved lateral manoeuvrability. He thought the 'b,' with its two 20mm cannons and four machine guns, would create more devastation than the 'a' with its eight .303 inch machine guns. Although the number of guns on the latter was exceptionally high and each had 300 rounds, the weight of fire was light rifle-calibre ammunition lacking the destructive power of shell-firing cannons.

They were now crossing the French coast, jinking[3] their aircraft and avoiding the cities that harboured most of the flak[4] guns. Don felt relaxed as he played follow-he-leader to Colby, enjoying the beauty of the French coast and enemy held territory. Suddenly he was shocked back to reality when the tranquil silence was broken by a frantic cry of, 'Flak! Flak

Squadron leader Thomas called, 'Whoever is yelling, stop it and stay off the radio! Only report enemy aircraft sighted and enough of that damned chatter.' Radio discipline was critical on combat missions. When someone was transmitting it meant the channel could not be used by anyone else, and once the R/T[5] silence was broken, the enemy would be aware of both their presence and location.

They had been slowly climbing and gaining altitude since their rendezvous with the Boston bombers in mid-Channel, and now were at 30,000 feet and settling down for the penetration into France. Because of their greater speed, the Spitfires would twist and weave around the bombers in pairs in order to stay in position.

According to British intelligence, the Abbeville Kids were being led by Major Gerd Schopfel. They had been issued the FW 190 A-3[6] in May. The 190 could react quickly for its size to any control commands. Fast, it could climb and manoeuvre with the best of the British aircraft and had an awesome gallery of firepower. It was operated almost entirely by push buttons; with the push buttons you could retract the landing gear and flaps and provide trim. A real sweet bird.

The twelve Boston bombers had a very successful run on Abbeville. As the squadron formed up on the bombers for the return trip, Don noticed what appeared to be the biggest and darkest thunderclouds he had ever seen in the vicinity of the airfield. The centre of these ugly clouds was pitch black, and the

Bombing of the Abbeville Aerodrome, home of the infamous Luftwaffe Sclageter JG-2600, the 'Abbeville Kids.'

sight of them made cold chills go down his spine; they had a frightening appearance. As they got closer to the base, he realised the clouds were not a natural arrangement of nature but a result of the Bostons' attack.

The base was a blazing shambles and the cloud formation was a result of a petrol dump[7] burning on the edge of the field.

Don heard excited quacking over the R/T. 'Bandit at six o'clock! Watch out Carter...two are trying to get on your tail! Break! Carter, break! They're coming in for the attack!'

Don was flying scared and excited on King's wing when...fruuump!...and an FW 190 went past him. He felt rather than saw him go by and when he looked to see where he had come from, he saw another FW 190 shooting down a Spitfire. The sky was full of the enemy. Suddenly eight Germans bounced them from the rear, while six came at them head-on.

The enemy opened fire and serpentine tongues of incandescent tracers licked around Colby's starboard[8] wing. Black smoke began pouring out of the engine and cockpit. Don could see Colby writhing in his seat, jerking his head frantically from side to side, trying to get away from the flames. The next instant there was a tremendous explosion and King's aeroplane blew up before Don's eyes.

Don shook off a near-overpowering urge to just sit and watch, as if mesmerised, without taking any action. As large chunks of fuselage and wing hurtled past him, he fought his nausea at the stench of death in the air and swerved instinctively and sharply to avoid the debris. Don found himself alone, without anyone to help. A gaggle[9] of Abbeville Kids surrounded him, figuring he was easy prey.

One of the Focke-Wulf fighters was getting ready to position himself on Don's tail. Panic! Don pushed his stick hard over and then back toward his gut and went into a deep, spiralling dive. Sky and threads of clouds went racing by. The orbit became tighter and tighter and his speed faster and faster. His guts slithered into his flying boots. He kept spinning, controlling his altitude with his rudder pedals. He continued spinning, crazily whirling through space like a centrifuge. The plane began to shake and strain and to vibrate from stem to stern. Don's body became heavier and his head lighter, until he felt as if he would lose consciousness. The world around him went black.

He had started the dive at 27,000 feet and when he came to he was at 4,000 feet. Reflexively, he kicked a rudder against the spin, the rotation ceased, and he went into an accelerated dive. The wings, shattered tail, and other parts of a Spitfire went spinning end over end past him looking like amputated limbs, as he continued his dive.

He cut his throttle and eased the stick back gently. Sweat bathed his hands and forehead and trickled down his back. His temples were throbbing and his chest pounded with every heartbeat. He pulled back slowly, easing the throttle forward, and the strains and vibrations of the aeroplane stopped. When he came out of the dive, he found himself flying just above a forest and a lake that stretched through the countryside. Miraculously, not a German had followed him. Either the enemy could not physically take the dive, or, when they saw him spinning down, they assumed he had been hit and was going to crash.

When Don got down on the deck,[10] he realised he had lost the enemy. He headed for England and landed at Gravesend.

From this flight three did not return.

The 133rd Squadron suffered a disaster. Three men were killed: Flight Lieutenant Colby King of Hollywood, California; Carter W. Harp of Columbus, Georgia, a veteran of nine months and one of the most experienced flyers in the Eagle Squadron; and Grant E. Eichan of Elgin, Illinois.

Jessie Taylor had narrowly escaped death but was severely wounded. Taylor had destroyed one FW 190 and damaged one Messerschmitt 109 F. Pilot Officer W.H. Baker also destroyed an FW 190. One of the leading German pilots on the Western Front at that time, credited with fifty-two kills, Lt. Col. Rude Planz was shot down and killed.

During the combat Gentile was too busy looking after himself to think about anything else, but when he returned to the airdrome his mind began to work.

It had happened!

As he walked towards his quarters he removed his helmet and a light wind ruffled his thick black hair, now matted with sweat. Don's dark, usually bright eyes were glazed and his young face like a gaunt mask, as if he had suddenly aged. He passed his fingers through his hair and rubbed his eyes. He stroked his cheeks where the oxygen mask had chafed them.

He threw himself on his bed, and as he lay there his hands began shaking. He closed his eyes and in his mind there flashed a vivid picture of disintegrating aeroplanes, white dots of chutes in the sky, and the sound of frantic calls for help on the R/T. He was not proud of today's performance, but he had got away - he had survived. He had cheated death once again, and Don began to thank God for saving him. As usual, the act of prayer helped to restore his self-confidence. Even if he could not keep pace in this game of death, at least he had a chance to go along with it - to survive it.

His thoughts turned to his friend and mentor Colby and his other dead comrades. For a long time he prayed for them as he stared at the ceiling over his bed. Everything that was pent up inside him...the loss...the fear...the frustration...the humiliation at being unable to save his comrades...all at once it all let go. He turned his head and buried his face in his pillow.

On February 14, 1942, the British issued a new bombing directive. It stated that the aims of the air offensive would focus on the morale of the enemy civil population and, in particular, the industrial workers. They would use the 'Douhet Theory'[11] to destroy the morale of the enemy.

In two years of war, the British had not only failed to make any real inroads in Germany's strength, but occasionally had been badly mauled themselves. In December, the Japanese attack on Pearl Harbor had brought the United States into the conflict. Now, not only was there additional manpower but the industrial might of the United States as well, to aid in bringing the enemy to submission.

The British air staff's belief in strategic bombing was assailed on all sides. The Navy wanted them to protect the coastal shipping, not only in Britain but in other theatres. Pressure from the other service branches continued to intensify until a March 30, 1942, report analysing the German attacks on British towns was released.

The report showed that one ton of bombs could make 100 to 200 people homeless. Based on an average operational life of fourteen sorties, a bomber could drop forty tons of bombs. The conclusion was that one bomber, during its lifetime, could make between 4,000 and 8,000 people homeless. It also informed that twenty-two million Germans were living in fifty-eight cities with a population over 100,000. The bombers, with only half a bomb load, could therefore render a third of the German population homeless. It further contended that this would ensure the moral collapse of the enemy and force him to sue for peace.

In the summer of 1940 talks had begun between the United States and the British to determine a co-operative arrangement in conducting the war should the United States enter. It was agreed that Europe was the critical area, and a combined bomber offensive was envisaged. At that time the R.A.F. advised the U.S. of their experience in unescorted daylight bombing: In three months they had lost twenty bombers. The Germans also had suffered heavy losses in daylight raids in the Battle of Britain. Both had turned to night bombing, which, because of the lack of accuracy and navigational techniques, still kept losses at a very high level.

The United States was determined to mount their offensive in daylight. This perturbed the British; they thought it was a squandering of the flower of American youth in a type of operation that experience had shown to be unwise. Despite such warnings, the U.S. believed the B-17 bomber, armed with ten strategically placed .50 calibre machine guns and able to operate at high altitudes (20,000 feet or more), would be able to defend itself from enemy aircraft and fly high enough to be out of the effective range of most of the German antiaircraft defences.

On February 20, 1942, a Douglas DC-3 transport landed in England with seven American Air Force officers, travelling in civilian clothes. Their leader, Brigadier General Ira C. Eaker, was no stranger to Britain and had spent a great deal of time in previous years studying the R.A.F.'s combat operation.

Despite their opposition to daylight bombing, the British from the beginning placed their facilities, experience, and personnel at the disposal of the Americans. One of the first acts of hospitality was the setting up of a headquarters for them in a former girls' boarding school at High Wycombe, Buckinghamshire.

'Pinetree' headquarters housed the 8th Air Force and was five miles from the R.A.F. Bomber Command headquarters and thirty miles from London. The Eighth was modelled after the R.A.F., both because the British had two and a half years of operational experience against the enemy and in order to facilitate co-operation. The British began constructing and developing, at their own expense, airdromes in East Anglia to the north of London for the American bombers.

The airfields consisted of three intersecting runways, the main being more than 2,000 yards long and the other two a minimum of 1,400 yards each. A fifty-foot wide perimeter track encircled the fifty-yard wide concrete runways. Branching from the tracks were hardstandings for the bombers. The various buildings for mess, housing, and administration were located in the neighbouring countryside in order to minimise damage in case of an enemy aerial attack.

During 1942 the British started construction of a new airfield an average of every three days. When they had completed the total project, sufficient for their needs and ours, they had used enough concrete to build a three-lane superhighway more than 4,000 miles in length. This was a phenomenal achievement considering the state of technology at the time.

By summer the preparation for the movement of the U.S. Air Force to England was well underway. The U.S. bombers and fighters went to Presigue Isle, Maine, on the first leg of their journey. They then headed to Goose Bay, Labrador, on to Greenland, and finally to Prestwick, Scotland.

The fighters did not have a means of navigating over water, so each B-17 escorted four fighters. These aircraft were flown and navigated by inexperienced young pilots in their late teens and early twenties, over a treacherous route, without the instruments and aids we have today. Despite this, the journey was accomplished with a minimum of incidents - less than four percent. The ground crews, gunners, and the support equipment were sent by ship through the enemy-infested North Atlantic.

August, 1942, found the Allies fortunes at a point lower than any other in the war. The Russians had been pushed back to Stalingrad. The Japanese had captured Bataan and were sweeping across the Pacific. The battle-fatigued British waited for a major attack by Rommel's tanks to drive them out of Egypt.

On August 15, 1942, the embryonic Eighth had twenty-four B-17s available for combat. The planned strength of the Eighth was put at sixty combat groups, made up of seventeen heavy, ten medium, and six light bombers; and seven observation, twelve fighter, and eight transport groups: a strength of some 3,500 aircraft.

The Eighth's confidence and determination had to be tested. On August 17, 1942, twelve B-17Es flew the 8th Air Force's first heavy bomber raid to the marshalling yards at Rouen, France. They operated under the heavy fighter protection of the Spitfires from the Royal Air Force. The 133rd Squadron of the Eagle Squadron was part of the fighter umbrella.

Gentile waited in his aircraft as a spare pilot at the field, hoping to replace anyone who might develop mechanical problems and abort. They took off without him.

This initial daylight raid by an American bomber squadron began a 995-day air war against Germany in which the Eighth would drop 4,377,984 bombs and 25,556,978 four-pound incendiaries, a total of 701,300 tons of explosives by 332,645 bombers. They would lose 41,786 men as dead or missing, until there were no more targets. The infantry, in all of the theatres, was the only branch of the United States Armed Services to suffer greater casualties.

The bomber formation was lead by Major Paul W. Tibbets, pilot of the command B-17E. This was his maiden voyage in combat. Three years later his destiny put him at the controls of a B-29 bomber making an even more historic mission, to Hiroshima, Japan, with the atom bomb. His co-pilot was Colonel Frank Armstrong, his immediate superior, and the man on whom the fictional General Frank Savage in the movie 'Twelve O'clock High'[12] was based.

In the second formation, on the aircraft Yankee Doodle, was Brigadier General Ira Eaker, head of the 8th Bomber Command. The aircraft was piloted by Lt. John P. Dowswell. General Spaatz, his staff, and members of the R.A.F. Bomber Command were present for their takeoff.

The bombers and their R.A.F. fighter escort crossed into France near St Valery and located their target ten minutes before release time. The 133rd Squadron and other R.A.F. units criss-crossed protectively above the formation. The twelve bombed at 23,000 feet while flying through light flak1313, but without meeting any enemy fighters.

Three of the bombers dropped 1,100-pound bombs on the locomotive workshop at Sotteville's marshalling .yards at Rouen, the largest railroad switching facility in France. Two thousand freight cars were there. The other aircraft carried 600-pound bombs which were dropped on the Buddieum rolling stock repair shops. At least half the bombs hit their respective targets. The damage to the rolling stock, track, and buildings was insufficient to cause the enemy much concern.

The Germans were caught by surprise, but they soon came to life with their antiaircraft fire, causing slight damage to two B-17s.

Back at the bomber base, the VIPs, thirty-odd pressmen, and the ground crews were sweating out their return. All ears were strained to hear the first drone of engines and then, when they came into view, all eyes strained to see which of their comrades had not made it. A watcher at the control tower shouted that he could see specks at twelve o'clock high[14] from the west. They counted and were relieved to see all twelve bombers had made it. Of the 111 men who flew this first bomber mission up the Seine from the port of Lahavre to Rouen, thirty-one were later killed or missing during the hostilities.

The success of the mission gave renewed vigour to high level precision daylight bombing. Afterwards, the British and Americans started their round-the-clock bombing, with the British raiding at night and the Americans during the day. These raids effectively tied down 900,000 Germans operating radar, antiaircraft, and fire fighting equipment, as well as pilots and the workmen repairing the damage the aircraft had wrought.

The enemy never knew what the bombers' targets were to be, so they had to alert defences for their homeland and all of occupied Europe. The Eagle Squadron, later to become the U.S. Army Air Force 4th Fighter Group, continued to support the heavy bombers until the Allies achieved air supremacy over Germany.

Gentile had tried valiantly to go as a spare, but he missed this mission. Whenever he was not on the board for a mission, he always hoped to muscle in as a spare, praying that someone would abort and make room for him. In the three years he served in combat, he allowed himself only three short two-day passes to London.

He never relaxed his single-mindedness. His determination and drive never wavered during his pursuit of acehood and his desire to return home a hero. He would occasionally irritate one of the other Eagles by his persistence, his eagerness to learn everything about combat flying, or by his serene peace with God. But it was simply that he had confidence in himself; there was nothing blatant or showy about him.

The 8th Air Force had to keep flying missions and get U.S. bombers into action in Europe with immediately favourable results in order to counteract the pressure from various quarters in the United States to send the majority of our airpower to the Pacific. If they had waited until they had several hundred aircraft instead of the small number then at their disposal, the Pacific deployment would most certainly have taken place.

They learned of the target shortly after midnight and started planning the operation: the size of the formation, who would be flying, route of bombers to target, route of fighter escort, and location of rendezvous with the escort and other bombers.

The bomber crews were up before dawn for the briefing and then off to breakfast at the mess hall. After eating they would go to their aircraft and check the bomb loads and ammunition before leaving the base.

Daybreak burst like a bomb right at takeoff time. The bombers began their slow, time-consuming climb to full cruising altitude before leaving the English coast, thereby reducing their vulnerability to enemy flak, and allowing the escort fighters and bombers from other bases time to group and get into formation. As they circled and increased the size of their formation, the air echoed with the full-throated roar of the many engines. They then tightened up their formations and headed out over the Channel. The tight formations allowed each bomber mutual supporting defensive fire. These neophyte raids were confined to German-occupied territory outside Germany, where the German air defence still had a limited interest.

The 133rd Squadron, including Gentile, was joined by the 65th R.A.F. Squadron flying escort to the Forts to Dunkirk. They were making a fairly wide detour inland, when they were attacked at 20,000 feet by ten FW 190s. At once the 133rd Squadron made a 360-degree orbit. The squadron leader, Flight Lieutenant Blakeslee, got behind a 190 and, blasting it with cannon and machine gun fire, caused the pilot to bail out. The other enemy aircraft took off, and no more combat took place. This was the second mission of the Eighth, and once again all twenty-two of the B-17s and their fighter escort accomplished the mission without any losses.

These early raids began General Eaker's three-prong mission plan for the 8th Air Force. First he would destroy the factories, docks, ports, and sheds in which the Germans built their submarines and from which they launched submarine assaults. Next he went after the aircraft factories and munition manufacturing facilities, and lastly their line of communications.

These early raids also pointed out that the flight crews were insufficiently trained. The pilots had little experience in high altitude flying on oxygen or in formation flying. Some of the gunners had never operated a turret in the air, and many of the radio operators could not receive and send

Morse code messages. These partially-trained crewmen were sent into combat due to civilian criticism of lack of action against the enemy.

Another big problem that had not been anticipated was the weather. England was subject to fluctuating high and low pressure areas, creating heavy, banked, cloud-covered skies which frustrated the Eighth's bomber missions. These overcast[15] skies affected aim and increased the danger of collision.

The Eagle Squadron and the other R.A.F. fighter groups were sent up day after day to allow the bomber crews a chance to practice gunnery and rendezvous with escort aircraft.

Each day when Don awoke, he went to the window to check the weather. This particular morning he was up earlier than normal, and as he studied the sky with its heavy overcast he wondered if he should go back to bed or try to cook up a Rhubarb[16].

These low level flights over enemy territory took full advantage of the low clouds and poor visibility, enabling a small number of Spitfires, usually two, to cross the Channel and let down below the clouds over the Continent undetected. The Spitfires would then search for targets of opportunity such as trains, staff cars, aircraft on the ground, and so on.

'I can't sleep all day,' thought Don, 'and when I do get up I'll be doing the same boring things I have been doing for the last few days - playing poker, billiards, or sitting in the mess and joining the usual bull sessions. I could write home but they would not be interested in who is winning in billiards or poker. Besides, they know how I hate to write. No, I have got to get something going. I can't stand this monotony.'

Rhubarbs were usually arranged on a voluntary basis, and Don liked these freewheeling personal shows flown low on the deck. They allowed him to pick his target and operate by instinct, rather than by orders planned by the commanders in a squadron mission.

Most pilots did not care for these flights. They had to contend with the severe weather, and flying on instruments in the overcast for sixty some miles in close formation was nerve-racking, to say the least. Then there was the hazard of making the let down over unknown territory, without accurate information on the cloud depth. And there was the light flak to worry about. Once you leave England, the Germans are tracking your aircraft on their radar. When you break into a clearing, they are ready and waiting with a deadly concentration of flak fire against your attack. The engine of a Spitfire is cooled by a liquid called glycol, held in a small tank under the spinner. If a bullet from ground fire penetrates this tank or the radiator, the engine will either catch fire or seize up in a matter of minutes. Hundreds of pilots have been lost in Rhubarb operations.

Don received permission for a two-man Rhubarb to the enemy-held Continent. As they rolled down the runway the sky was dark, with streaks of blue trying to break through the gloom. When they broke through the overcast over reasonably flat French countryside, they searched for something to destroy - anything that would hurt the enemy's war effort.

They spotted a train travelling at top speed several miles away. Gentile estimated the distance and charged down on it, squeezing the trigger and raking the entire length of the train with a two-second machine gun burst. They jerked up and began a climbing turn to starboard. As they continued to climb Don looked back to survey the damage. The train appeared to be barrelling along with the same speed it had before they strafed it.

They turned to port and attacked again, this time point blank on the engine. Suddenly the train skidded to a stop, the engine blowing steam like a geyser. They circled the train and watched as civilians and soldiers jumped out windows and doorways and ran to the protective cover of ditches and brush in the surrounding fields, looking to hide from the expected bullets. After circling one more time they headed home; they did not want to take the chance of wounding French civilians.

Making a tight turn on the deck, they unknowingly had flown over a flak nest. The air filled with flak of every description, tracers from machine guns and white puffs from exploding 20mm shells flying from all directions. The sky was full of death, and their only escape was to get back into the overcast. Don rammed his throttle wide open, weaved, twisted, and turned as he made for the clouds. His heart was beating wildly as he raced, so low to the ground that the trees and bushes swayed as he passed over them. The German gunners were still pumping away at them with their guns as they slipped thankfully into the clouds. They could hear and feel the concussion of the exploding flak in the darkness of the overcast as they winged their way home.

The English coast came into view and as Gentile checked his map he realised they were several miles off course. Now a new terror gripped his heart, barrage balloons. The steel cables that anchored the balloons could shear a wing off in a matter of seconds, and in this foul weather it was impossible to see them until it was too late. Don corrected his course to lead them inland, away from the areas with the menacing balloons. They hedgehopped and skirted obstacles on the ground until they reached the airdrome.

After landing Don sat in the cockpit for a few seconds to regain his composure as his ground crew came out to meet him. The R.A.F. British crew chief leaped up on the wing and said, 'Are we glad to see you, sir. We were worried about you getting back in this thick pea soup. How did it go?'

'Fine, just fine.' There was no way Don could describe the terror and the relief he felt on this mission. He was glad to get out of the cramped Spitfire cockpit. He always felt crowded in that narrow space; he was broad shouldered and almost six feet tall. Seated on the dinghy and parachute, his forearms rubbed uncomfortably on the sides and his head almost touched the top of the canopy. Boy, what a relief to get out of that aeroplane and on the ground again.

The next day twelve B-17s from the 97th Bomb Group, led by Major Tibbets with Colonel Armstrong as co-pilot, took off to bomb the Longueau railroad marshalling yards at Amiens. They were escorted to the target by twelve Spitfires from the 31st Fighter Group. To confuse the enemy as to which was the main body of bombers, three diversion sweeps were instituted. The first consisted of twelve Spitfires escorting the R.A.F.'s Boulton-Paul Difiant. These aircraft were unique, the only single engine, two-seat, turret-mounted fighter planes to see action in World War II. German fighter pilots would occasionally mistake them for the Hurricane craft, and employ the classic attack from above and behind, only to be promptly greeted by fire from the Difiants four .303 browning guns on the aft turret gunner.

One of the other two diversion groups was the 133rd Squadron led by Flight Lt. Don Blakeslee. Gentile and the rest of the squadron flew over the St Omer area. They did not encounter any combat or casualties. The main body, with eleven B-17s, successfully reached the marshalling yards, a key point in the flow of war materials to the German army in France.

Operation Jubilee

In the spring of 1942, the British and American armed forces were working on various plans to establish a second front. It became increasingly evident that neither the troops nor equipment yet existed to accomplish successfully such an operation. It was thought a reconnaissance in force could obtain the technical information needed to plan it.

The problem was discussed again and again, and everyone agreed to establish a second front. The invading forces had to capture a port in good working condition. It was further felt that one division with two brigade groups in the assault and one in reserve, supported by tanks and naval and air bombardment, could accomplish the task. But no matter how strongly the theory was held, it had to be tested for soundness.

After a thorough evaluation of all the ports on the Continental coast, Dieppe was concluded to be the best prospect. It had an excellent harbour, with rail and roadways to vital inland areas. The initial plan was to avoid a frontal assault and land tanks and a battalion of infantry at Quiberville, six miles west of Dieppe. There Churchill's tanks and troops would defend the high ground Southwest of the port and capture the airfield. Two miles west of the harbour, two battalions of infantry would go ashore; two more would land a mile east of the harbour, with two battalions in reserve in ships off the port.

The tank landings were separated by two rivers and six miles from their objective. If the bridges across the rivers were destroyed, the tanks would be isolated and out of the forthcoming battle. This landing would also alert the enemy and the element of surprise would be lost. It was finally concluded the only plausible plan was a frontal assault with tanks on Dieppe itself.

On June 5, a fateful decision was made to forego the heavy bomber attack. It was thought the debris created from the destruction would prevent the tanks from operating in the streets, and the raid the night before would alert the enemy prematurely.

The troops were originally embarked on July 2 and 3 and sealed aboard ships. They were fully briefed on the raid, but adverse weather conditions delayed it and the troops disembarked. Once these fully informed troops left the ships, there was no way to maintain security and keep the knowledge of the forthcoming raid from the enemy.

The raid was postponed time and time again, either by changes in the plan or while waiting for proper weather. These cancellations were a bitter disappointment to the troops and the planners. There had to be one final change in order to prevent further unforeseeable delays. Three commando units would replace the parachutists, eliminating some of the delays they caused by their sensitivity to bad weather. Now, six weeks later, the operation was on again.

The night of August 18, 1942, 252 ships carrying 6,086 officers and men, primarily Canadians, crept out of the Solert, Shoreham, and New Haven ports. The ships sailed out of these English ports with escort craft and destroyers protecting them until they could later rendezvous with the rest of the armada.

In mid-Channel there was an enemy minefield one hundred miles long by seven miles wide. The mine sweepers cleared a path for the ships to safely pass to Dieppe.

The eleven-mile coastal area would be neutralised by air and sea bombardment. With the commandos, they were supposed to destroy defences and leave before nightfall.

The landing craft passed through the minefields and landed safely at 4:50 a.m. at six selected beaches. As the cover of darkness disappeared, twelve Boston bombers dropped smoke bombs to blind the German gun batteries on the cliffs overlooking the beach and port area. The bombers came in low on the deck and discharged their loads, placing 150 one-hundred pound bombs on the target area. The smoke created a screen some 900 yards long. A light wind drifted the screen into the placements of the German gunners and also carried it out to sea almost five miles, giving the invaders excellent cover.

In accomplishing this mission, the bombers were subjected to intense and accurate flak so effective that nine of the twelve aircraft were severely damaged. Throughout the day the Bostons bombed and strafed the enemy positions in support of the ground troops. The Royal Navy kept up a constant bombardment of the enemy shore positions. The German shore batteries put up a heavy retaliatory fire. As the enemy guns hit the ships, flames shot up, followed by heavy black smoke and sometimes an explosion.

The sky was blanketed with planes diving and twisting, engaged in intense dogfights. As the R.A.F. maintained their protective umbrella, they were flying through a fierce barrage of armour-piercing, incendiary, and explosive flak, with intermingled tracer rounds from the Bofors.

Paul Tibbets led most of the missions during the late summer and early autumn of 1942, even though Frank Armstrong went along. Two days after the Rouen raid they learned their target would be the German Drucat airfield at Abbeville. They started the detailed planning for the mission shortly after midnight. They had to decide on the size of the formation, the route to the target, where they would rendezvous with the fighter escort. There were hundreds of details to be worked out before the mission jumped off.

Tibbets led the 8th Air Force's effort in the Dieppe raid by bombing the Abbeville airfield, thereby keeping the Luftwaffe pinned down and occupied, taking the pressure off the British while the commando troops were completing their attack on Dieppe. They launched twenty-four B-17s and twenty-two reached the target, two having to turn back with mechanical trouble. They caught the Germans by surprise and did a great deal of damage. All twenty-two B-17s returned safely to England.

The R.A.F., with French, Canadian, Polish, and other squadrons, provided a force of seventy-six squadrons, or more than 1,200 aircraft forming an air umbrella over the ships and beachhead. They were to destroy Luftwaffe resistance and to silence German ground fire. The enemy called up air reinforcements from all parts of Belgium, France, and Holland to meet the challenge. The three Eagle Squadrons were a part of the R.A.F. squadrons engaged in this, the biggest combined operation carried out on the European Continent since the evacuation of Dunkirk.

Several days before the raid, Flight Lt. Donald Blakeslee became squadron leader of the 133rd. He joined the squadron in mid-June and had flown thirty-three missions with the group, twelve as squadron leader. A few days before the Dieppe landing the 133rd flew from Beggin Hill to an advanced air base at Lympne near the English south coast, to reduce the flying distance to Dieppe.

They were briefed for the mission in the baronial banquet hall of an abandoned castle by the sea. They listened attentively, almost solemnly, as the commanding officer informed them they would go in before dawn and stay over Dieppe for half an hour. The order was specific; the planes were to remain in the skies over France for a full thirty minutes, even if they were out of ammunition. Anyone returning to base before the half-hour had lapsed would be court-martialed. It was essential that an air umbrella be there to protect the attacking commando forces from the enemy, and it had to be done at all costs.

At 3:00 a.m., Gentile was awakened by the batman[17], who handed him a cup of tea and said, 'Good morning, sir. It looks like a beautiful day for flying. It sounds like they are planning to have a jolly good show today.'

Don hurriedly dressed, and by 3:30 he was having a breakfast of eggs and bacon, toast, canned peaches, and tea. A pilot had to watch his diet carefully, avoiding fried foods, beans or any other gas-producing foods. At extreme altitudes, where the air pressure is eight times less than normal, intestinal gas can cripple a flyer. He enjoyed the fresh eggs, which were very hard to obtain in wartime England.

As he made his way through the darkness to his Spitfire, he could hear the ground crews giving the planes their final checks. He buckled on his parachute, and checked his Mae West and pistol. When he started the Merlin engines of his Spitfire, he told himself he was ready to go on the offensive. He now had the confidence not only to avoid being killed, but also to annihilate the enemy.

Flight Lieutenant Brettell walked over to Don and placed a hand on his shoulder. 'Gentile,' he said, 'there has been a mix-up in the flight plan, and you will fly the second patrol. Nelson will fly your Bm 530 aircraft. Sorry, old chap.' Brettell noted Don's disappointment and the change in his composure. The colour drained from Don's swarthy cheeks and a pained expression appeared in his deep-set eyes.

Operation Jubilee, the Allied beach landing at Dieppe, was now in progress. The 133rd Squadron had been told to be at readiness at 3:50 a.m. to take off for the first patrol. This, however, was not necessary since the Canadian Squadron 65 was assigned the job. The 133rd finally took off at 7:20 a.m. with orders to orbit Dieppe at 7,000 feet and to form an air umbrella to protect the landing party. They took off for their first patrol and flew across the Channel just above the choppy sea so as not to be detected by the enemy's radar. At twelve miles off Dieppe they began the climb to the assigned height of 7,000 feet.

They circled the beach area and could see a heavy pall of black smoke hanging over Dieppe. Blakeslee saw four FW 190s carrying bombs at six o'clock, heading for the ships in the harbour. He called them out and lead the squadron in a dive, engaging the enemy in dogfights. The squadron destroyed two FW 190s and scored one probably destroyed, with all men returning safely to base at Lympne at 8:40 a.m.

Gentile sadly watched the pilots climb down from their aircraft. They were immediately surrounded by the flyers who had missed the first sortie, excitedly asking questions machine-gun style about their encounter with the enemy. They could tell by the broken tape over the gun muzzles and the black smoke around the barrels that they had been fired. Some of the flyers acted the way they always did, outwardly excited and wildly gesticulating, while others tried to cover their excitement by placidly engaging in small talk. All eyes turned as Blakeslee's propeller quit turning. He ripped open the canopy of his Spitfire and said ecstatically, 'Boy, what a day I'm having.'

The whole group wandered over to the refreshment truck manned by the

Women's Auxiliary Air Force. W.A.A.F. members took care of everyday tasks for the R.A.F., such as driving trucks, cooking and serving food, manning switchboards, and crewing for the Balloon Command (whose job it was to raise and lower the barrage balloons over important targets). They served some of the pilots sandwiches and tea, engaging in small talk or innocent flirtations with the men.

Gentile acted the way he normally did, quiet and calm and smiling as usual, but he could feel the strain. He had waited and waited and had flown nothing but those damned forsaken, endless patrols, and now his great chance had arrived and he had missed the first sortie. He tensed; maybe he would not fly at all in this big show? Could that happen? He began to get depressed as he mulled over this new possibility. But once again his despair turned to renewed hope as soon as he began to pray. Shortly the word came down to be ready to take off with Nelson's Spitfire.

The 133rd Squadron took off again at 10:15 a.m. with orders to fly top cover over Dieppe at 12,000 feet. The enemy's fighter support had been light on the first sortie, but the feeling was that the Germans would now realise this raid was a big show and come out in force to protect their turf. The squadron flew low and close to the sea in a fast, tight formation, like a bunch of killers going on - the town, spoiling for a fight. As Gentile looked down on the white-capped sea, he recalled what the older pilots had told him about the hungry sharks that cruised the water over which they flew. He wondered if any of his comrades had become shark bait.

Don mentally reviewed the procedures for ditching into the sea, just in case he might be so unlucky. First, unstrap the safety belt, push back the canopy, and jump clear of the plane. Just before hitting the water, release the parachute so it will not land on top and drown you. The pilot sits on the dinghy, which is packed in the shape of a cushion. He inflates his Mae West by blowing on the attached tubes and detaches the dinghy from the chute. He inflates the dinghy with gas from an attached bottle. He takes the fluorescent dye and pours it into the sea, making a large, green patch, which is phosphorescent and can be seen more easily by rescue ships. The high-walled, pear-shaped dinghy has a repair kit, a flashlight, a whistle, and a red distress flag. The pilot can either lay in the boat and wait to be picked up, or paddle with the square paddles that attach to the hands.

When they reached Dieppe it was like flying through fireworks. The Luftwaffe was out in force. Enemy aircraft from JG-2 in western France, JG-26 in Northwest France and Belgium, JG-1 from Holland and northern Germany, and JG5 based in Norway on airfields in Oslo and the Trondheim area were there, all engaged in the battle. The air above Dieppe was thick with enemy and Allied planes. Don flew through the cluttered wake of this desperate air battle. Disintegrated aircraft were commonplace, and the white dots of parachutes in the air were hardly worth a second look. At 12,000 feet, he had a panoramic view of the fierce fighting. The casino, hotels, and business district of Dieppe were gutted by fire. Canadian troops, with tanks in support, fought their way into the centre of the town. Explosions could be seen all over the area, as the demolition boys went about their work, destroying ammo dumps and strategic targets.

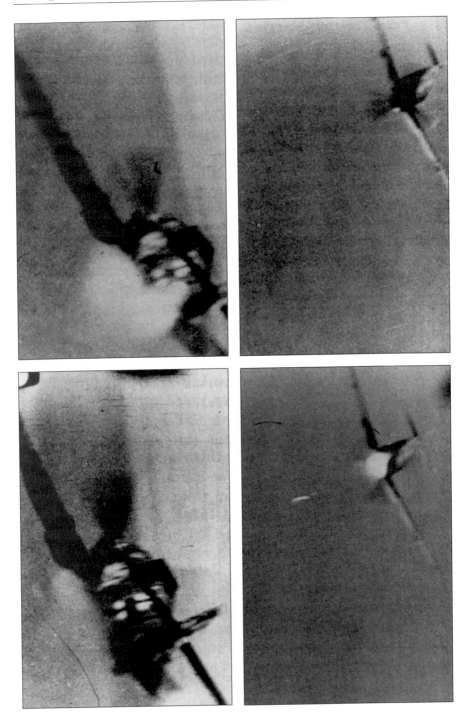

*Gun camera film showing Gentile's first victory over a Focke-Wulf
190 during Operation Jubilee, August 19, 1942. (Clockwise from upper right.)*

Gentile potted two Abbeville Kids in their yellow-nosed Focke-Wulf 190s on the tail of Wing Commander Thomas. He pushed the tit[18] and dove down on them, rolling over to the port and getting on one 190's tail. He gave the enemy a one-second burst of machine gun fire at 300 yards and watched the 190's engine belch black smoke, while parts of the wing and fuselage flew off. He closed to 200 yards and gave a second burst of gunfire. Now glycol could be seen seeping out; this white stream told Don the German could only last a few more minutes. The German pilot headed straight for the beach with Don right on his tail, blazing away. The enemy plane began to smoke badly now and started to roll in a spiralling turn. It finally disintegrated, splashing all over the beach with a tremendous explosion. The other FW ran back toward Berlin like a scared rabbit.

Flushed with confidence and pride and a feeling of invincibility, Don went looking for more prey. He saw a gaggle of Junker 88s[19], one diving toward the beach at fantastic speed, bomb bay doors open to release more death and destruction on the troops pouring from the landing craft. Don dove under, surprising the enemy on his tail, and sprayed him before the tail gunner realised he was there. The startled rear gunner returned the gunfire and began spraying deadly lead all around Gentile's Spitfire. Don returned the fire, as casually as if he was watering the lawn. The tail gunner died immediately; the bomber's wings and motor started smoking profusely.

Left without a tail gunner the bomber was totally helpless; now it was like shooting clay pigeons, and all Don had to do was give it another squirt. As the distance between them shortened, he thought about the poor devils in the bomber. He knew they would be just sitting there, waiting helplessly, waiting for their death. All he had to do was push a button and he would blow away their lives. He broke out in a sweat, and his trigger hand began to get numb; he felt giddy. He vigorously shook his head and snapped back to the reality of the situation. He pressed the button. The enemy aircraft finally rolled over to the starboard, smashed into the ground and exploded, burning on the beach with its crew of four.

Don pulled up sharply to 12,000 feet to give cover to the commandos. He was completely out of ammunition now, and there was nothing he could do except fly around in tight little circles, breaking away from one attack after another, assaulted by Germans anxious for the kill. The seconds ticked by slowly as he circled the combat area. The seconds slowly turned into minutes and finally the minutes formed the half-hour he had to stay over France.

With the throttle wide open, Don now turned and headed, low on the deck, for his home base in England. He circled the base before he started a thunderous dive, then pulled back up and ended with two victory rolls. As he taxied off the runway to the parking area, the ground crew ran out to meet him, waving and jumping up and down as he pulled into the revetment. He was their personal weapon, and he had scored two victories for them. Before the propeller stopped running, the crew leaped on the wing and pounded him on the back, repeating, 'Good show, sir. Jolly good show.'

As the other pilots returned to base, they passed the ships returning with the first batch of wounded. All the aircraft returned and landed safely by 11:35 a.m. As the pilots sat eating, tallying the day's activities, it became clear that their squadron was the star performer, with three destroyed - one Ju 88 and two FW 190s - and seven damaged - four FW 190s and three Do 217s[3] - without any losses.

By midday, all the objectives of the raid were attained, and the withdrawal was carried out only six minutes after the scheduled time. All the tanks and mechanised equipment were blown up before the total evacuation.

Five Boston bombers flew their final mission of the day, braving intense fire from the enemy cliffs in order to lay their smoke down right over the water and cover the withdrawal of the commandos. They went in over the North Beach and dropped their 100-pound phosphorous bombs. They made eleven low-level sorties, laying smoke first by phosphorous bombs and later by a spray that came out in a cloud behind the aircraft. The latter operation was extremely hazardous, because they had to fly straight and level and could not take any evasive action. In the rapidly deteriorating weather, one Boston went down in the sea, while the others, severely crippled, landed at the first airfield they could find.

The squadron was ordered up again at 12:25 p.m. with orders to orbit Dieppe. Nelson took the Bm 530 Spitfire from Gentile for this, the third sortie of the day, when the air battle was the most intensive. The Germans had been waiting for this time, when the troops were concentrated on the beaches for evacuation. The Germans had everything they could muster flying, and their intention was to inflict mass destruction on the troops and ships involved in the reembarkation. The R.A.F., with the 133rd Squadron, kept the Messerschmitts and Focke-Wulf 190s so busy defending themselves they had little time to strafe them.

In the ensuing combat Pilot Officer Nelson, flying the lucky Bm 530, destroyed a Do 217. Pilot Sergeant Alexander claimed a Do 217 destroyed, and Flight Lieutenant Blakeslee claimed an FW 190 as damaged. At this time the evacuation of troops was seen to be in full progress. Large and small boats were being dive-bombed by the enemy, and two ships, one a destroyer, were seen to receive direct hits. All the aircraft landed safely at 1:45 p.m.

Immediately after landing, the ground crews began to repair, inspect, re-arm, and refuel the planes. The strain of the day's missions could be detected in the pilots and ground crews, but that strain was allayed with a buoyant, triumphant spirit. As they were gulping tea and wolfing down sandwiches, the pilots were given orders to go up for a fourth sortie, to provide air cover for the convoys returning from Dieppe.

The squadron took off for the fourth and last patrol at 7:55 p.m. Gentile was given Spitfire Vb EP 167, flown by Pilot Sergeant Slade, because Nelson would also be flying this sortie. They met the armada ten miles Southeast of Eastbourne on the coast of England. The homeward bound ships carried the wounded ahead, the damaged ships limping immediately behind, followed by the Royal Navy deployed far behind, patrolling and guarding their rear. The enemy was about, but not willing to engage in combat. They made only feeble attempts to harass the armada. From high above, Gentile looked down and watched the convoy push its way homeward. Mine sweepers were far out in front. Destroyers were twisting around, leaving queer patterns in their wake. Rescue launches were speeding about, looking for downed pilots. Visibility had, by now, deteriorated considerably and all the aircraft were ordered to return and land. It was a great ending to a perfect day for the 133rd Squadron.

It was very difficult to judge whether the raid was a success or a failure. The military operation was a disaster. Of the 6,086 officers and men, 5,000 were Canadian, 1,000 of whom were killed, 2,000 (including many wounded) were captured, while only 2,000 (most of them wounded) made it back. The naval operation had 550 casualties, with the destroyer Berkeley and thirty-three smaller craft lost. The R.A.F. had 190 men missing or killed, with 106 aircraft destroyed. The Germans had only 591 casualties and forty-eight planes destroyed.

The German bombers suffered heavy casualties and were able to inflict little damage on shipping, but the losses inflicted on the British squadrons made it the most costly single day of the war for the R.A.F. Fighter Command.

Of the enemy pilots, Oblt. Siegfried Schnell claimed five victories, raising his total to seventy, but the hero of the day for the enemy was Ltn. Josef 'Sepp' Wurmheller. Wurmheller had already claimed twenty-two victories during May and June, when he crash-landed following the destruction of several Spitfires. Although he suffered a brain concussion and a broken leg, he got patched up and took off again to destroy a total of seven for the day. Oblt. Egon Mayer claimed his fiftieth victory, and Felduebel Emil Babenz scored three.

The R.A.F. was up against a force of aces and the FW 190 A-3. This aircraft was vastly superior to the Spitfire Vb and gave the Luftwaffe the edge. The Spitfire IX, with a more powerful Merlin engine, was the answer to the FW 190 A-3, but it would not be available in sufficient quantities until the beginning of 1943.

What was the lesson learned from this grim experience? Mistakes were certainly made, and one of the biggest was a frontal assault on a defended port. This was impractical, and the Allies never tried it again. If it was too costly to capture a port, it was decided, then the invaders must bring one with them.

This conclusion fostered the operation to create artificial ports, code-named Mulberry. For D-Day, two such harbors were constructed. Each port consisted of four main components; all had to be towed by some 132 tugboats from England, and then either anchored or sunk in place. These structures were composed of 105,000 tons of steel and eleven and one-quarter tons of concrete, and were several miles long.

Another lesson learned was that they should have put their tanks ashore on a flank, where there were no obstacles to hinder their movement. A school was later set up to teach servicemen how to breach obstacles, even underwater obstructions.

Still other lessons were learned from Dieppe. The plan was too rigid; the absence of parachutists was a mistake, as was the failure to utilise heavy air and sea bombardment. The use of capital ships and heavy bombers in addition to something extra, which would drench the enemy with fire and reduce him to a state of shock, was lacking at Dieppe, but would be needed at the next invasion. It was decided that some of the landing craft would contain two 4.7-inch guns, while others were to carry tanks and artillery and would be constructed so they could fire their weapons during the landing. Perhaps the most brilliant idea was the mounting of 1,000 sixty-five-pound rockets in LCT[20]. It was felt that this certainly would reduce the defenders to babbling idiots.

There were many more lessons learned from the Dieppe raid which saved many lives, not only in the European invasion, but in amphibious landings in the Pacific as well.

That night Gentile had another fitful sleep, tossing and turning until dawn. He thought of home - oh, how he was homesick and lonely for his family. He thought about his buddies back home, what they might be doing, about the simplicity of life in the States, of a girl he knew in Columbus, of what had happened today and what...he...had... done.

It had happened.

His first emotion was one of satisfaction, satisfaction at a job well done, and elation and excitement at his two victories, his start toward acehood. Then, all of a sudden, he felt sick, and a cloud of depression overcame him. He was deeply ashamed for the lives he had taken today, young vigorous lives of men just like himself, whose deaths would be mourned by their loved ones. Oh, how they must hate him for what he had done. This was no game he was playing, but a life and death struggle. He, like nearly all other fighter pilots, was an automaton behind the gun barrels of his aircraft. He never thought about killing an individual, only of shooting down enemy aeroplanes. He had no personal animosity; he would have been delighted to see them bail out and escape with their lives.

But they were dead and he was alive. It could have been the other way around, and somehow that would have been all right too. He was glad he was a fighter pilot, killing the enemy as a duellist - dignified and impersonal. How lucky he was to not be an infantryman with rifle and bayonet, charging the enemy, confronting him eyeball to eyeball, in this fantastic death battle. He was privileged to kill in an impersonal way. He had killed five young men in the prime of their lives, yet he had long ago promised the Lord he would not kill if he could avoid it. He had never realised how difficult that promise would be to keep. Don took out his little statue, placed it on the bed, and got down on his knees to ask the Lord's forgiveness for destroying those lives, and to thank Him for bringing him safely through the day's terrible ordeal.

August 22-August 31, 1942. During this period the squadron was detached to R.A.F. Martlesham for a course of air firing training, and no operational work was carried out.

Blakeslee, the new C.O. of the 133rd Squadron, was demoted and removed as the commander. The demotion was the equivalent change, in American rank, from major to first lieutenant. He was also banished from combat and sent to a training unit to tow targets for recruits in training. The rules in the R.A.F. were strict, and Blakeslee had violated them by entertaining two females in his quarters in the early morning hours.

Morlaix

On September 7, 1942, an operational order was cut requiring three squadrons of fighters to escort the 97th Bombardment Group. The nineteen B-17 bombers were to destroy the railroad yards and Focke-Wulf factory in Morlaix. The 133rd of the Eagle Squadron along with the 401st and 402nd Squadrons of the Royal Canadian Air Force were to rendezvous in mid-Channel and escort the bombers on their mission. The operation was postponed several times because of adverse weather but finally, on September 26, the mission was a go.

They flew the new Spitfire IXs two hundred miles to the English coastal base, Bolt Head. The squadron was the only one flying the Spit IX. They were given them because of the fantastic effort by the 133rd during the Dieppe raid.

Gentile rode his bicycle the mile distance from the BOQ[21] at Sampford to the mess hall. As he rode in the cold, nasty weather he said his rosary aloud. This was a routine he followed religiously whenever he had to fly a mission.

Don attended the mission briefing as the ground crew gassed, armed and gave his new Spit IX, serial number BS 445, its final tune-up. When he was ready to take off, the British air controller came on the radio and said, 'The oranges are sour. To all pilots: The oranges are sour.' This, in R.A.F. code, meant they would experience severe weather. They took off and flew from Sampford to Bolt Head through a grey, murky sky thick with clouds almost touching the ground. The squadron was under the temporary command of Flight Lieutenant Brettell, an Englishman with limited leadership experience whom the R.A.F. had sent to the

133rd to tighten up internal discipline.

The overcast was as solid as a brick wall, and the farther they flew the worse it got. They flew on instruments, and every so often Brettell would let down through the storm to check his location. The clouds seemed to melt into the terrain. They flew on, buzzing over treetops, skirting around church steeples and balloon barrages, in some of the worst weather they had ever seen. Don thought, 'Boy, even the birds are walking.'

It was like a nightmare, and they began to have doubts about Brettell's leadership and his ability to fly on instruments. They thought he was lost most of the time, but eventually they arrived at Bolt Head. Don didn't like the approach end of the runway, which was located at the top of a sheer limestone cliff. He was coming in too fast for a normal landing but he did not want to go around again to try another approach. He lowered his gear, chopped his throttle, put on full flaps, and hit his brakes, finally coming to a grinding halt just short of the end of the runway.

They received a final briefing from the wing commander of the R.A.F. It was supposed to be a routine mission, the same as dozens they'd flown before. They would take off at 4:00 p.m., meet the B-17s at 25,000 feet over the Channel, escort them to the target, and then back to England. The weather officer reported a tail wind of forty-five miles an hour at 28,000 feet with some overcast. This would be routine...no sweat...no problem...duck soup.

The Spit IXs were being fitted with small teardrop belly tanks loaded with fuel that would extend their range. Don sat waiting to take off when Flight Lieutenant Brettell informed him there would be a last minute change. Gentile would be bumped off this mission and his plane would be flown by George Sperry, whose ship had developed some carburettor problems. Don was terribly disappointed he could not go along. He had flown all this way through this incredible weather as a spare, in case someone had to abort the mission. It was the old familiar pattern he followed throughout his combat duty; if he wasn't on the mission he would be ready to go as a spare if needed.

Don had been flying wingman to Brettell, and now he watched sadly from the ground, as Sperry's Spit and the other eleven aircraft slowly disappeared into the overcast. The takeoff had been delayed due to a tire blow-out on Brettell's plane. When they arrived at the rendezvous point, the bombers were nowhere in sight. They combed the area and still no B-17s. Deciding the bombers had missed the rendezvous, they proceeded to the target. As they continued to fly through the solid overcast, they were unaware they were being shepherded along by a 125-mile per hour tail wind instead of the forty-five miles per hour they'd expected. The solid front prevented them from seeing the ground and its reference points. When they arrived at where they thought the target was and did not see the bombers, they decided to turn and head back to base.

They were getting low on fuel, and so Brettell, the acting squadron leader, went down through the overcast to fix their position. Through some mix-up the entire squadron followed him. They came out over a city which they thought was in England but, in fact, was the enemy-held Brest, France. The heavily fortified port city opened up with antiaircraft fire and dispatched its fighter planes. The inadvertent encounter turned into a field day for the Germans, with eleven of the twelve Spits lost. Four pilots died, seven were captured, and one crash-landed in England, out of fuel.

Back in Bolt Head Gentile was sitting by himself on a wooden bench in a corner of the squadron's ready room, while the other pilots lounged about, some reading, some drinking tea, some grouped in corners shooting the breeze.

A small radio had just finished playing a Glenn Miller tune on the Armed Forces Network when a pilot turned to another station and a voice in a precise British accent began the 'news.'

'This is Lord Haw Haw, speaking to you from Berlin.' There was a rustle of reading material being tossed aside and then silence as the pilots' attention turned to the glib voice on the German propaganda network.

'Tonight I bring a special announcement to the few remaining members of the infamous Eagle Squadron. Your 133rd Squadron was, this afternoon, totally annihilated by the victorious Luftwaffe forces. Their bodies are floating in the Channel. Do you American gangsters think you can be successful against the superior race of the Third Reich? Oh, by the way, your gangster cousins from Canada, the 401st and 412th Squadrons of the R.C.A.F, also suffered a disaster. They lost six planes, which gives us a total of twenty-two of the thirty-six aircraft you sent over today. So good luck on your mission. We will be waiting for you.'

All eyes swung to Gentile. Don sat bent over, his head cupped in his hands, in a state of shock. How could this be, the whole squadron, all twelve of the new Spit IXs... incredible.

As Don flew back to Great Sampford, he began to realise how lucky he was to have not gone on this mission. He knew the Blessed Mother had heard his prayers and was looking after him and had spared him once again from death.

Gentile landed at the satellite airfield at Great Sampford. As he walked alone across the grass field towards the wooden huts which were used as officer barracks, he closed his eyes and prayed tearfully to himself. All gone. He was the only one left.

He dragged himself wearily down a dark narrow corridor of the barracks to his room at the far end. He threw his gear on his bed and began walking into the deserted bedrooms. The sight of his comrades' personal effects, a half-squeezed tube of toothpaste, the shaving gear, photographs of loved ones, was more than he could bear. He left this desolate sad scene and returned to his room, slumping onto his bed. He stared up at the ceiling as he tried to hypnotise himself to sleep. Everything was swirling dreamily in his subconscious mind. He could see all the faces of the men who did not return, their neat rooms, their gear, the mementoes of the lives they wouldn't be returning to.

Fear and frustration gripped him, and the same questions kept popping back into his subconscious. 'What am I doing here? Why don't I go home?' But gradually his mind, grasping like a drowning man at a straw, clung to the thought that had sustained him for as long as he could remember. He had to go home an ace and a hero. That was what he had set out to do. That was the destiny he would die trying to fulfil. He got out his flight log and listed the pilots of A and B flights, and made one final notation at the end, 'So long, fellows.' Then he prayed himself to sleep.

R.A.F. t o the USAAF

On December 8, 1941, the day after the infamous Japanese attack on Pearl Harbor, the Eagle Squadron sent representatives to the American Embassy in London to volunteer to fight for the United States. The Ambassador told them that their experience and service would be needed. As soon as possible the squadron would be transferred into the United States Army Air Force. America urgently needed experienced fighter pilots.

It was not until August 22, 1942, that the three R.A.F. Eagle Squadrons were transferred into a new unit, the 4th Fighter Group, and simultaneously into the service of the United States.

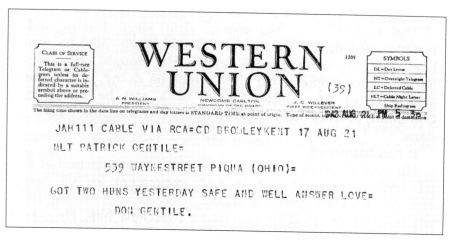

[[?]] On September 16, 1942, Don sent home this telegram:

September 29, 1942 - December 20, 1942

On the cold and rainy morning of September 29, 1942, the Eagles stood at attention on the parade grounds at Debden. This fighter base was located forty miles north of London and fifteen miles south of Cambridge. A unit of the R.A.F. regiment and a company of W.A.A.F.s flanked the three squadrons of Eagles. As the R.A.F. band played a march tune, the enlisted men took their positions behind the Eagles. These airmen were British R.A.F. riggers, fitters, radiomen, and mechanics. They swung their arms straight from their shoulders, and with their heads held high made a smart turn into their respective positions. All assembled faced a reviewing platform where generals of both the English and American air forces stood.

As the rain soaked Gentile's blue tunic, Air Chief Marshal Sir W. Sholto Douglas spoke:

I would have wished that on this, my first opportunity of addressing all three Eagle Squadrons together on one station, that my words should have been other than words of farewell. We, of Fighter Command, deeply regret this parting, for in the course of the past eighteen months we have seen the stuff of which you are made, and we could not ask for better companions with whom to see this fight through to a finish. But we realise as you too must realise that your present transfer to your own country's air force is in the long run in the best interests of our joint cause. The United States Army Air Force's gain is very much the Royal Air Force's loss.

The losses to the Luftwaffe will no doubt continue as before. In the eighteen months which have elapsed since your first unit became fully operational, Eagle pilots have destroyed some seventy-three enemy aircraft - the equivalent of about six squadrons of the Luftwaffe - and probably destroyed and damaged a great many more. The actual official total of destroyed is, I believe, seventy-three and one-half, the half being part of a Dornier shared with a British squadron as a symbol of Anglo-American co-operation. Of the seventy-three and one-half enemy aircraft destroyed, forty-one have been claimed by the senior Eagle Squadron 71 - a record of which they may very well be proud, but one which I understand the other two squadrons are determined will not long remain unchallenged.

It is with great personal regret that I today say goodbye to all you boys whom it has been my privilege to command. You joined us readily of your own free will when our need was greatest and before your country was actually at war with our common enemy. You were the vanguard of that host of your compatriots who are now helping to make these islands a base from which to launch the great offensive we all desire. You have proved yourself fine fighters and good companions and we shall watch your future with confidence.

There are those of your number who are not here today - these sons of the United States who were the first to give their lives for their country. We of the R.A.F. no less than yourselves will always remember them with pride. Like their fathers who fought and died with that American vanguard of the last war, the Lafayette Squadron, so will those Eagles who fell in combat ever remain the honored dead of two great nations.

And now I have some news for you. The Air Council, anxious to give tangible expression to the gratitude which we all feel for the great work you have done, is going to ask each of you to accept a small personal memento of your services to the Royal Air Force. The memento will take the form of a medallion, and though it has not been possible in the short time available to have this medallion struck and ready by today, it is hoped that its presentation will be made in the very near future.

I hope that these emblems will serve as a pleasant reminder of your comradeship with the Fighter Command of the Royal Air Force, a comradeship which we have been very proud to share and which I, as your Commander-in-Chief, shall always remember with gratitude and affection.

Goodbye and thank you, Eagle Squadron of the Royal Air Force. And good hunting to you, Eagle Squadron of the United States Air Force.

General Carl Spaatz, the Commanding General of the 8th Air Force, also spoke: 'The operational experience of the Eagle Squadron is a most valuable asset to the fighter units of the American air force. I welcome you with a great sincerity.'
The band played 'The Star Spangled Banner' and British airmen hoisted the American flag alongside the blue flag of the R.A.F.

The three Eagle Squadrons turned left and marched off the parade grounds. The 71st Squadron was led by Squadron Leader Gregory A. Daymond; the 121st was headed by Squadron Leader William James Daley, and the 133rd by Squadron Leader Carroll W. McColpin. These units became the 334th, 335th, and the 336th Fighter Squadrons of the 4th Fighter Group.

As Gentile headed back to his quarters he thought sentimentally of the passing of his year in the R.A.F. He could not forget that all the services of the United States turned him down because he lacked the two years of college. The R.A.F. had accepted him with open arms, and after he was posted to the Eagle Squadron, four months ago, he had flown thirteen combat missions and destroyed two enemy aircraft. Now he would become a second lieutenant, the equivalent of his R.A.F. rank of pilot officer. The other Eagles who were flying officers would become first

Transfer of the Eagle Squadron from the R.A.F. to the 4th Fighter Group of the U.S. Army Air Force's 8th Air Force. Forefront, left to right: Brigadier General Monk Hunter, U.S. Army Air Force, and Sir W. Sholto Douglas, Royal Air Force.

lieutenants; the flight lieutenants would become captains; the squadron leaders, majors. In his quarters Don changed from his soaked blue uniform to the brown one of the U.S.A.A.F. He studied himself in the mirror. They had sewn the knitted R.A.F. wings over the right breast pocket of his tunic. His new American silver wings and his British decorations were placed over his left pocket.

Another Eagle entered quarters, stopping to study the figure Gentile cut in his new uniform. He found himself also studying the young lieutenant's individual features - his black wavy hair, the handsome and youthful face, the long-lashed dark eyes, his dimples and full lips. It was a stronger face than he had previously realised, almost too good looking. Don reminded him of Robert Taylor, the movie star.

'You look great, Gentle,' he said, calling Don by his affectionate nickname. 'That brown seems to be your colour.'

'Thanks. I'll miss the R.A.F., but not the bubble and squeak[1] for breakfast,' Don laughingly replied.

'Boy, you can say that again. Hey, what do you think of the pay? As pilot officers we got seventy-six dollars, and now we will be getting two hundred and seventy-six. That's a big improvement!'

As Gentile followed the other Eagles from the BOQ, he found himself thinking that they had trained as pilots in the R.A.F. system and technique, and flew Spits with British personnel. He, like the rest of the Eagles, had loved to fly the British Spitfire aeroplane. They had been weaned on this battle-tested, compact fighter which looked and flew like a racer. But rumours said they would soon be piloting the seven-ton P-47 Thunderbolt. They were disturbed that this huge milk-bottle-shaped aircraft would not match the challenge of the Messerschmitts in the deadly contest in the sky. As it turned out, they had a seven-month reprieve during which they would continue to fly Spits. The 'jug' had not yet begun to be ferried from the States in sufficient amounts.

Many changes had to be made. The R.A.F. personnel stayed for several months, acquainting the Americans with the operation of the Spitfire equipment and British Fighter Command. Thirty-nine year old Colonel Edward Anderson, the new American commander, had the most difficult job. He had to retrain the former R.A.F. pilots in U.S. military customs.

The former R.A.F. pilots saluted him in the British style of showing their palms; they marched with their arms swinging straight from the shoulders and with their heads held high, and completed all facing movements by stamping their feet down. He had to go back to the basic fundamentals, instructing them in close order drill, the customs of the service, and acquainting them with the reams and reams of paperwork characteristic of the U.S. Armed Forces.

Weekly since the first flight of bombers on August 17, the 8th Air Force bomber strength had been increasing, becoming most formidable on the 9th of

October. The first full-scale raid with 108 heavy bombers, twenty-four of them B-24 Liberators on their first mission plus seven on diversion, were dispatched to attack two targets in the city of Lille. The targets were the Compaignie de Fives - Lillie, a steelworks, and Ateliers d'Hellemes, a locomotive and freight car factory. The bombers were escorted by a heavy force of fighters, thirty-six Spitfires of the 4th Fighter Group and thirty-six P-38s from the 1st Fighter Group. This was to be the last mission of the First, which was being transferred to the 12th Air Force for the North African invasion, 'Torch.'

Early in the morning the bombers began to climb into a clear October sky. The B-24s were to bring up the rear of the bomber stream. The bomb groups included some inexperienced B-17 and B-24 airmen on their maiden mission.

This was an important mission, the first time the Americans had put more than 100 bombers in the air at one time, something they would not be able to do again for another six months. The lead bomber was flown by Major Paul W. Tibbets.

The Eagle Squadron was now the Fourth Fighter Group of the United States Army Air Force, but their ground crew and commanders were still members of the Royal Air Force.

Gentile and the 133rd took off from Debden at 8:51 a.m. under the leadership of R.A.F. Wing Commander Duke Woolley. They were to rendezvous with seven B-17s at 24,000 feet over Beachy Head for a diversion raid and lead the bombers to Abbeville. The Fourth reached the rendezvous point and joined two British squadrons from Tangmere and two from Kenley, but only three B-17s showed up. Because of mechanical problems, only seventy-nine of the 108 bombers dispatched in the main bombing force made it to the target.

As the Forts got within twenty miles of Dunkirk, Lieutenant Dempsy manoeuvred his B-17 to tighten up the formation. His tail struck the right wing and starboard engines of Lieutenant Wiley's bomber. The force of the impact sheared off the entire tail and pitched Dempsy's Fortress into a steep dive. There was a frantic effort to regain control of the aeroplane. It dove from 23,000 feet until finally it levelled out at 1,000 feet, and they were able to return to base and make a safe emergency landing. Wiley's B-17 jettisoned its bombs and landed at Detling, England.

At Lille, ten B-24s and fifty-nine B-17s bombed their primary targets between 9:30 and 9:48 a.m.; the other ten went on to hit targets of opportunity, including the St Omer Airdrome. The Luftwaffe was out in force. Fifty enemy aircraft made seventy passes at them. A Fortress caught fire and went down five miles south of Lille, with eight of the crew bailing out. These fighter attacks were especially deadly and accounted for a B-24 and two more B-17s going down in the sea.

One of the Forts was on fire and plunging in a 1,500-feet-a-minute dive. The pilot, Lt. Donald Swenson, knew they could not make it to base and would have to ditch in the sea. They hit the water hard, into fifteen- and twenty-foot waves; the crew was pitched around in the aeroplane like so many bowling pins. They managed to free themselves from the craft, which sank in less than one minute. Now they were faced with only one inflatable life raft. Swenson ordered three of the gunners into the raft while two other crew members clung to the sides. The remaining five held on to a partially inflated raft. The violent pitching of the cold sea made their prospects for survival very poor.

The R.A.F. Air-Sea Rescue had heard their Mayday[2] call and within fifteen minutes of the plane hitting the water, they were at the spot trying to pick them out of the frigid sea. The rough waters made rescue very difficult, but after nearly an hour all were finally picked up.

Gentile and the other Spitfires on the diversion mission set their course for France, crossing the coast east of La Treport around Euvermen, then proceeding south of and over Dieppe. They returned six to ten miles off the French coast, passing Berche, La Touquet, and Boulene, and recrossed the English coast at Dungeness. Don spotted FW 190s in the distance, but they were too far away to attack. When they landed at Debden at 9:32 a.m. they discovered there were a large number of aborts, no less than thirty-three, including fourteen B-24s. Four bombers were lost, three B17s and one B-24, and forty-six suffered moderate battle damage. One Fort had more than 200 holes of various sizes from fighter and flak fire.

The bombers and the escort and enemy fighters totalled more than two hundred aircraft engaged in the melee around Lille. Traffic control over the target was terrible; some bombers never even got the target in their sights. Consequently, the bombing was ineffectual.

Throughout the war, the bombers would make greater claims of planes destroyed than were fact. In the heat of battle, more than one gunner would often claim the same enemy fighter shot down. In spite of this duplication, one fact remained: The 8th Air Force bombers could defend themselves from concentrated enemy fighter attacks without exorbitant losses and release their bombs on the target. The fighter escort also assured the Eighth the opportunity to carry out its campaign of daylight strategic bombing. The diversion raids would confuse the enemy's radar as to which force was actually the main raiding party.

As winter approached the 4th Fighter Group became part of the 8th Air Force but under the control of the R.A.F., who still issued their orders. The weather began to deteriorate, creating serious problems for the pilots, who continually developed colds when they used their oxygen masks for high altitude flying. The inclement weather cancelled most of the missions until December 20, when it allowed the Eighth an opportunity to make a serious bombing effort against the enemy.

One hundred-and-one bombers were dispatched to Romilly-sur-Seine, sixty-five miles upriver from Paris. This was the Luftwaffe's major aircraft servicing centre for all of France and the Low Countries. It was an excellent choice, with ease of location and importance, but also risky because it was more than 100 miles further inland than any previous target they had bombed.

Gentile and the Fourth provided fighter escort to the French coast, but as soon as they departed the bombers came under frontal attack by sixty enemy fighters from G-26. In fifteen minutes the Abbeville Kids destroyed two B-17s, and when they were low on fuel and departed they were replaced by the FW 190s from the G-2 Squadron. These two German fighter groups kept their shuttle going against the bombers, to and from the target, until the bombers were met again by a Spitfire fighter escort from a British squadron. Seeing the Allied withdrawal escort the enemy disengaged, but not until they had destroyed six B-17s and severely damaged another twenty-nine.

On this same day, Lt. General James Doolittle was authorised to form the 12th Air Force for the forthcoming North African landing, 'Torch.' He took the two most seasoned combat B-17 groups, the 97th and the 301st, and five of the six fighter groups. The Eighth, soon to be the world's mightiest air force, was now reduced to less than one hundred bombers, and the Fourth was the only fighter unit in the United Kingdom. The Fourth was still flying the British Spitfire Vb.

And so the year of 1942 came to an end, with the Eighth and the Fourth providing a pioneer clinic for the future planners who would design the gigantic raids of the coming years. In the four months the Eighth was operational, it had carried out twenty-seven missions; only 421 of the 1,053 bombers dispatched reached the target, with a loss of thirty-three. But a start had been made, a great deal had been learned, and much had been achieved.

Debden Air Force Base

Debden Air Force Base

January 13, 1943-July 29, 1943

The Beginning of 1943 witnessed a turn in the fortunes of the war in Stalingrad, Midway, Alamein, and Guadalcanal. The Allies still had a long way to go, but they were on the offensive. The Eighth was hitting its stride with new aircraft, equipment, techniques, and a slowly increasing strength.

But in the Atlantic and the English Channel the decisive battles were yet to come. By the end of January the U-boats had reached their full strength and had sunk 117 ships or 814,000 tons, the worst month of the war. The British and American Bomber Commands were called into the battle at the insistence of the Navy, and much against their wishes.

Gentile was assigned to convoy patrols off the Channel, boring, dangerous, and difficult duty, particularly with the land-based Spitfire. It was easy to lose your sense of reference when the sea became calm and the sky and water merged into one. When patrolling a convoy day after day, seeing nothing but sky and water, a pilot could lose his sense of position and the relationship of the sky to the sea. He must constantly refer to the ships to regain this relationship. The monotony and strain were tremendous, but the patrols had to continue to protect the ships and the shipping lanes.

On January 13, Don was promoted to first lieutenant, and flew as element[1] leader with the 336th Squadron, providing rear cover for the Forts bombing the 'Fives' locomotive works at Lille. As element leader, he had more of an opportunity to look around, rather than worry about an enemy getting on his tail. On this mission the wingman looking out for Gentile was Second Lieutenant Nee.

When the squadron met the bombers at the rendezvous they noticed they were flying a staggered eighteen-aircraft group formation. These new three-aircraft 'Vs' afforded the best concentration of firepower with the greatest manoeuvrability and most effective bombing pattern. They were more effective against fighter attacks and gave the enemy fighters a much warmer reception, thanks to the increased concentration of firepower.

The bombing of the 'Fives' locomotive works was so effective, the 8th Air Force never had to return to bomb that target again. The bombers lost three aircraft. Two of them collided over Belguim after the bombing; Second Lieutenant Bishop, of the 336th, developed engine trouble and crash-landed at Manston, England.

February 1, 1943, marked two new arrivals, one welcome but the other faced with trepidation. The Officers' Mess changed from British personnel and rations to American; no more sprouts, cabbage, kippers, or imitation sausage. They did, however retain the tea time; the pilots still enjoyed tea at 4:30 p.m. as was the custom under the British.

Less well received were the Republic P-47 Thunderbolts, the first to arrive in England from the United States. The pilots had been hearing for weeks about this new aeroplane, and when they first saw it they were filled with contempt. They felt it a dubious honor to have been selected as the group to give the P-47 its combat baptism.

Gentile stared in amazement, for this was the biggest and heaviest fighter aircraft he had ever seen - 14,000 pounds. It was more than twice the size of most combat fighters and yet it could fly at speeds in excess of 429 miles per hour. He went over to the Officers' Mess, sat by the fire, and immersed himself in the 'Pilot's Flight Operating Instruction Manual', fascinated with the specifications of this bull-necked monster. He thought that if he had to live with this bowlegged 'jug,' with its twelve-foot diameter four-blade propeller, he had better familiarise himself with it. As Don read on, he learned the 'Bolt' had eight 50-caliber machine guns, four in each wing, with a potential maximum load of 425 rounds per gun. The desired load with six guns was quoted at 300 rounds, or 200 rounds for the eight guns. The 300 rounds of ammunition delivered a firing time of approximately twenty seconds.

The other pilots around the mess were playing ping-pong or chess. Someone sat at the piano, playing Chopin's 'Polonaise'. Seeing Don by the fire, welded to that thick manual, one of the chess players said, 'Hey, Gentle, with that 2300

Thunderbolts, the 'jugs,' lined up at the runway for another sweep into France.

horsepower radial engine, she resembles a milk bottle. And I hear she flies like one, too. Sure not like the jockey feeling you get from the Spit.'

'And what about those wide apart, hawk-like legs that give her the 12' 8' height? Crazy looking, hey?' piped in the other chess player.

Pierce McKennon, the piano player, said, 'I hear the propeller turns the wrong way - clockwise. Sure will be different from the Spit. It's going to give you a different torque and a different feeling for sure. I can't see any sense in all those guns. My God, they got eight...give me a couple of cannons anytime. I like to see my strikes on the plane, it makes me feel I am tearing it to bits. I don't care about the fifties' greater range or that they can carry more ammunition. Give me a cannon anytime. It has larger and more explosive shells.'

'I hear it will out dive any German plane,' replied Don.

'By God it ought to,' snorted one of the ping-pong players. 'It sure as hell can't out climb them.'

The conversation drifted into a sentimental discussion of their beloved Spitfire. Don went back to reading about the Thunderbolt. He discovered it had two self-sealing tanks installed in the fuselage. The main tank had a capacity of 205 gallons, while the auxiliary tank only carried 100 gallons. It required forty-five gallons to warm-up, take-off, and climb to 5,000 feet, giving the aircraft an approximate range of 450 air miles, more than the Spit's 395-mile range. While it did not allow enough penetration into occupied Europe, it was still better than anything else. And it had a speed of 429 miles per hour compared to the Spitfire Vb's speed of 369 miles per hour.

Later that day several of the pilots flew the P-47 to gain some familiarity. They had a lot to learn about handling this big brute. It was almost like learning to fly all over again. The transition from the Spitfire was a difficult one, with most pilots finding the Thunderbolt sluggish and unmaneuverable. The aircraft did not perform as well in the wintry skies of England as it did in the United States. The high humidity caused the engines to occasionally cut out completely. Radio communication was another difficult problem that had to be solved. The equipment had to be modified to allow communication with the British controllers and the R.A.F. aircraft. The powerful engine ignition system created interference that plagued the communication between P-47s.

These and similar aggravations caused the Fourth some hair-raising close calls. One pilot found that when the time came to drop his flaps, only one would extend. Another had his cockpit fill with smoke and the pilot was almost forced to bail out before he got the situation under control. But the worst was experienced by Second Lt. John Michellwies, Jr., of Rockford, Illinois. He took up a P-47 and put it in a spin in order to learn its flying characteristics. As he started his dive the speed built up alarmingly. He tried desperately to bring it out but it continued to gain in speed, and when he realised the plane had entered the realm of compressibility, he decided to jump. He tried to open the canopy by pulling the latch release lever on the forward edge of the canopy, but it would not slide back. He rotated the emergency release handle up and aft 180 degrees until it snapped into place. He finally threw himself clear of the aircraft, but the terrific force of the dive tore his parachute and clothing. The aircraft crashed eight miles north of Debden, and his body was discovered at the bottom of a deep crater in a farmer's field, one mile from the site. After this the Fourth never completely trusted the Thunderbolt.

Upon his return from a convoy patrol, Gentile was ordered with the rest of the pilots of the Fourth to the parade grounds. There Major General Frank Hunter, Chief of the 8th Fighter Command, passed out the Royal Air Force medallions. These had been awarded by the Air Council and promised by Sir Sholto Douglas, back in September, 1942, when the pilots transferred from the R.A.F. Eagle Squadron to the U.S.A.A.F. 4th Fighter Group, for their service to the Royal Air Force.

He said, 'Five months ago I came here when the first group of you were transferred to the 8th Fighter Command. You will never know what it meant to us to receive a group of fully trained operational pilots. It has formed a nucleus around which we have built our fighting machine. We have been able to select men from among you to send to other units to train and lead them. All this, and everything the R.A.F. has learned in three years of fighting the Hun, has been of invaluable aid.'

Gentile flew No. BL 255 Spitfire Vb, which he named 'Buckeye Don,' with the group on the monotonous convoy patrols for several months during the winter of 1943. These patrols and the boring routine of them were driving him up the wall, but by the end of March he would see the end of the convoy missions.

On March 3, Major Oscar H. Coen, the 336th Squadron's commanding officer, was transferred to command the 334th Squadron. Captain John DuFour became the 336th's new squadron commander.

It had always been Gentile's main aim in life to shoot down five enemy aircraft and join the ranks of the aces, but this was a formidable task. The Fourth could only boast of two pilots at this time with such a distinction: Chesley Peterson, who had a score of five, and Gregory Daymond, the leading ace, with nine. These pilots were held in awe, and occasioned whispers and requests for autographs. Gentile was almost consumed by his pursuit of acedom. He still had only two scores from Dieppe after being in combat for almost a year. In fact, he did not think he had much of a chance to increase that score, especially when they traded in their Spitfires for the new seven-ton monsters, the P-47 Thunderbolts.

The pilots had to fly fifty hours with the Thunderbolt before they would be considered combat ready. They painted the noses and tails white after their British planes and antiaircraft fired on them because they resembled the German FW 190s. The Group became operational with the P-47 on March 10, 1943, when Peterson led fourteen 'Bolts' in an uneventful sweep along the French coast.

On March 12, 1943, at 4:50 p.m., led by Lieutenant Colonel Peterson, the 335th Squadron took off from Debden and the 336th from Martlesham, bound for St Omer, France. The two squadrons rendezvoused over Bradwell Bay, then headed out to France just over the waves. As they approached the coast of the Continent they increased their altitude to 16,000 feet. When they made landfall near Dunkirk, the 336th Squadron was some fifteen miles behind the 335th. Gentile's squadron came under attack by a gaggle of FW 190s. Lt. Stanley M.M. Anderson, the squadron leader, ordered the A Section to attack the enemy, but before they could get organised for the attack, Don, in Section B, broke away and dove in a solo head-on attack.

Thirty of the 190s came streaking toward him out of the setting sun. He continued on his collision course, took in a deep gulp of oxygen, and felt his hot blood course faster through his veins. He knew they could clearly see him; he was silhouetted against the clouds. The enemy's wings were blinking like Christmas lights and the air all around him was filled with corruption. Their guns were spitting fire, and Don was looking into a fiery line of tracers that he could see streaming his way.

They broke in every direction. Don swung around and rolled on his side, and pulled back into a series of deep turns until he was positioned on the tail of a 190. He rolled, yawed, skidded, kicked his rudders, and pulled back on his stick, flinging himself into aileron turns, all the while remaining on the 190's tail and blazing away with all eight of his guns. The 190 shook and shuddered, smoke and flames rolling out from its engine and starboard wing. Don broke off the attack when he realised he was getting low on fuel. As he flew back to his squadron he looked back, over his left shoulder, and saw the FW going from a shallow to a deep spiralling dive, thick black smoke trailing behind.

Shortly after he got back in formation, he heard Lieutenant Anderson on the R/T, reporting he was twelve miles Northwest of St Omer. He had been hit and was getting ready to bail out. The other squadron saw him rapidly lose altitude and disappear, but no one saw a chute. When they landed Don turned in his claim for a Probable[2].

From this flight Lt. Stanley M.M. Anderson did not return. He died in the crash.

On April 1, 1943, Don flew both his last convoy patrol and his last flight with the beloved Spitfire 'Buckeye Don.' Although they were supposed to have been operational with the P-47s on the first of March, because of the mechanical and radio problems they missed the date by a month.

Don with his Spitfire V6, serial No. BL 255, 'Buckeye Don.'

The 17th of April, the 8th Air Force dispatched 115 B-17s for their first penetration raid into Germany, but only 107 made it to the Focke-Wulf aircraft factory in Bremen. The 4th and the 78th Fighter Groups sent fifty-nine P-47s on a diversion raid.

Bomber Command began utilising diversion sweeps to confuse the enemy radar as to which was the main bombing force and what their ultimate destination was. The German fighters had only a ninety-minute fuel supply, and if they were deployed to the wrong location they could not be committed to another sector until they first returned to their airfield and refuelled. This greatly decreased the effectiveness of their defence. The Allies had over 1,000 miles of coastline they could penetrate when making a bombing raid, and this created a serious tactical problem for the enemy, leaving them with no choice but to disperse their fighters. This further attenuated the defenders combat effectiveness. However, if the enemy anticipated correctly, the results were devastating to the bombing force with excessive losses of men and aircraft. This constant chess game continued until the very end of the conflict.

As the main body of bombers crossed Europe, a German observation aircraft was tracking them just out of gun range and eventually alerted the Luftwaffe of their approach. The enemy fighters arrived and kept up a savage and concentrated attack to and from the target at Bremen. Sixteen B-17s with 160 men never returned and forty-six other bombers sustained serious damage. The Focke-Wulf plant was so severely damaged, however, it was never rebuilt at Bremen but moved deeper into Germany at Marienburg.

Gentile and eleven other members of his squadron flew the diversion sweep to the Walsh-Flushing area. Shortly after takeoff they heard on the R/T that Lieutenant Fuchs had developed engine trouble and was forced to return to Debden. While flying at 26,000 feet they sighted enemy aircraft, but they were again too far away to engage in combat. They returned and landed safely at Debden at 8:10 p.m.

It certainly was a day of records. The Bremen raid marked the most savage attack experienced to date by the Eighth from the Luftwaffe. It also proved that unescorted bombers, even with all their firepower, were still vulnerable to attacks from a determined foe. The losses this day were twice as large as any previous raid and they shook the advocates of the Fortresses, who had believed they had the ability to hold their own in a conflict with interceptors.

When the bombers returned to base there was a party in progress, 400 people celebrating the first American raid into Germany. The revellers included base personnel and civilian and service guests; some were invited by the crews that did not return. The festive occasion soon degenerated into a wake and the party broke up, with only the survivors left to lick their wounds and grieve the loss of their comrades.

On April 18, Don Gentile, wingman Second Lt. J. Goodson, and four other Thunderbolts took off on a freelance to St Omer but it was uneventful; no enemy sighted or action taken.

At the end of April Duane W. Beeson and Spiros (Steve) Pisanos were promoted from second to first lieutenants. First Lieutenant Gentile added the Oak Leaf Cluster award to his Air Medal, while Second Lieutenant Goodson received the Air Medal.

May 3 saw Old Glory fluttering over Debden, England, the first fighter station to be transferred to the United States Army Air Force. In a brief and simple ceremony at noon, Group Captain L.G. Nixon handed over the station to Col. Edward W. Anderson, Commander, 4th Fighter Group.

Group Captain Nixon said, 'Colonel Anderson, Commander 4th Fighter Group of the 8th Fighter Command, U.S. Army Air Corps, on the third day of May, 1943, it is with pleasure that I have the honor to hand over to you Royal Air Force Station, Debden. Debden, among other stations, performed its share in the defensive fighter role of this island. Now that the tide of battle has turned in favour of the United Nations, Debden will be well to the fore, under your command, performing an offensive fighter role. When the time comes for you to return to your native country we shall be happy to receive back this station, knowing that history has been made affecting our respective countries and sealing a bond of friendship that must endure for all time.'

Colonel Anderson replied, 'I am deeply honored to have the privilege of accepting the first fighter station to be transferred to the United States Army Air Force. We are fortunate to receive such a finely equipped and organised station. I hope when the time comes to transfer this little bit of England back to you, we can do it proudly in the knowledge that the operations we have conducted here have been worthwhile.'

Two platoons, one from the R.A.F. Regiment and one from the U.S.A.A.F., presented arms as the R.A.F. ensign was replaced by the American flag. At the conclusion of the dedication they retired to the Officers' Club with their R.A.F. guests for a dance and buffet supper.

The next day there was a sign over the bar of the Officers' Club which read, 'Free Beer On Steve Pisanos - American.' First Lt. Spiros Nicholas 'Steve' Pisanos of Athens, Greece, and Plainfield, N.J., became the first American soldier in the British Isles to become a U.S. Citizen under the provisions of the modified overseas naturalisation laws.

It was not until the fourth of May that the Thunderbolts were used on a fighter sweep. The Fourth and the 56th accompanied the Forts attacking Antwerp, the first escort mission with the P-47.

Debden England, Air Force Base transferred to the United States Army Air Force.

Seventy-nine bombers were dispatched; sixty-five made it to the target, the Ford and General Motors works at Antwerp. The presence of the escort fighters accounted for the mission success, for all of the bombers returned to England. They encountered some flak and sighted FW 190s and ME 109s but evasive action was taken. The only combat experienced was by Lieutenant Carpenter of the 335th Squadron, who claimed one FW 190 destroyed.

The Fourth rendezvoused with the bombers over Flushing at 28,000 feet. The pilots were increasingly unhappy with the P-47 and its teething problems. First Lieutenants Braley and Foster from the 336th had to abort and return to base because of engine trouble. Lieutenants Lutz and Care of the 334th Squadron were approaching the Dutch coast at 27,000 feet, two miles south of Flushing, when Lieutenant Lutz's aircraft started smoking and losing speed. 'Pappy' Lutz had borrowed a pair of expensive handmade boots that First Lieutenant Howard 'Deacon' Hively had bought in London. Lutz was wearing these boots, Deacon's pride and joy, on this mission. He was overheard on the R/T saying, 'Sorry, Deacon, kind of looks like I am going to get your boots wet...' Lutzs aircraft went over on its back, straight into the Channel, fifty-five miles east of Clacton, on the English coast. Care circled the area and saw Lutz in the water, noting that his face was frequently awash as he lay motionless in his American Mae West. The former Eagle pilots preferred the British Mae West to the American jackets because they felt they had more buoyancy and could give greater support to an injured pilot even when not inflated.

The visibility was excellent but the Air-Sea Rescue Walrus aircraft never found Lutz. From this mission Lieutenant Lutz did not return.

Captain Clark Gable, Hollywood's most celebrated male star, went to the 303rd Bomber Group at Molesworth and flew as an observer in the lead bomber, Eight Ball II, on this raid to Antwerp. On the mission Clark had to man the radio room machine gun when an enemy aeroplane attacked and inflicted slight damage to his bomber. While overseas he flew eleven missions and came under attack in seven. His greatest fear during his combat tour was of being captured and exhibited by Hitler in a cage.

The Forts went back to Antwerp with the Fourth providing general support. Forty-two B-17s were dispatched but only thirty-eight reached the industrial area of Antwerp. The thirty-nine aeroplanes in the fighter escort moved to Bradwell Bay on the coast of England for refuelling. As soon as they crossed the coast of the Continent they were jumped by a gaggle of enemy aircraft. These Abbeville Kids had their yellow-nosed aircraft's undersides smeared with lamp black to give them some camouflage. The 334th Squadron gave high cover while the 335th and 336th dove on the enemy. Major Blakeslee and Lt. Aubrey C. Stanhope each destroyed an FW 190; Lieutenant Colonel Peterson scored one probable and one damaged;

Captain Stepp and Lieutenant Hobert both claimed a damaged aircraft. Some of the pilots sustained damage to their own aircraft. Lt. Kenneth J. Peterson made a forced landing; Lieutenant Both had his 'Bolt' fired on by an excited B-17 gunner; Lieutenant Foster developed engine trouble and had to leave before he even saw the enemy. Gentile didn't even get an opportunity to fire his guns and was terribly disappointed. They all were low on fuel and had to land at various emergency fields, Don landing at Bradwell Bay.

Thirty-six aircraft from the Fourth crossed the enemy coast on this 16th of May, 1943, at 30,000 feet. They saw four yellow-nosed FW 190s and A Section was ordered to investigate. As Don and the other pilots in A Section closed to 800 yards, the enemy dove for the deck. Major Blakeslee ordered them to rejoin the formation because he thought it was a trap.

The Fourth flew on for another fifteen minutes when suddenly they were attacked by fifteen red-nosed FW 190s. The sky was filled with individual dogfights. Three FW 190s were damaged by Lts. Aubrey C. Stanhope and K.O. Bentie, and Capt. Gilbert O. Halsey, all from the 335th Squadron.

Two P-47s received some damage, while the 336th saw no action and returned to base.

The next day Field Order 23 sent twenty-four P-47s from the Fourth on a high altitude sweep. At 4:55 p.m. the 334th Squadron bounced[3] four FW 190s 5,000 feet below them. The enemy took evasive action, ducked into the clouds, and got away. Before the 334th could get back into formation twelve Messerschmitt 109Gs appeared astern, coming toward them. The squadron promptly turned into them and two of the enemy were shot down.

Don and the 336th engaged in combat but made no claims.

From this mission Lieutenant Boock did not return.

On May 20, for another sweep, Don and two other pilots in his squadron were issued the all new P-47 D Thunderbolt fighter instead of the P-47 C. The D model was similar to the P-47 C, except that water injection was made standard for more prolonged combat power, permitting 2,300 horsepower at 27,000 feet, and a top speed of 433 miles per hour at 30,000 feet. It also had more armour plate, added to better protect the pilot, and modifications in the supercharger exhaust system. These improvements made the aircraft an ideal fighter to provide top cover for the B-17 and B-24 in their raids on Europe. Don named his new steed 'Donnie Boy.'

Don's wingman, Lieutenant Nee, and Captain Stepp had to abort the mission because of engine problems. The Fourth did not sight the enemy and landed at 12:45 p.m.

The next day they were off again on the 'old bus run' to Belgium. They saw several groups of enemy aircraft flying. As usual, the 334th carried out the attack while the 335th provided high cover, and the 336th positioned itself to prevent the enemy from dashing back into France. During this combat Lt. Spiros (Steve) Pissanos, of 334th Squadron, damaged an FW 190.

Don and his wingman, Lieutenant Millikan, did not even get an opportunity to turn on their gun safety switches.

Three pilots, Lieutenants Morgan, MacFarlane, and Whitlow, failed to return from this flight.

General Order No. 10, dated May 28, 1943, awarded Don S. Gentile the second Oak Leaf Cluster to his Air Medal and James A. Goodson his first.

On behalf of Britain's Royal Household, the Duchess of Kent came to Debden on June 2 to present plaques commemorating the part played by the American Eagle Squadron in the R.A.F. to the commanders of the 334th, 335th, and 336th Fighter Squadrons. At the ceremony officers and enlisted men of the three squadrons marched in review.

In presenting the plaques the Duchess said, 'Nearly three years ago you, as volunteers, first spread your wings in defence of this country, and by doing so wrote not only American history, but history in the annals of the Royal Air Force. By your great deeds, courage, and self-sacrifice during these years you won eternal gratitude from us all, and we felt then that, sooner or later, your example would be followed by thousands of young men from the United States. And now, when your great country and ours are fighting in the same cause, the three Eagle Squadrons of the Royal Air Force have become part of the United States Army Air Force, and are winning new triumphs. To commemorate forever the part the Eagle Squadron played in those critical days, the King has gladly given permission for the R.A.F. crests to be designed for each Squadron and has approved and signed them. I have the greatest pleasure and honor today to hand over the crests to you, and in so doing I wish you good luck, and may God bless you all.'

Following the presentation ceremony, the Duchess had lunch in the Officers' Mess and inspected the enlisted men's barracks and mess. She surveyed the Thunderbolt P-47 fighter and looked on from the station watch tower as the Thunderbolts, piloted by former R.A.F. airmen, passed overhead in formation.

July 2 saw the Bob Hope, Francis Langford, Tony Romano, and Jack Pepper USO Show presented on the parade grounds at Debden.

The July 4, 1943, mission was cancelled due to poor weather, but this did not prevent the base from having a typical American Fourth of July, with a parade, speeches, and other festive activities. The 336th Squadron was victorious in the tug-of-war contest, winning a case of beer. And the enlisted men beat the officers by a score of ten to five in softball.

A fighter sweep to Courtrari, Ghent, Flushing, was staged with the 334th and 336th Squadrons on July 25. It was a no hits, no runs, no errors mission, with the

July 2, 1943, Bob Hope converses with Don Gentile during a USO show on the parade grounds at Debden.

Germans eating breakfast and unwilling to be bothered. The 335th did not participate because they were test dropping the new belly tanks off the coast of England.

The next day a diversion raid was sent to Rotterdam and the Hague. The lead squadron, the 334th, bounced four FW 190s flying south and Lt. Henry Mills claimed one probably destroyed. Several more FW 190s were seen by the 334th who attempted a bounce, but the Germans evaded. Don and the 336th saw no enemy aircraft or action because they were so far back in the formation, in 'tail end Charlie,' as it was called.

By mid-May of 1943 the twin engine B-26 medium bomber served operational in the 8th Air Force. It was the most controversial aeroplane of its time. The Martin B-26A Marauder had four-bladed propellers turned by two Pratt and Whitney Double Wasp engines, which gave it 3,700 horsepower and a maximum speed of 315 miles per hour. It had an impressive bomb load of 3,000 pounds to a target more than 500 miles away. Its streamlined circular shape caused it to be nicknamed the 'flying torpedo,' but this soon changed when it racked up excessive training and combat casualties. The pilots then started calling it the 'flying prostitute,' because the small amount of wing area disallowed the aircraft a 'visible means of support.' Most bomber pilots had been trained in aircraft with large wings like the B-17, which had a wing area of more than 1,400 square feet, in sharp contrast to the 602 square feet of the B26.

The B-26's 27,000 pounds of aeroplane and bombs demanded a landing speed of 135 miles per hour, much like the jets of today, rather than the slower eighty-five miles per hour needed to land the Fortresses. The Martin Aircraft Company eventually lengthened the wing by six feet, enlarged the tail area, and made many other improvements which helped reduce the aircraft's early casualty rate and redeemed her much maligned reputation.

On July 27, Major Halsey led a B-26 diversionary mission into France. The fighters met the bombers on time at Dungeness and supported them in a series of wide orbits until they were thirteen miles off St Valery-en-Caux, when the B-26s turned back. They made a wide orbit, touching the enemy coast in the vicinity of Dieppe, when lack of fuel caused them to withdraw. This was a frustration they would not have to endure much longer.

As the Eighth gained in strength and range, the Germans pulled their fighters farther eastward, away from the coast, to get beyond the range of the fighter escort. The Germans would wait for the escort planes to turn back to England because they were low on fuel, then attack the unescorted bombers and wreak havoc. Up to this time the protection given to the bombers was limited to twenty or thirty minutes; the fighters had only internal fuel tanks and their range was limited by their capacity.

In a combat mission the Thunderbolt, with its 2,300 horsepower engine, could consume 100 gallons per hour from its 305-gallon tank. This allowed it a range of only 175 to 190 miles, although it was somewhat of an improvement over the Spitfire, which burned forty-five gallons an hour but whose tank capacity limited it to a combat radius of 150 miles.

During the Spanish Civil War the Germans were the first to utilise external auxiliary fuel tanks slung under the wings of their aeroplanes, extending the range and flying time of the fighters. Later, during World War II, the Allies used similar tanks to aid them in ferrying fighter aircraft from the United States to England. These belly tanks were called 'babies' by the personnel of the Fourth.

To extend the range of fighter escorts, the 8th Air Force directed its Air Technical Section to devise a method of utilising external tanks for the P-47. They were confronted with many problems. First, it took several months before they received the tanks used in ferrying aircraft from the United States. Then, when they finally did arrive, they were 200-gallon resonated paper tanks that proved unsatisfactory because they were not pressurised, and therefore fuel could not be drawn from the tanks above 23,000 feet. Other problems included leaking and poor aerodynamics, which decreased the aircraft's manoeuvrability and speed.

They did design an acceptable pressurised 100-gallon tank, but because of an acute shortage of sheet metal in England they could not start construction for several months. The need for an external tank was urgent, as it could extend the range of the fighter an extra seventy-five miles to and from the target. It was decided they would use the formerly unacceptable ferry tank, with a restriction: They would not extract fuel from the tank above 22,000 feet, so the tanks were used only at the beginning of a journey into enemy territory.

At 1340 hours[4], July 27, 1943, at Pinetree, headquarters for the 8th Air Force Bomber Command, General Eaker and his staff held their daily bombing conference. The general turned to the weather officer.

'You say there may be a weather front passing over Europe tomorrow? Can you be more definite on the conditions?'

'No, sir, at this time I can't.'

'Well, let's plan the targets, the Fieseler FW 190 parts factory at Kassel and the AGO FW 190 plant at Oschersleden, Germany. I want to dispatch 300 heavies for this operation and I don't want them mauled by the Luftwaffe. Can I count on fighter escort, General Kepner? How are you coming with the problem of the auxiliary tank? We are really going to need your fighter cover, Bill. How does it look?'

'You can count on us. We will be ready, sir.'

Once the target selection is completed by Pinetree, the intricate machinery of destruction is set in motion. The teletype machine in the message centre of the 91st Bomb Group started ticking at 0120 hours, July 28. At the 92nd Bomb Group and at the 303rd, 305th, 306th, 351st, 379th, 381st, and 384th, the heavy bomber bases scattered throughout England, the teletypes clatter out the pertinent details of the day's mission, planned and worked out by Bomber Command. How many aircraft will be dispatched, the targets-primary, secondary, targets of opportunity or targets of last resort, amount of flak and location, weather, routes to and from the target, the bombing altitudes, rendezvous with the fighters and time, time of takeoff, time of bombing. These and dozens of other important details are dispatched to the bomb groups for Mission 78.

At 0140 the bomber bases began to bustle with activity. Tractor trailers transport the bombs from the ammunition dumps to the bombers. The armourers load the machine guns, while the crew and crew chiefs gas and service the B-17s for the impending mission. The oxygen systems are tested, filled, and made ready. At 0230 the base is dark and silent except for the mess hall, where the cooks and kitchen crews are busy preparing the morning meal. At 0300 hours the bomber crews are awakened and don their flying outfits. By 0330 hours the combat crews are filing into the mess hall for breakfast. At 0405 hours the briefing for this mission begins.

By the time the briefing ends almost twelve hours have passed before the general's intent has been translated into a program of assault. The men leave the briefing to give their aircraft and equipment its final check. The gunners have cleaned and checked their weapons. The bombardier has checked his instruments and bombs. The navigator has laid out the routes and targets on his maps. The pilot has checked the instruments and aeroplane. All is ready for the assault. The only thing left to do is wait. A tense immobility settles over the field.

At 0640 hours, all the bombers start their engines, then stand by on the interphone frequency. The lead bomber checks with the other planes in his formation. After confirming they are set for takeoff, he calls the tower and clears his formation for taxi and takeoff instructions. The control tower orders the takeoff. As the lead aeroplane starts rolling, the second aircraft pulls into position. When the first is airborne the second starts his takeoff; time elapsed, thirty seconds. The lead aircraft flies straight ahead at 150 miles per hour, climbing at a speed of approximately 400 feet per minute, for one minute plus thirty seconds for each aircraft in the formation. The other planes form on the leader a three-unit 'V' formation, then turn back over the airfield to collect the rest as they become airborne. They then turn on their heading for the target and begin their climb to attack altitude.

Formation flying created both advantages and disadvantages. The primary disadvantage was that more fuel was needed for the form up and the constant changes in speed necessary to maintain position in the formation. This in turn made the fuel-and-bomb-laden aircraft heavier and more difficult to fly, increasing pilot fatigue. However, proper formation provided controlled and concentrated firepower, manoeuvrability, cross-cover, and better fighter protection. When attacking a formation, the assailant would have to concentrate his fire on a single aircraft, making himself more vulnerable to cross-cover fire from the other bombers in the formation and thus more easily destroyed. And formation flying allowed a more precise bombing pattern.

The 8th Air Force was making more frequent deep penetrations into Germany, and it became apparent the structure of the formations needed alterations for greater protection from attacking enemy fighters. The eighteen-aircraft group was changed in April, 1943. Three of these eighteen- aeroplane groups were formed in a closer formation to form a fifty-four bomber combat wing.

The bombers from the various groups met at the rendezvous point and orbited in a circle as they formed up into two Combat Wings. The First Bomb Wing led, the Fourth Bomb Wing following, as they slowly headed out into the English Channel on their way to the North Sea. Here they encountered extreme weather conditions, including towering cumulus clouds reaching up to 30,000 feet. The First Bomb Wing started with 182 aircraft but was reduced to fifty-eight; the Fourth had dispatched 120 but only thirty-seven were still airborne over the North Sea. Mechanical, electrical, weather-related, and other problems created serious difficulties in maintaining a high percentage of effective aircraft from those dispatched.

At 0855 they passed the East Frisian Islands and were surrounded by bursting flak, the concussions knocking the Forts around as the blasts came closer and closer. They turned and headed inland over Germany. The two Wings split, the First heading for Kassel and the Fourth for Oschersleben. Immediately, they came under attack by between forty-five and sixty FW 190s, Me 109s and Ju 88s. They fought their way to the target.

Back at the 78th and the 4th Fighter Group bases, the ground crews were experiencing real problems in fuelling the 200-gallon ferry tanks. In order to keep the mission on time they only partially filled the tanks, allotting approximately seventy-five gallons of fuel. This would be enough to take the planes to the coast of occupied Europe. At 1040 hours the two groups were supposed to put up 123 fighters for the mission, but during the takeoff at the Fourth's base two aircraft's belly tanks dropped off and exploded all over the runway. They had to abort this show.

The two fighter groups were to penetrate, for the first time, beyond France into Germany and provide escort cover for the bombers coming out of Germany on their way home. The rendezvous was to take place in the vicinity of Emmerick, just inside the German border. The two groups were able only to put up 105 of the 123 fighters planned for this operation, and only forty-one aircraft from the

Fourth made it to the rendezvous area.

Colonel Edward W. Anderson, the 39-year old commanding officer of the 4th Fighter Group, was flying as wingman to Captain Carl H. 'Spike' Miley. The average age of most fighter pilots was in the early twenties, but on the tough missions the 'old man' went along for moral support. This was one of those, with the unpredictable drop tank slung precariously under the belly of the P-47 only a few inches off the ground.

The group, led by Major Halsey, could not find the First Bomb Wing, returning from Kassel, Germany, at the rendezvous point. They continued to fly farther into Germany and finally sighted some of the Forts from the Fourth Bomb Wing returning from the Oschersleben raid. The bombers were under intense attack by more than 100 enemy aircraft.

Major Halsey's voice came over the R/T. 'There's some big friends[5] at six o'clock.' The formation of bombers he was referring to were being attacked by Luftwaffe fighters who were dropping parachute bombs and regular bombs from above onto the formation. One bomber was hit, exploded, and its fragments hit two other Forts, causing all three to plunge toward the earth.

Gentile saw a new battle innovation: rockets. Because a formation of twenty-seven B-17s could bring to bear 200 50caliber machine guns on an attacking aircraft, they had to come up with a way to stay out of range. German FW 190s and Me 110s were positioned out of range of the B-17s' guns (more than 1,000 yards), firing rockets. These rockets, an adaptation of an infantry weapon, Wfr. Gr 42 spr., had their launch tubes mounted under the wings of the aeroplanes. Each tube contained a 250-pound missile with a twenty-one pound warhead. It was difficult to fire accurately, but a direct hit could completely destroy a bomber, while it took twenty to twenty-five hits with 20mm shells to bring down a Fortress.

The group broke up into its three squadrons, the 335th going over and in front of the bombers, while the 334th broke to the starboard and the 336th to the port. The Fourth caught the enemy completely by surprise because they were operating beyond their normal range. A frantic battle ensued in the skies over Germany and the Netherlands. The group destroyed nine enemy aircraft: Colonel Anderson claimed two; Captain Miley had one probable, and Lieutenant Mirsch racked up one damaged for the top-scoring 336th Squadron. The group with the 'babies' estimated they had flown a total of 520 miles-the farthest penetration into Europe accomplished to date by escort fighters.

When the group landed, the majority of the pilots were pleased and excited about the day's mission, but not Gentile. He was slowly becoming one of the older boys, yet he had not downed an enemy plane in almost a year. With only two kills he continued to worry about becoming an ace. When he stepped out of his fighter, his ground crew knew he was down but he didn't show it. Despite his disappointment, Don's dark, deep-set eyes were as cheerful and undefeated as usual. The pilots stowed their flying gear and walked over to the mess hall. Don did not join them but headed instead for his quarters. He lay on his bed and it was then that he felt the depth of his tiredness. As he lay back, his hand on a pillow, a blanket drawn up under his arms, the midday sunlight poured through the window, spreading its July warmth over the expressionless Gentile.

He lay awake with thoughts of a triumphant return home as a hero. He knew unequivocally that God would hear his prayers, hadn't He always? He could go home now; he had more than fulfilled the necessary number of missions for rotation. 'No, I won't go home,' he thought. 'I'll take a second tour. I have made up my mind. I will not go home until I fulfil my goal, even if I have to stay until the last bullet is fired.'

Physically and mentally exhausted, Don slowly sank into a deep sleep. He did not dream about his triumphant return home, but instead of a vast gaggle of German fighters that stretched for miles in a line across the sky. Don would position his aircraft behind the 'tail end Charlie' and blast away with his 50-caliber machine guns. The burning enemy plane dove straight to the ground in a red ball of flames. He would position himself behind the next aircraft and repeat the performance, over and over again. Later he dreamed of home and his family. A feeling of loneliness and despair, such as he had never known before, engulfed him. His mind struggled to free itself from these depressions and fears. When he finally opened his eyes and came back from the long way away, his self-confidence returned.

During the Casablanca Conference in January the Eighth had been issued directives authorising the elimination of Germany's war production capabilities by March 31, 1944. Although there were 1,500 major military objectives in occupied Europe, some were so small or inaccessible they were not practical for destruction from the air. A careful analysis of the German war economy revealed the enemy's ability to make war depended on about fifty key German industrial centres, all within a 600-mile radius of England.

On July 29, the First Bomb Wing continued strikes on one of the key targets within 400 miles, the U-boat yards at Kiel, while the Fourth Bomb Wing attacked the Heinkel aircraft factory which produced FW 190 parts at Warnemunde, Germany. The B-17s of both Wings were the new bombers with additional wing tanks, increasing their fuel capacity from 2,730 to 2,810 gallons.

The Third Bomb Wing, composed of nineteen B-26s, flew a diversion raid to bomb the St Omer airfield. They were escorted by 118 P-47s from the 4th, 56th, and 78th Fighter Groups. Gentile and the Fourth met the bombers on time and provided close escort until they turned back. They did not sight any enemy planes.

Later that day all the base personnel were assembled on the parade grounds, where General Hunter introduced Captain Eddie Rickenbacker, the famous Ohioan who was America's 'Ace of Aces' in World War I with twenty-six kills. He gave an inspiring speech describing the situations in the other theatres of war he had visited. And then he extended to the fighter pilots his offer of a case of Scotch for the first person to beat his record of twenty-six.

July 31, 1943 - August 17, 1943

On July 31, the big B-26 bombers were sent on two missions, the 386th Bomb Group to Abbeville and the 322nd Bomb Group to Triqueville airfields. The 4th, 56th, and 78th Fighter Groups provided 108 fighters as escort on the diversion mission of the 386th. The Fourth, led by Lieutenant Colonel Blakeslee, provided top cover for the B26s from their rendezvous at Clacton until the bombers turned back to England. Gentile took off with them as a spare.

Several generals and senators from Washington D.C. who were making a tour of the European Theater of Operations visited Debden August 2. Later in the day, Don and the group took off on a diversion sweep with the 387th Bomb Group's B-26, but the mission was aborted due to inclement weather.

The maiden combat mission of the 353rd Fighter Group, flying in the place of the Fourth's 334th Squadron, took place on August 9. The 386th and 332nd Bomb Groups' B-26s were to bomb St Omer, but intensive cloud cover caused the formations to become so scattered they were unable to obtain good results. They also missed their escort by the 4th, 56th, 78th, and the 353rd Fighter Groups.

When the B-26s returned, they were missing one aircraft. It was determined later that it had strayed into a restricted area in England, was mistakenly identified as an enemy, and shot down by two R.A.F. Spitfires. The entire crew was lost.

Two hundred and forty-three B-17s took off on August 12 to bomb the Ruhr valley. This highly industrialised area was accurately referred to as 'Flak Alley' or as the 'Valley of Death.' The primary target of the mission was the industrial city of Gelsenkirchen. When the group reached the city heavy clouds obscured the target; they headed for the secondary target at Bochum and met with similar results.

The attacking formations then headed for Reckling-hausen, their tertiary target. Here, when they found a break in the clouds, the target was obliterated by a dense smoke screen sent up by the Germans. During these circling movements over the three targets in the Ruhr, the enemy had not ignored them. Deadly flak of every description filled the sky. It was so thick and dense it appeared as one solid black cloud of destruction. The group was finally forced to turn and head south for their slated 'targets of opportunity,' the marshalling yards at Cologne, Germany. In the lead bomber, Clark Gable was filming the event for a training film on gunnery.

The 4th, 56th, and 78th Fighter Groups dispatched 131 fighters to provide shuttle escort cover for the Forts. The Fourth was to provide withdrawal support from the Sittard, Holland, area.

Lieutenant Colonel Blakeslee led their takeoff at 8:25 a.m. When they rendezvoused with the returning Forts at 29,000 feet, the B-17s were under attack. At this point Lieutenants Nee and Fuchs were having serious difficulty trying to drop their belly tanks and had to return to base.

Silently, in pairs, a gaggle of FW 190s peeled out of the German sky, twisting and turning for a frontal attack on the lead formation of B-17s. The Fourth's 334th Squadron moved from the rear to the front of the formation and broke off the attack. First Lt. Cadman Padget, completing a 180-degree turn to port, positioned himself behind and above the bombers as they flew west of Duren, Germany. One FW 190, mistaking him for a friendly aircraft, started to form up on his starboard side. Padget slowly turned to the starboard, then back to port, and manoeuvred to 150 yards behind the unsuspecting enemy. He delivered a two-second burst of gunfire. He saw a series of hits on the 190's fuselage and watched as it was engulfed in flames. Padget closed to within fifty yards and fired another burst. The aeroplane exploded and plummeted to the earth.

Captain James A. Clark also destroyed one FW 190 and damaged an Me 109 with the help of Captain Hopson and Lieutenant Hively.

Again Gentile and his squadron saw two enemy aircraft but never were close enough to engage.

General Order No. 22, dated August 12, 1943, awarded Don S. Gentile a third Oak Leaf Cluster to his Air Medal for meritorious service.

The morning of August 15 at 8:30 a.m. Blakeslee led an uneventful sweep to the St Inglevort, Ypres, Kocke area of Belgium. Lieutenant Simon had to return almost immediately after takeoff because of a defective undercarriage; the rest of the 336th landed at 10:00 a.m.

Blakeslee took the group airborne again at 6:30 p.m. The seventeen P-47s were to provide withdrawal support for 120 B-17s returning from a bombing raid on the Brussels airdrome. The air controller recalled the bombers because of adverse weather but neglected to notify the Fighter Groups. The 56th Fighter Group arrived 30 minutes early at the rendezvous and therefore could not locate the bombers. The Fourth located them off course, near Roulers, and escorted them out over Nieuport to Bradwell Bay. Two FW 190s tried to attack the bombers when they reached Nieuport, but the 336th forced them to break off their attack. The Fourth landed at 8:40 p.m. without further incident.

August 16, 8:05 a.m., Blakeslee led the group in providing general support for the B-17s bombing a Paris airfield. They crossed the coast of Continental Europe just west of Dieppe, arriving at their rendezvous point at 9:12 a.m. The Forts were under attack and so the group orbited to port, coming in from behind and meeting the attackers head on. The group moved up and over the B-17s while the 334th bounced the enemy aircraft. The Germans kept up their assault on the fighters and bombers all the way to and from the target, and virtually all the sections of all the squadrons were engaged in combat.

Gentile was Green 1 in Green section of the 336th Squadron, and First Lt. Phillip H. Dunn, his wingman, was Green 2. They were flying in an easterly direction slightly to starboard and a little ahead of the bombers when they saw an Me 109 dive down out of the sun and commence a frontal attack on the B-17s. As he dove, the German fired on a P-47 which was below and to the front of the bombers. The strikes were connecting and the P-47 was starting to smoke. Don broke to port and dove down on the enemy. He started his firing at 400 yards, hoping to scare the enemy into breaking off the attack.

Suddenly Don's gun sight went out, forcing him to guess as he continued his firing. White smoke poured out of the German plane and it flipped over to the port on its back and started spinning lazily out of control. Don and his wingman followed it down from 30,000 to 24,000 feet, watching the smoke pour out of the aircraft, until they had to break off and return to position to protect the bombers.

They landed at 10:55 a.m. and Don put in a claim for one Me 109 as damaged, subject to gun film assessment.

On this show, the P-47 piloted by Lt. A. Rafalovitch, 334th Squadron, was attacked by an FW 190. Cannon shells shredded his starboard wing and forced his ammunition door to fly open. The constant banging of the door badly damaged the vertical stabilizer and tail plane. He lost control and began to go into a dive; as he prepared to bail out at 19,000 feet, he managed to regain control of the aeroplane. He took evasive action and lost the enemy in the overcast. Despite the considerable damage to the tail plane and starboard wing and a punctured gas tank, Rafalovitch made it back to England and landed at New Rommey on the coast.

From this mission First Lt. Joseph G. Matthews did not return.[1]

In early 1943, President Roosevelt and Prime Minister Churchill and their top military and civilian advisors had met in Casablanca, Morocco, to decide the future strategy of the war. The fruit of those many conferences was the Casablanca Directive. One portion of the directive stated that the aim of the British and American air forces would be the destruction of the German military, industrial, and economic systems and the undermining of the enemy's morale. This would be accomplished by 'around-the-clock bombing.'

Britain's night bombing was intended to kill and displace the enemy from their homes, consequently having a profound effect on their morale.

The Americans, with precision daylight bombing, were to destroy specific military and industrial targets which would eventually lead to the collapse of the enemy war machine. In order to achieve these objectives, the Allies had to gain air superiority. Initially it was believed that the B-17 could, with its twelve guns, defend itself, but later it became painfully clear that fighter cover was a necessity in holding down the bomber losses. General Eaker pleaded for belly tanks for the P-47 and the new P-51b.

The P-51 originally was an American aircraft designed for the R.A.F., but because of the poor high altitude performance of its 1,200 horsepower Allison engine it was never employed as a fighter. Later the British replaced the American Allison with the British Rolls Royce Merlin 1,600 horsepower engine used in the Spitfire. This so improved its performance it made it the best aircraft of its time.

Winston Churchill and other British brass had always been sceptical about the potential of daylight bombing and impatient with the Americans for not yet having dropped many bombs on Germany. In the United States, Roosevelt and the Navy were mounting pressure to divert future bombers to the war in the Pacific against the Japanese. The daylight precision bombing concept had to be proven immediately, with or without long range fighter support.

The 8th Air Force planners began work on the details of a raid against the ball bearing factories at Schweinfurt. The five factories, clustered around a railroad yard, were considered a prime target, as they were responsible for two-thirds of Germany's ball and roller bearing production.

While gathering all the intelligence available and constructing a plaster model of Schweinfurt, the planners became aware of a new problem. The Germans had successfully expanded their fighter aircraft industry to such an extent that they now posed a serious threat to future bomber raids. Two factories, the Messerschmitt plant at Regensburg, Germany, and the Focke-Wulf plant at Wiener Neustadt in Austria were responsible for forty-eight percent of the German fighter production.

With the hope of dividing and confusing the German defending forces, raids on all three targets, Schweinfurt, Regensberg, and Wiener Neustadt, were initially planned for implementation at the same time. The Schweinfurt and Regensberg raids were to be launched by the 8th Air Force from England while the 9th Air Force attacked Wiener Neustadt from its bases in North Africa. However, the 1,000mile distance between the two air forces and the unpredictable weather over Europe made it impossible to co-ordinate. The Wiener Neustadt end of the operation was executed independently on August 13; sixty-four B-24s made a successful foray, with only two bombers failing to return to the base in North Africa.

The combined raids from England were code-named 'Alabama' for the Schweinfurt assault and 'Haymaker' for the Regensberg portion. The mission called for the bomber force heading for Regensberg to take the lead, reaching the Continent at 8:30 a.m. The Schweinfurt force would follow fifteen minutes later along the same route. The lead Regensberg force was supposed to act as a decoy and attract most of the German opposition. After they passed Frankfurt the Schweinfurt bomber force would swing left toward their target, the lead force continuing straight on to Regensberg.

Both would be bombing at precisely the same time, 10:12 a.m. After bombing their target, the Schweinfurt force would have to fight their way out along the same course they had taken to the ball bearing factories. The Regensberg bombers would turn south and fly to North Africa and after resting and refuelling would return to England, attacking a target on the return flight. This mission was the biggest bombing operation and the deepest penetration into Germany the United States Air Force had attempted since America's entry into World War II. The raid to Schweinfurt would involve 231 B-17s; there would be 146 Forts in the Regensberg force. They would be escorted part way to and from the targets by 183 American P-47s and ninety-seven R.A.F. Spitfires. Four diversionary raids would take place using medium bombers, 108 B-26s and thirteen B-25s, escorted by 152 R.A.F. Spitfires.

On the evening of August 16, the ground crews loaded the bombers with 787 tons of bombs - 307 tons for Regensberg and 480 tons for Schweinfurt. The bombers' fuel tanks were filled with a million and a half gallons of fuel. Normally an individual B-17 would carry 8,000 rounds of 50caliber machine gun ammunition, but because of the gunners' apprehension over this particular mission they loaded more than 10,000 rounds for the 4,700 machine guns, a total of three million rounds of ammunition.

The first diversionary raid, composed of thirty-six B-26s escorted by ninety R.A.F. Spitfires, bombed the German airfield at Bryas, France. A total of 232 300-pound bombs were dropped, sixty percent of which landed on the field, making it unusable for several days.

The next two raids were carried out by the R.A.F. Typhoon fighter-bombers. These aircraft possessed awesome firepower: four 20mm cannons, and launching rails which held eight three-inch rocket projectiles fitted beneath the wings. Although it was ineffective as a high altitude fighter, at low altitudes the Typhoon was more than a match for the FW 190 or any other plane the Luftwaffe pitted against it. The first of the Typhoon raids was carried out with eight aircraft and an escort of twelve additional Typhoons. They bombed the enemy fighter airfield at Lille while another Typhoon force hit a German airfield in France at Poix. The raids cratered the fields, but no one was home. The targets had been bombed two days earlier and the Germans had moved their fighters to an auxiliary field. Unfortunately these raids did nothing to prevent action against the Schweinfurt-bound bombing force.

The remaining diversion raids would be on the railroad yards at Dunkirk and Calais. Calais was bombed by six R.A.F. B-25s escorted by forty-eight Spitfires and Dunkirk by seven R.A.F. B-25s similarly escorted. The Calais raid caused minimum damage to the rail yard, while the Dunkirk force was recalled before they reached their target.

After many delays caused by bad weather, the Regensberg bomber force finally took off at 6:21 a.m., Colonel Curtis

LeMay in command. A bomber stream of 139 B-17s, flying at a cruising speed of 165 miles per hour, extended over fifteen miles in length, from Le May's lead 96th Bomb Group to the tail-end Charlie position occupied by the 100th Bomb Group.

Ten minutes after reaching the coast of Belgium the 353rd Fighter Group, consisting of twenty-four P-47s, overtook the bombers at ten o'clock. The fighter escort had reached the rendezvous a little early and was now sweeping backward to try and pick up the formations of B-17s. This new Fighter Group, operational for only a week, had lost their commander on a raid to Le Bourget the previous day. The 56th Fighter Group sent the experienced Major Loren G. McCollom to lead them. They had left England with thirty-seven fighters but belly tank and radio problems compounded by the inclement weather reduced their number to only twenty-four. This force was insufficient to adequately protect the fifteen miles of bombers, but it did perform a useful spoiling action on some of the enemy. Several times the Germans would dive down out of the sun to find the P-47s positioned between them and the bombers.

The 353rd Fighter Group checked their fuel and decided they had just enough to make it home. As they were departing, the 56th Fighter Group, with forty more Thunderbolts, arrived to relieve them. They could only remain as escort for another sixty miles, to just inside the German border, and then they too would have to return to England. The Germans' ploy was to wait until the American fighters had been forced to turn back and then they would 'escort' the bombers the rest of the way.

The two departing Fighter Groups had been itching for battle and were upset that they did not have the range to escort the bombers any further. Now the Regensberg bomber force would be alone and on their own. They had come more than 125 miles but still had 325 miles to fly before they would reach the target.

Several weeks prior the enemy had recalled fighter units from Norway, Russia, and Italy and deployed them in depth along a 150-mile corridor. They now had more than 300 fighters stationed at airfields rimming the corridor which would take off as the American bombers approached their area of protection. As the besieged B-17s droned steadily deeper into enemy territory they flew through a gauntlet of enemy aircraft. As soon as one enemy force expended its ammunition against the passing bombers and left, a fresh new group from the next airfield would continue the attack.

The 100th Bomb Group was especially vulnerable as it was the last group in the formation. The hapless men, fighting desperately, watched as half of their bombers plunged burning to earth. One 100th bomber, piloted by Captain Robert Knox, was being torn to ribbons by German fighters. A 20mm shell tore into the wing, shattering tubing, and knocking out the hydraulic system and one of the engines. As the plane began to lag and drop out of the formation a second engine went dead. The crippled aircraft with its reduced power became a near-stationary target. Suddenly the wheels of the Fortress lowered. When Captain Knox and his co-pilot John Whitaker looked out from the cockpit, they were amazed to see a dozen enemy aircraft flying alongside as if they wanted to fly in formation with them. Every man who could get to a gun opened fire and several German fighters were blasted out of the sky. The surviving fighters pulled out of range, regrouped, and dove on the floundering bomber. The Germans attacked with a vengeance, placing salvo after salvo of cannon fire into the stricken Fort. It too went down.

From this incident grew the infamous legend of the 'Bloody 100th.' Lowering the wheels of an aircraft was a sign, internationally understood, that the aeroplane had surrendered. Once done, attacks upon the surrendering aircraft were supposed to cease. The enemy fighters flew alongside the Fort to escort it down to an airfield, but the bomber's gunners took advantage of the situation and shot down some of the escort. After this violation of the Code of the Air, or so the story goes, the 100th Bomb Group was sought out for extinction by the Germans.

At 11:37 a.m. the battered Forts reached the IP[2] and started their bombing run on Regensberg. Although the force had been reduced to 122 aircraft from the 139 that crossed the French coast, it released 230 tons of bombs with results better than excellent. The reconnaissance photographs showed that all of the released bombs fell on the Messerschmitt factory, totally destroying it and thirty-nine new Me 109 fighters just off the assembly line.

The formation left Regensberg and headed south to North Africa, catching the Luftwaffe by complete surprise. The Germans had expected to catch the remaining bombers on the return trip back to England. While Colonel LeMay's force crossed the Alps, the Schweinfurt bomber force was just leaving England after a weather delay of six and a half hours. Instead of LeMay's force acting as a decoy, they alerted the enemy, who replaced spent ammunition and fuel and waited for them.

The two large forces, each over ten miles long, headed out over the North Sea. The first was 116 bombers strong, the second consisted of 114 bombers. They met over the coast of Holland and formed into four combat wings stretching out over sixty miles. Of the 230 B-17s who had started on the mission, eight developed mechanical problems and had to turn back to England. The remaining 222 bombers crossed into Holland at 22,000 feet and met ninety-six R.A.F. Spitfires who would escort them for just fifteen minutes to Antwerp, Belgium. The Spitfires positioned themselves to provide top cover and stayed out of range of the nervous B-17 gunners. Accidental firings on friendly escorts were not unknown.

The R.A.F. squadrons were flying the new Spitfire IX and weaving back and forth above the stream of bombers. During the fifty-mile escort not a single enemy aircraft got close enough to the bombers to initiate an attack. The R.A.F. returned home with four Me 109s and four FW 190s destroyed and no losses.

By now LeMay's force had crossed the Alps, reached the Italian coast, and headed past the Mediterranean over the Ligurian Sea. In the crossing six more damaged B-17s went down and only 117 landed at Bone, North Africa, at 4:32 p.m.

The 4th Fighter Group led by Lieutenant Colonel Blakeslee took off from Debden, England, at 1:10 p.m. The 4th and 78th Fighter Groups were to take over the escort duties from the R.A.F. at Antwerp and stay with them until they reached Eupen, Belgium, on the western border of Germany. The 78th was to protect the rear two wings of bombers while the Fourth was to provide support for the leading wings.

The Thunderbolts of the 78th Fighter Group arrived at the rendezvous eight minutes late and missed the bombers, but after heading east of Antwerp made contact and took their assigned position on the rear two wings. The 78th had left England with forty-eight fighters but seven had to abort because of defective belly tanks. The group was led by Lt. Col. James J. Stone, who ordered partial coverage of the leading wings all the way to Eupen when it became apparent the Fourth had not yet arrived.

The Fourth arrived on time but could not find the formation of bombers. A frantic search was initiated and the pilots had spent a frustrating twenty minutes searching north almost to Eupen, the limit of their fuel supply, when Gentile called out he could see contrails south at six o'clock. They wheeled and as they approached enemy aircraft were seen attacking the bombers. When the Luftwaffe saw the approaching Americans they withdrew, knowing their fuel supply would not allow them to remain on the scene for long.

The P-47s made one sweep down the long bomber stream before turning to the port and heading home. They had arrived just in time to depart. Gentile wigwagged his wings, an inadequate gesture of support, but the only one he could offer. Don felt helpless and sick in the pit of his stomach. He knew all the fighter pilots wished they were able to go all the way to the target and back with the bombers. Don could feel hundreds of eyes watching forlornly. The intercoms were silent as the bomber crews contemplated that soon they would be all alone, staring death in the face. Feeling the terror and agony of these men who would soon die, an awful empty feeling came over Don. He prayed for them and made a solemn promise to always protect the bombers whenever he could.

He stole one last glance back and observed German fighters arriving as soon as the P-47s left. Instead of the usual method of attacking alone or in pairs, they were in phalanxes of twelve abreast, firing all at once with cannon and machine guns. Don could feel the sweat trickle down his back as groups of four Me 110s approached the B-17s from the beam, each firing all four of their rockets at once, then diving under the bombers only to be replaced by four more 110s who would repeat the performance. In two years of combat Don thought he had seen everything, but he had never witnessed such ferocity and intensity. He watched in admiration as the crew of the bombers courageously pressed steadily forward at 165 miles per hour towards Schweinfort, in spite of the frightful bites being taken out of the formation. Don adjusted his oxygen mask to free it of ice and fastened it a little tighter. He pushed the throttle forward to keep up with his squadron, who had set a heading for home.

The bomber force passed Eupen, ten miles from the German border, at 2:15 p.m. and had travelled more than 240 miles from the airfields in England. They still 190 miles, requiring sixty-eight minutes of flying time, before reaching Schweinfurt. They encountered the fiercest part of the battle in this last stretch, meeting more than 300 enemy fighters.

At 3:50 p.m. they were over the target and dropped 435 tons of bombs on the five ball bearing factories. They did such severe damage that ball bearing production in Germany was reduced by thirty-four percent for several months. The raid lasted eleven minutes. At 4:15 p.m. the bombers circled near the target to reassemble and tighten the formation, then banked and headed west for home. Schweinfurt was a blanket of smoke and fire and in shambles, and they had a short respite as far as the Rhine River, when the B-17 crew members enjoyed their first relaxed look at the beautiful Bavarian countryside.

When they passed the Rhine at 5:00 p.m. they were only eighteen minutes from Eupen, where the Thunderbolts of Colonel Hubert Zemke's 56th Fighter Group were to meet them and provide escort to Antwerp. From there, the R.A.F. Spitfires were to take over the last leg of the return journey. The bomber crews were now frantically searching the cirrus-covered sky for their P-47 escort, when someone noticed masses of small dots in the distance. An excited voice yelled out on the intercom, 'Little friends at eleven o'clock.' All eyes stared intently in that direction and smiling, relieved faces lost their tense appearance. The little dots quickly enlarged and spread out ten to fifteen abreast, coming at the bombers head-on at a rapid closing speed. The intercoms chattered loudly as everyone called out the presence of the enemy fighters. An abject silence and a sense of hopelessness settled over the bombers.

When the fighters got into range the bombers' 50-caliber machine guns began their deadly chatter, spitting out about fourteen bullets per second. When the enemy fighters came within 600 yards their guns started firing, looking like winking lights on their wings.

The enemy attack was being led by Major 'Wutz' Galland, a veteran of two years of combat and credited with fifty-five kills. He was one of three brothers in the Luftwaffe; the others were Adolph, a lieutenant general in the fighter arm credited with 104 kills, and Paul, a lieutenant with seventeen kills who had died in combat over the English Channel in October, 1941.

The 56th Fighter Group, who had provided support earlier in the day for the Regenberg force going to the target, had had three hours to rest, refuel, and re-arm. Now the forty-six P-47s released their belly tanks over Belgium and climbed to 27,000 feet. They had nursed the leaky belly tanks, squeezing from them all the vital fuel possible, so they could penetrate fifteen miles farther east of their rendezvous at Eupen.

As the American fighters approached the B-17 formations they observed Major Galland's Focke-Wulf 190s completing their first attack on the bombers leading low group. After this attack Galland turned to starboard and led his gruppe[3] back into a frontal position for a second attack. Captain Walker H. Mahurin, who later shot down twenty-one German aeroplanes, one Japanese bomber, and three and a half MIGs in the Korean War, flew out of the sun, 5,000 feet above the enemy, leading a flight of P-47s to break up the Galland attack pattern. In the great battle which ensued eleven German fighters were destroyed, plus two probables and one damaged. Mahurin shot down Galland, to the shock of his gruppe, and all of Germany grieved the loss of their fine young ace. The B-17s lost only one bomber during the battle while the 56th Fighter Group lost three.

The dogfights lasted for eighteen minutes and continued almost to Antwerp. Zemke's P-47s had to withdraw and were replaced by forty Thunderbolts from the 353rd Fighter Group. These American fighters were later relieved by eighty-two R.A.F. Spitfires. In this part of the action the British shot down four Me 110s and one FW 190 at a cost of two Spitfires.

Back at the American bomber base in East Anglia, England, the ground crew in their fatigues mingled with the white uniformed cooks and mess helpers, all of them anxiously scanning the horizon for the bomber force. Someone yelled that he could hear a deep, low rumble of aeroplane engines in the distance. Every man among them watched as the group came in fast and low - some of the planes skimming the rooftops, some with gaping holes, some with one or two props feathered, others yawing jerkily across the field. The spectators gasped, apprehensive, searching desperately for 'their' aeroplane.

The 8th Air Force had paid a bitter price. Thirty-six Fortresses were shot down and twenty-seven were so badly damaged they would never be airborne again; another ninety-five had varying degrees of damage. Some 550 crew men were either killed or captured on the Schweinfurt mission. The Regensberg operation dispatched 146 bombers but only 119 had relanded in North Africa. Twenty-seven bombers were lost and 240 crew men were killed or reported missing.

Although the price paid was high indeed, the damage inflicted on the enemy hurt where it counted most. And one small but very important result of the raid on Regensberg was not realised until after the war. The raid destroyed most of the jigs for the fuselage of a secret jet fighter - the Me 262. The destruction of this aircraft most certainly aided the Allies in shortening the war.

The day after the raids a joint conference of bomber and fighter commanders was held. Lt. Col. Donald Blakeslee was severely criticised for his failure to provide the 4th Fighter Group escort for the bombers from Antwerp to Eupen, Belgium. In a heated exchange he was blamed for their loss of fifteen bombers. In fact, the wanderings of the Fourth could be attributed to a number of things, from faulty navigation to poor timing. It also could have been a result of the last minute change of the rendezvous to a lower altitude, of which the Fourth was not informed.

The damage in lost men and bombers was devastating, and consequently the Eighth would have to temporarily retrench and rebuild before launching another massive raid into Germany. It was decided to carry out only short range missions by a limited bomber force with fighter escort the next two and one half weeks.

August 19, 1943 - October 8, 1943

The 4th Fighter Group, led by Lieutenant Colonel Blakeslee, took off from Debden at 5:50 p.m. to provide withdrawal support for forty-five B-17s that were to bomb the German airfield at Woensdrecht, the Netherlands. The bombers orbited the target twice but because of the weather could not bomb the airfield. On the way home they rendezvoused with the Fourth mid-Channel at 6:40 p.m. It was then that a fire broke out in the top turret of the 96th Bomb Group's aircraft 'Black Heart Junior.' Fires of this nature were a prevalent problem with the B-17s at the time; the electrical and oxygen cables passed through the central spigot of the turret and would in time fray from the revolving action.

The oxygen bottles exploded as the fire reached them and the aircraft seemed to stop in mid-air. Flames spread through the front of the Fortress. The pilot, Second Lieutenant Attaway, fearing another explosion, dropped out of formation in a diving turn. He managed to level the plane, but a great stream of blue smoke filled the aircraft and eventually the bail-out signal bell rang. Attaway set the aircraft on automatic pilot, put on his chest pack parachute, and with the crew jumped out the front hatch right through the flames. The co-pilot, Second Lt. Matthew Vinson, and the bombardier, John Miller, were the only ones left in the burning bomber when Vinson discovered his chute had been destroyed by the fire. Miller suggested they jump with one chute, clinging together. But Vinson declined and forced Miller to jump alone, while he went back to attempt to land the burning aircraft.

Vinson returned to the fiery smoke-filled cockpit, released the auto-pilot, and put her into a steep dive, hoping to blow out the flames. He was badly burned on his face and hands and could not see through the blackened windshield, so he opened the side window. With only partial visibility he located the English coast, 2,000 feet below. He brought her down, steep and fast, and sparks flew as the aircraft skidded along the beach. Vinson, afraid the sparks might ignite the leaking fuel, ran from the burning bomber just as the bomb load exploded, spilling debris over the beach area. For this extraordinary feat of survival he was awarded the Distinguished Service Cross, America's second-highest award for valour.

Gentile and the 336th Squadron witnessed this drama and marvelled at the courage and tenacity of the bomber pilots. Don silently reaffirmed his vow to do whatever he could to help, whenever possible, those brave airmen.

On August 31 the Fourth, led by Major Duford, provided general support for a bomber run to the Romilly-sur-Seine airfield in France. The air commander of the bomber force, Colonel William Gross, was a strong advocate of VHF radio in aiding control of formations during missions. Since its inception the Eighth had adopted the R.A.F.'s rule of radio silence to maintain secrecy during a mission. Gross felt the radio could add little to what the enemy already knew, since his radar had been tracking the bomber force from their takeoff.

Colonel Gross decided to test his theory when he found the raid's target obscured by clouds. He immediately radioed the situation to the combat wings following, saving them needless miles over enemy territory. They were redirected by radio to the Amiens/Gilisy Luftwaffe airfield. He gave them directions and other information for the attack and this became the first mission VHF was used to accomplish an improvised and controlled attack on a target.

On this outing the Fourth saw few enemy planes. Captain Miley claimed one probable and one damaged. During the month of September a new bomber, the B-17G, arrived equipped with the new 'chin' turret. This was a twin 50-caliber machine gun, power-operated turret installed in the nose almost directly beneath the bombardier's position. Now the bombers were more capable of meeting the head-on attacks of the German fighters. Most of the B-17s prior to this were the

F Model, with two 50-caliber machine gun installations, one mounted through a window on both sides of the bombardier's compartment. They were manned by the bombardier and the navigator, one on each side of the nose, but they were hand held and not as manoeuvrable and effective as the chin turret in the G-model B-17s.

On a September 2 mission, Lt. John W. Voght of the 56th Fighter Group introduced an improvement in rear viewing on the P-47 fighter after he was almost shot down by an enemy who dove and approached him low from the rear without being seen. He placed two rear view mirrors, one on each side of the fuselage, just forward of the cockpit. This dual mirror system much improved the rear viewing and the innovation eventually appeared on all the P-47s in combat.

The 336th Squadron was divided into two flights, A and B, each flight composed of eight aircraft. On September 3, 1943, First Lt. James A. Goodson was designated 'A' flight commander and First Lt. Donald S. Gentile was 'B' flight commander. The two flights took off with the Fourth at 7:20 a.m. to provide penetration support for 140 B-17s which were to bomb the Romilly-sur-Seine air depot. Lieutenant Nee had to return early due to troubles with his tachometer and belly tank. Later Lieutenant Braley developed radio trouble, Lieutenant Millikan had trouble releasing the belly tank, and Flight Officer Ingold's engine repeatedly cut out. These men all returned to base early.

The bombers, late at the rendezvous as usual, forced the group into a wide slow orbit until they arrived. At 8:39 a.m. seventy FW 190s attacked the bombers and the 336th Squadron engaged and dispersed the enemy formation. Captain Miley and Lieutenants Fuchs, Gentile, Goodson, and Stephenson fired on the enemy but made no claims.

September 15 saw 139 B-17s sent to bomb the Renault and Hispano-Suiza factories in Paris, France. Lieutenant Colonel Blakeslee led the Fourth in the escort but it turned into a milk run, with thirty or forty enemy aircraft sighted and some combat but no claims.

When they returned to land at Debden Don Gentile's engine cut out just as he was making his final approach and he had to make a dead stick landing.

General Order No. 159, dated September 15, 1943, awarded Don S. Gentile, 0-885109, First Lieutenant, Army Air Force, United States Army, the Distinguished Flying Cross.

The Fourth had lost many men, and experienced replacements were constantly needed and added to the group. Most were American boys trained and serving in the R.A.F. for whom the United States paid the British Government $100,000 per man to allow the transfer to the American Armed Services.

On September 21, 1943, Major Carl H. Miley, commander of the 336th Squadron, introduced the newest replacements to Gentile. He was particularly impressed with two, Second Lt. John T. Godfrey and Pilot Officer Ralph K. Hofer.

John Godfrey, 6' 2', tall, dark, and good looking, with darting, gypsy-black eyes, was from a prosperous family in Woonsocket, Rhode Island, who were troubled with his refusal to attend college. He had been moody and reckless, seemingly without ambition, and ran away to avoid attending college. On August 19, 1941, he ran away and joined the Royal Canadian Air Force in Canada.

On October 9, 1941, his commanding officer handed Godfrey a telegram. His brother Reggie, while sailing to England as a civilian employee of the R.A.F. assigned to man their radar system in England, had been killed. The vessel, Vancouver Isle, was torpedoed off the coast of Greenland and went down with all hands. Flying curbed his recklessness and rebellion and gave him something he enjoyed and could take seriously. Now his brother's death hardened his character and gave him a goal in life-vengeance.

Ralph Hofer, of Salem, Missouri, was assigned to the 334th Squadron. In 1940 he had won a trophy boxing in a Golden Gloves tournament. Later he boxed professionally under the name of Kid Hofer. In 1941 he travelled to Windsor to check out Canada. There he joined the Royal Canadian Air Force.

On September 27, the Eighth launched the first mission utilising H2S, a radar device developed by the British which scanned the ground under the clouds and could be read like a map by a trained technician. The Americans designated the device H2X, or 'Mickey,' and hoped it would guide them to the targets at the important seaport of Emden, Germany. The radar would give contrasting reflections of land and water and Emden's location should show up more distinctly on the instrument.

For this mission four H2S-equipped B-17s used the radar to aim and drop marker bombs when clouds covered the target. The other B-17s could then drop their load of bombs on the smoke trails of the markers. In this way 242 B-17s bombed Emden with a fair amount of accuracy despite an overcast sky.

Back at Debden the pilots of the group enjoyed ham and eggs for breakfast, a ritual held over from their R.A.F. days.

Gentile was to lead today's 'B' Flight with John Godfrey as his wingman. This would be John's first mission and he had butterflies in his stomach.

Don was flying the P-47 'Donnie Boy' and John was alongside him with a P-47 lettered VF-P. They left Debden at 8:30 a.m. for a forward base at Hardwick, on the coast of England. They had a new belly tank, 108-gallon capacity and pressurised, which had replaced the old seventy-five gallon paper tanks, so now the fighters could escort the bombers up to a range of 350 miles.

Godfrey maintained his position on Don's wing and did not take his eyes off it for fear of losing him in the mass of fighter aircraft. The sky was filled with 262 P-47 fighters from the 4th, 56th, 78th, 352nd, 353rd, and 355th Fighter Groups.

When the bombers entered northern Germany the enemy scrambled its fighters to intercept the incoming raid. FW 190s and Me 109s dove in and barreled through the formations, trying to break them up. Another group of German fighters approached the bombers and lobbed rockets at them. Thanks to the new belly tanks, the P-47s were there, able to go all the way to and from the target. The Luftwaffe were taken by surprise, and the deep penetration cost them dearly: twenty-four aircraft lost to the Americans' loss of one P-47 and seven B-17s. The 353rd scored eight kills, the 78th got ten, the 56th scored five, while the Fourth got only one, an FW 190 scored by Willard Milligan at 10:00 a.m. The Fourth was upset with their low score, since they felt they had done a better job of escorting.

On the return flight they ran into a solid front of weather extending up to 20,000 feet. They stayed on top of the overcast until it came time to let down over the Channel. The planes up ahead slowly vanished into the billowing mass of cumulus clouds. Don called for a tight formation and 'B' Flight closed up and started the descent into the clouds.

Godfrey clung tightly to Don's wing as they hit the dark overcast. He had a premonition something was wrong but he was too close to take a chance and glance at his own instruments. He had to rely and trust Don, even if they might spin into the ground. He was tired, completely fatigued, from the tension created by this mad charge through the darkness. John had heard of pilots with even more combat time than Don who had been lost trying to fly by instruments in bad weather. He felt his flight suit filling with sweat; they continued to lose altitude every second. He was still sweating when a moment later they broke out of the overcast seventy-five feet above the choppy sea. As they headed across the Channel they passed through clouds that dipped down and merged with the ocean. At other times they were flying just above the waves with the visibility next to zero. All at once, land loomed up ahead. With their fuel diminishing rapidly, they had to land at the nearest airfield. Now they were skimming along the ground, while the top of their canopies seemed in the clouds. They found an emergency airfield and landed. Don walked to over Godfrey, grinning a grin that would not quit.

'Are you all right, John?'

'I think so.'

'Man, that sure was a close one!' Don said in his high-pitched voice.

'What do you mean?'

The grin faded. 'We almost played submarine. My instruments went haywire and I lost our bearing. Lucky we found a break in the clouds.'

'Well, we made it anyway.'

Don doubled over with laughter, put his arm around Godfrey, and said, 'Let's go borrow some gas, Johnny, you have had quite a first day.'

Special Order No. 271, dated September 30,1943, promoted First Lt. Don S.

Gentile to captain.

The second of October saw 339 B-17s pay a second visit to Emden. Once again they used two H2S-equipped aircraft because the target was obscured by clouds. The smoke bombs dropped by one of the aircraft were not on the target, and the wind blew the marker smoke from both aircraft away from the target area. The effect on the aim of the bombers following in the formation was cataclysmic.

At 3:00 p.m. the Fourth was led by Lieutenant Colonel Blakeslee to Hardwick for staging. The group rendezvoused with the bombers at 24,000 feet at 3:53 p.m. Gentile flew with Flight Officer Hughes as his wingman. Six Me 109s attacked the lead box of Fortresses but the 336th drove them off, with Major Miley and Lieutenant Peterson scoring some hits. On the return journey ten FW 190s were sighted; the 334th Squadron attacked and First Lt. Duane Beeson got one.

After finally rebuilding its numbers to the strength it had during the Schweinfurt mission, the Eighth Air Force started a new series of raids deep into Germany. Three hundred and twenty- three heavies (B-17s and B-24s) were sent to Frankfurt, and more fighters than ever before escorted them. They encountered strong enemy fighter opposition, but the 223-strong P-47 escort kept the losses down to twelve bombers. The 4th, 56th, 78th, 355th, and the 353rd Fighter Groups again provided shuttle escort for the heavies, with the Fourth's withdrawal support.

Gentile, leading 'B' Flight of the 336th, eased the stick back gently and started a steep climb into an unresisting blue sky flecked with dull red. The group, led by Lieutenant Colonel Blakeslee, arrived on time at the 28,000-feet rendezvous over Eupen at 1:24 p.m., but the bombers were not there. They did a slow orbit for sixteen minutes but finally had to return to base. When they landed at 3:00 p.m. from this October 4 mission, they learned that the 56th had shot down sixteen German fighters, and the 353rd and 355th had scored one each. But the Fourth did not even see the bombers, let alone the enemy.

On October 8 the 8th Air Force launched a three-pronged attack on Bremen and Vegesack, Germany. The First Bomb Division's 174 B-17s made a direct approach across Holland to Bremen. The Second Bomb Division, with fifty-five B-24s, took a northern route across the North Sea to Begesack. The Third Bomb Division, 170 B-17s strong, flew Northwest over the North Sea to Bremen also. This was the largest mission to date, sending out 399 bombers in a shrewdly timed, triple approach. Unfortunately, the enemy was not deceived. This raid deep into Germany and beyond fighter escort range cost the Eighth dearly - thirty bombers.

This mission also marked a first for its use of a British radar device, code-named 'Carpet.' This was an airborne transmitter which jammed the radar that operated the enemy antiaircraft guns. Forty Forts were so equipped, and the Bomb

Groups utilising them suffered the least from the enemy flak.

These bombers were escorted by 274 P-47s from the 4th, 56th, 78th, 352nd, 353rd, and 355th Fighter Groups. The Fourth left Debden at 3:00 p.m. led by Blakeslee; the 336th Squadron was commanded by Major Miley; Captain Gentile was Flight 'B' commander and Captain Goodson, the 'A' Flight commander. Flying Officer Hughes served as Gentile's wingman.

The enemy also paid a tremendous price, losing thirteen aircraft to the American escort, among them two of Germany's top aces: Lt. Col. Erwin Clausen, holder of the Knight's Cross of the Iron Cross with Oak Leaves, 132 victories, including fourteen four-engine bombers, and Lt. Col. Hans Philipp, holder of the Knight's Cross of the Iron Cross with Oak Leaves and Swords, 206 victories. The Swords award was won by only 154 military men during the entire war.

The Fourth shot down six enemy aircraft, the 56th scored five, and the 353rd, two. First Lt. Duane Beeson got two, bringing his total score to six, and Major Ray Evans got five. They shared the distinction of becoming the 4th Fighter Group's first aces, and on the same day. F/O Ralph 'Kid' Hofer, on his first mission, shot down an FW 190. This was unusual; most pilots were lucky to return in one piece or just see the enemy, let alone annihilate him. In a few months the 'Kid' was destined to become an ace, with five swastikas painted on his P-47.

From this flight Lieutenants Clyde D. Smith and Rufus L. Patterson did not return.

October 10, 1943 - December 31, 1943

October 10, 1943. Two hundred and thirty-six B-17S headed for Munster, Germany, a rail centre handling most of the traffic north of the Ruhr. The intent of the mission was to drop bombs on the city itself, disrupting the working population by depriving them of life and home.

The Americans put 216 P-47s from the 4th, 56th, 78th, 352nd, and 353rd Fighter Groups in the air. The Fourth took off at 1:45 p.m.; at 2:53 p.m. they dropped their belly tanks as they crossed over the Continent. They met the bombers at 3:06 p.m. and took up their position on the last box of B-17s. The 56th Fighter Group was assigned to protect the lead bombers but they arrived late due to a navigational error.

Enemy aircraft attacked the bombers but the 56th, low on fuel, could do nothing but turn and head home, ten minutes from the IP. Blakeslee led the 336th Squadron forward to protect the lead bombers but the Forts were too strung out for effective cover.

When Gentile and his wingman Godfrey landed at 4:20 p.m., they were told the 56th scored ten, while the 78th and the 353rd each scored five. This was John

Godfrey's third combat mission and the second one as Gentile's wingman; it was the first time he had the opportunity to fire his guns.

Despite heavy flak and attacks by approximately 200 German fighters, the bombers dropped their bombs on the city but in so doing lost thirty aircraft. One of the bombers to go down was piloted by Lt. John Winant, son of the U.S. Ambassador to Britain. Winant bailed out of his crippled plane and was captured and became a prisoner of war.

October 18, 1943. This day marked the end of 'Black Week,' with the 8th Air Force and the Luftwaffe each suffering severely from the slugging match. The cost to the Americans was near catastrophic: 143 B-17s and five B-24s were destroyed and 121 aircraft more were damaged. These losses were more then the ten percent considered acceptable. The raids demonstrated the enemy's growing ability to break up the tightly knit bomber boxes by concentrating on one bomber formation at a time. Their strategy was to fire rockets just outside the shooting range of the bombers, then continue to press the attack with their single-engine fighters. The Americans also dealt some critical blows with the destruction of 102 German aircraft and fine strategic bombing on key industrial targets.

It was now painfully clear that the concept of a selfdefensive bomber formation was not feasible. The Allies needed more and longer-ranged fighter escorts to keep down the bomber losses. It was therefore decided the bombers would not venture so deep into Germany again until they could be escorted all the way.

Captain Gentile and his wingman Flying Officer Richards took off with the Fourth for a bomber escort to Duren, Germany at 1:40 p.m. Due to the deteriorating weather, the bombers were recalled over the North Sea and the mission scrubbed. Don landed with the Fourth at 3:35 p.m.

October 20, 1943. The mission was to escort 282 bombers to Duren, Germany. The fighter escort was composed of 321 P-47s from the 4th, 56th, 78th, 352nd, 353rd, 355th, and 356th, and thirty-nine P-38s from the 55th Fighter Group. The twin engine P-38 Lockheed fighter aircraft, with its two seventy-five-gallon wing tip drop tanks, could escort bombers a distance of 520 miles, but they were less manoeuvrable than the single-engine fighter aircraft. The P-47s were to escort the bombers to the limit of the fighters' range in shuttles; the P38s would accompany them to the target and back to the P47s, who would continue the shuttle back to home base.

Captain Gentile, his wingman Flying Officer Raphael, Lieutenant Messenger, and his wingman Lieutenant Godfrey took off at 1:20 p.m. At 2:20 p.m. the Fourth took over escort from another P-47 group and at 2:47 let the P-38s handle the withdrawal support.

Green Section of the 334th Squadron was detailed to accompany a crippled

Fort back to England. The section broke off and headed back, constantly weaving over the Fortress in pairs. First Lt. Duane Beeson (Green 3) and Flying Officer Nickolas Megura (Green 4) were on the port side of the bombers when Captain Mills (Green 1) reported two aircraft approaching rapidly from the rear. They made a turn to the port and observed the two aeroplanes behind their section, about 700 yards and closing fast. The planes were P-47s, and so it was presumed they were Green 1 and 2. Continuing the port turn, Green 1 called to break. Just at that moment the lead aircraft opened fire. Immediate evasive action was taken, but Megura's aeroplane sustained considerable damage from the encounter.

Lieutenant Nee and his section of the 336th Squadron, consisting of Lieutenants Garrison, Messenger, and Godfrey were likewise detailed to escort a crippled Fort back home. Lieutenants Messenger and Godfrey were also bounced by 'friendly' P-47s.

November 3, 1943. Captain Gentile and his wingman Flying Officer Van Wyk took off from the forward base of Halesworth at 11:35 a.m. to provide escort on a mission to the German seaport of Wilhelmhaven. The Fourth and six other Fighter Groups comprised the largest escort to date - 333 P-47s and forty-five P-38s. The P-38s, having superior endurance, provided escort the last leg of the journey and made the escort continuous throughout the bomber route. This was the second time the P-38s saw combat in the European Theater of Opeations (E.T.O.), and they enjoyed their first victory, claiming three enemy aeroplanes without a single loss.

The mission boasted other firsts. It was the first to use more than 500 bombers - 566 were dispatched and 539 reached the target. It was also the first to utilise the new improved H2X, the American version of the British H2S.

Due to the 10/10[1] cloud cover over the target area, eleven bombers were equipped with the H2X radar devices. They dropped 1,448 tons of bombs, creating extensive damage to the ship-building facility.

A P-47 crashed on takeoff, splitting up the 336th Squadron, but they regrouped and crossed the Dutch coast at 12:15 p.m. At 12:30 p.m. the 334th Squadron was attacked; in the ensuing battle they scored one Me 109 but lost two P-47s. Overall the Fighter Groups destroyed fifteen aircraft: the Fourth, one; the 55th and 56th, four each; the 78th, one; the 353rd, five. They sustained two losses, both from the Fourth. Their scores would have been higher had their orders not required them to remain in close support of the bombers warding off attacks rather than engaging in independent combat.

November 13, 1943. The Fourth and two other groups made up of 345 P-47s and forty-five P-38s were to escort bombers to Bremen, Germany. Captain Gentile, with wingman Lieutenant Garrison, and Captain Bishop with his wingman, Lieutenant Godfrey, took off with the Fourth from Debden at 11:15

a.m. The group staged their mission from the forward base of Hardwick in order to escort the B-24s back from Bremen. But the bombers were thirty minutes late and the Fourth missed them entirely.

The weather got progressively worse with the onset of winter and made flying very difficult. Cloud layers extending from a few hundred feet above the ground to an altitude of 30,000 feet necessitated long periods of tedious and exhausting instrument flying. This prolonged blind flying on instruments alone could cause one to become vulnerable to a temporary loss of control or vertigo, often resulting in a fatal spin. On this raid the inclement weather caused many bombers to abandon the mission either during assembly or in flight; only 143 of the 272 dispatched made it to Bremen.

Sixteen bombers crashed, most of the losses attributable to the weather rather than enemy fire.

While the American fighters were credited with the destruction of nine enemy aeroplanes, seven for the P-38s and three for the P-47s, this mission was unlucky for the P-38s. The extremely cold European weather caused considerable physical discomfort to the pilots and a host of both mechanical and performance problems for their aircraft. The pilots would suffer from frostbitten faces, hands, and feet in the inadequately heated cockpits and become so numb and weak they would have to be lifted out of the aircraft. And though the P-38s could perform admirably at 18,000 feet or less, at 30,000 feet they were no match for either the Me 109 or the FW 190. At high altitudes not only did their performance diminish, their engine problems increased.

Lieutenants Fuchs and Godfrey were hit by flak but sustained only minor damage to their aircraft. They returned at 1:55 p.m.

November 26, 1943. Six hundred and thirty-three bombers, 100 of which were B-24s, departed England on two separate raids. One hundred and twenty-eight of this force were to attack Paris, but due to the overcast they had to abort. The rest of the bombers headed for Bremen, Germany, escorted by 353 P-47s, including the Fourth, and twenty-eight P-38s. Fourteen H2X-equipped bombers guided the 1,205 tons of bombs from the 440 bombers that made it to the German target. Over the target they encountered 100 enemy aircraft, including the FW 200[2] which unsuccessfully attempted airto-air bombing 4,000 feet above the formation.

Gentile and his wingman Garrison left Debden for the forward base at Hardwick at 11:10 a.m. As part of the Fourth, they were to provide withdrawal support to the bombers returning from Bremen. They rendezvoused at 12:21 p.m. and found the B-17s in a tight box formation, but the B-24s were strung out for several miles, making effective escort next to impossible. The 56th was responsible for destroying twenty-three enemy aircraft, the highest one-day score of the war.

The Fourth shot down only one plane. The total for the day counting all groups was thirty-six destroyed, three probably destroyed, and nine damaged. Captain Mahurin shot down three, giving him a total of eleven victories and making him the highest scoring ace in the Eighth. Six other pilots of the 56th shot down two each: Lieutenant Colonel Schilling, Majors Gabreski and Graig, Captains Cook and Johnson, and Flying Officer Velenta.

November 29, 1943. Three hundred and sixty B-17s were to return to the port city of Bremen with 352 fighters in support, including thirty-eight P-38s. All but 154 of the bombers aborted due to various problems with their aircraft caused by the extremely cold weather (46 degrees below zero centigrade) at 30,000 feet. They did drop more than 457 tons of bombs.

Don and his wingman, Lieutenant Braley, flew with Lieutenant Messenger and Lieutenant Godfrey, his wingman, to the forward staging base at Bungay to give themselves an extra fifteen minutes of flying time. Braley developed difficulty dropping his belly tank and Gentile had to continue to lead the flight without a wingman, while Godfrey left Bungay late because of belly tank siphoning problems. He could not find the 336th so he joined up with the 335th Squadron of the Fourth.

This was a difficult day for the American fighters. They lost sixteen aircraft and seven P-38s were destroyed, while only fifteen kills were scored against the Germans. Six of the fifteen were shot down by the lead Fighter Group, the 56th, while five kills were scored by a new group, the 356th, in its first major battle with the enemy. Captain Fonzo D. Smith, 335th Squadron, shot down an Me 109.

Major Carl H. Miley, commander of the 336th Squadron, received the Silver Star medal for completing more than 200 hours of combat flying. He was scheduled to leave for the States, turning over the command of the 336th to Major Edner.

November 30, 1943. Three hundred and eighty-one bombers, including thirty-two B-24s, were dispatched to the industrial area of Solingen, Germany, in the Ruhr. The weather conditions were so severe only eighty reached the target, with poor results. Major Evans led the Fourth.

Lieutenant Colonel Blakeslee led the newly formed 354th Fighter Group, which had just become operational, flying the all new P-51B Mustang. He and the other pilots in the group had been taking turns familiarizing themselves with this new aircraft on the two 6,000-foot runways at the Boxted airfield near Colchester. The Mustang consumed less than half the fuel of either the P-47 or the P-38. Its internal wing tanks, with a 186-gallon capacity plus an eighty-five-gallon tank in the fuselage behind the pilot, gave it a range of more than 475 miles. It also could be fitted with two external seventy-five-gallon drop tanks which then gave it the amazing range of 650 miles. These new aeroplanes were assigned to new units which would become the 9th Air Force. The Ninth was primarily a tactical force, to be used in support of the ground armies in the coming D-Day invasion.

The Mustang fighter could reach speeds of 455 miles per hour at 30,000 feet. It outperformed all other aeroplanes in the Allied and Axis arsenals, at all heights. It was superior to the enemy's planes in manoeuvrability, excepting the rolling rate, in which the FW 190 excelled. Use of its external drop tanks only resulted in a speed loss of thirty-five miles per hour. It was the first truly offensive fighter and could escort the bomber formations all the way to their target.

Gentile and wingman Lieutenant Nelson took off with the Fourth at 10:20 a.m. They observed bombers on the way to the rendezvous but did not sight the formation they were supposed to escort. The latter was attacked by unmarked P38s diving through the box formations. One of the P-47s from another group finally drove the attackers away after he realised they were captured American aircraft being used by the Germans. The bombers dropped 225 tons of bombs, with poor results, but only three aeroplanes were lost. Their escort suffered the loss of six aeroplanes without destroying a single enemy craft.

December 1, 1943. Major Carl (Spike) Miley, who was waiting for passage home and had been relieved of his flying duties, took Don Gentile aside.

'Don, I have kept a tight rein on you. I know you have been restless, and the more restless you got the stricter my control was. All right Don, you're red hot, and it is natural you should want to be a firecracker over here. I have recommended you for squadron commander of the 336th. Now you will be leading green, inexperienced men who have a great deal to learn before they too become red hot and can survive and take care of themselves. They are going to follow you wherever you take them. You can either get them killed or hold them down until they are ready and teach them how to survive. The choice is yours, and it is a terrible responsibility you now have. Before you only had your 'B' Flight to worry about, but now the lives of the entire squadron are in your hands. Don't waste them. Good luck, Don, and good hunting.'

Gentile found himself shaking hands with Miley. Then he raised his head expectantly, for he could hear the muffled drone of the Thunderbolts' engines, getting ready for today's mission to the 'Valley of Death.'

Don's forehead furrowed in thought. At last, he was in command. The R.A.F. had trained him to fly and to fight as a combat pilot, but his responsibility in this war had been divided and parcelled out in military directives from higher-ups until now. Finally he was on his own, he would have some latitude in making decisions. For the first time he thought about being responsible for the lives of the other men. He was not afraid of being responsible for himself, that he would willingly do, but the others... He would have to think about that...that was something he would have to give some real thought to.

Gentile could feel Miley's eyes dissecting him, but before he could speak Spike put his arm around him and said, 'Don't worry, Don, you can do it. I had the same pangs of fear when I was asked to take over the 336th.' For a second more Don hesitated, whispering to himself that he would do just what Spike did to him, he would keep the men in his squadron under a tight rein.

In almost two years of combat, Don had brooded over the loss of friends, but he was determined to do his job well and not be responsible for the loss of any of his men.

'Spike, thanks, I'll take care of them.'

As he departed Don scarcely notice the arrival of his crew chief, John Ferra.

'Captain, the planes of the squadron are ready, sir.'

Two hundred and ninety-nine bombers returned to the industrial complex at Solingen. The Ruhr had an extremely high concentration of flak guns, more, in fact, than any other area in Europe.

Don and his wingman, Lieutenant Hughes, led the squadron's takeoff at 10:20 a.m. Godfrey, wingman to Lieutenant Garrison, was piloting a brand new P-47. Letters four inches high in front of the cockpit spelled out 'Reggie's Reply;' and on the cowling there was a picture of his dog Lucky looking out from a horseshoe.

When they crossed the coast of the Continent, Lieutenant Braley's belly tank froze and would not detach. Don sent him home with Lieutenant Bonds as an escort. Normally, another aeroplane would not be sent home as an escort, but today Gentile was leading the squadron and he was not taking the chance of losing anyone. The bright sky of the morning was giving way to frontal weather, and now as Don looked around he could scarcely see the other aircraft in the squadron. He had them fly on their own instruments rather than close up on his wing.

When they emerged from the overcast they were approaching the Fortresses, but they were all mixed up. Don made a wide arc to the left and ordered them back into formation. As they formed up one of the sections of the squadron slid in front of Godfrey, forcing him into a sharp turn to the right. He found himself alone when he attempted to rejoin the formation, then noticed a lone crippled Fort heading home with an Me 109 getting ready to attack from up sun. Godfrey dove on him from 15,000 feet, and when he was 250 feet dead astern he gave the German a short burst. The enemy was flying with a belly tank and when John's bullets hit, red and white flames totally engulfed the plane and threw debris fifty feet in all directions.

The 336th rendezvoused with the bombers at 11:23 a.m. and at 11:45 a.m. the Fourth broke escort and headed home. All returned to base safely at 1:05 p.m.

December 11, 1943. Five hundred and eighty-three bombers, including ninety-three B-24s, were dispatched to attack Emden, an industrial area in Germany. They dropped 1,407 tons of bombs with poor results and encountered intense enemy fighter opposition. Major Roy W. Evans led the 4th Fighter Group, consisting of the 334th, 335th, and 336th Squadrons, with twenty-five to thirty P-47s in each.

Each squadron was now composed of seventy-five to eighty pilots backed up by the necessary ground crew, administrative, and support service personnel. During a normal combat mission each squadron would put up four flights of four aircraft, while four more manned aircraft were held in reserve in case of aborts. As temporary squadron commander Gentile led many missions, but occasionally he would permit a flight leader or even an element leader to take over in order to gain experience.

Don took off at 10:25 a.m., but he developed radio trouble and turned the command of the squadron over to his wingman Lieutenant Mirsch and returned early. The squadron was attacked by eight or ten Me 109s and the engagement lasted until 12:07 p.m., when the P-47s' endurance limit was reached, forcing the Fourth to break off and return home. The bombers were late and were not encountered on the way to Emden.

Two P-47s of the 56th Fighter Group collided when preparing to attack, but the 56th still managed to destroy seventeen enemy fighters. The Fourth destroyed one enemy with no losses and all of the Fourth landed safely at 1:15 p.m.

December 13, 1943. The Eighth undertook a three-point attack, sending 117 B-17s against Bremen, 355 B-17s and B-24s to Kiel, and 111 B-17s to Hamburg. Major Edner led the Fourth as general support for the Forts to Bremen, Germany.

The 336th Squadron, led by Captain Goodson and his wingman Lieutenant Simon, took off from the forward base of Bungay at 10:30 a.m. with Gentile and wingman Lieutenant Braley leading 'B' Flight and Lieutenant Milliken and wingman Lieutenant Godfrey leading 'A' Flight.

The 336th's takeoff was not without mishap. Lieutenant Wiggin's belly tank connection broke; Dunn's belly tank would not function; Sooman's engine cut out, and Norley cracked up his aeroplane. Despite these, at noon the group rendezvoused with the bombers twenty miles north of Bremen, and escorted them to the target and back to Groszenkeneten, where two other P-47 groups took over at ten minutes past noon.

The bombing of Bremen yielded poor results, but no bombers were lost.

December 16, 1943. Five hundred and thirty-five bombers returned to Bremen, Germany, to drop 1,508 tons of bombs. The day was hazy but there was no actual overcast; the forecast for Europe was clear. The Fourth took off at 11:50 a.m. with a fifth (purple) section added to each squadron. As part of an experiment, each squadron flew 2,000 feet apart, spread out over a thirty-mile front, while the Purple Sections flew 500 feet above their respective squadrons. They did not meet the bombers at the rendezvous point at the designated time of

1:23 p.m. so they made a slow wide turn to starboard and found them at another altitude, 27,000 feet, at 1:45 p.m.

While cruising at 27,000 feet, First Lt. Vermont Garrison sighted a JU 88 diving at 17,000 feet. He radioed to First Lt. Louis Norley and they both dove on the enemy, but because of their speed they could not get proper deflection shots. They turned to port and went down for another attack. Gentile spotted this action at 1:15 p.m., diving to catch the enemy at 12,000 feet, but his excessive speed and his opponent's turn into the attack caused him, too, to overshoot. He fired a short burst from 150 yards then pulled back up and made another attack from above and astern. He was firing a special British incendiary ammunition which made red flashes as it struck. He made strikes on the tail gunner's position and around the engines, causing the left engine to burst into flames and the right engine to smoke. Garrison and Norley made several more attacks with Gentile and when the JU disappeared into the clouds they could see flames spreading over the wings and left side of the fuselage.

Gentile claimed one JU 88 destroyed, shared with Lieutenants Garrison and Norley.

December 20, 1943. Four hundred and seventy-two bombers again headed to Bremen, Germany, to drop 1,099 tons of bombs. On this mission they lost twenty-seven bombers, including a B-24 which collided with a P-47 from the 356th Fighter Group.

The Fourth was airborne at 10:45 a.m., led by Major Evans. While over the coast of Europe Flying Officer Ralph Hofer developed engine trouble and had to turn back for home, only to be attacked by six Me 109s. They chased him all the way back to England, but thanks to his exceptional flying ability Hofer eluded them.

Flying at 28,000 feet, Gentile was attacked head-on by an FW 190 coming at him on his starboard side in a thirty-degree dive. Don broke to the right, the enemy following, then rolled onto him at 800 yards, but the German sped away from him. Don followed him down to 14,000 feet but he was not able to get close enough to fire. Major Evans gave the order to break all contact with the enemy and return to base. All returned safely at 1:00 p.m. First Lt. W. Millikan claimed one Me 109, scored after a terrific fight.

December 22, 1943. One hundred and ninety-four heavies were sent to bomb Munster, Germany, with 354 tons of bombs. The Fourth was to provide withdrawal support, led by Lieutenant Colonel Blakeslee, who had just returned from readying the 354th Fighter Group combat for their maiden missions with the new P-51s. Each day he would return to the Fourth, supposedly because the 354th Nissen Hut accommodations were more primitive than the facilities at Debden. But there was some suspicion his real motivation was to show off the new 'bird' to his pilots. They would crowd around the Mustang, goggle-eyed and spellbound by his enthusiastic account of its combat ability.

Gentile, wingman Hughes, Captain Goodson, wingman Braley, Lieutenant Messenger, and his wingman, Godfrey, took off with the 336th at 12:25 p.m. They rendezvoused with the bombers at 1:59 p.m., at 26,000 feet and fifteen miles west of the target area. The group circled the target area until 2:15 p.m. and then followed the bombers home, leaving them at 2:22 p.m..

First Lts. V. H. Wynn and J. T. Godfrey shared an Me 109 destroyed. Gentile did not even get to switch on his gun sight. Despite his prayers, he was on the wrong side of the bombers. Once again he was only a spectator, and when they returned to base he listened with envy to the excited combat accounts of the other pilots. Don wondered if he would ever get the five kills he needed to become an ace.

December 24, 1943. Six hundred and seventy bombers went to Pas De Calais and dropped 1,745 tons of bombs. Captain Gentile and his wingman Flying Officer Van Wyk led the 336th Squadron again, departing at 12:25 p.m. It was an uneventful mission and all returned safely at 3:20 p.m..

December 31, 1943. The end of the year found Germany on the defensive and fighting on three fronts. Bombings by the 8th Air Force would be joined increasingly by efforts from the 15th Air Force in the south. Initially raids by the 15th were sporadic, and were either unescorted or covered by a small number of P-38s.

The Luftwaffe was far from being defeated. Its ground radio regularly jammed the Allied fighters' radios. When the fighters approached the enemy coast they would hear a high-pitched whine in their earphones that continued all the time they were flying over the Continent. The Allied forces instituted countermeasures which lessened the disturbances but did not entirely remove them. The enemy understood the radio was the lifeline of the fighter, the communications link with the bombers they were escorting and the other fighter aircraft. The radio also aided in their safe return to base when adverse weather, combat, or low fuel supplies required 'homings' to help them.

The last mission of 1943 saw 464 bombers attacking nine Luftwaffe airfields in and around Paris, France. One thousand two hundred and fourteen tons of bombs were dropped, but twenty-five bombers were lost. More than 548 fighters from the Fourth and twelve other groups provided escort support for this force. Lieutenant Colonel Blakeslee led the Fourth through dense cloud conditions extending to 25,000 feet over the English Channel and France. The fighter escort groups lost four aircraft while destroying nine enemy aeroplanes.

As the year came to a close, things were changing. The first American-trained pilots were joining the Fourth. The strength of the fighters for escort had trebled in the last few months of 1943 and the enemy's fighter strength had increased to some 1,500 aircraft. While the British raids against Germany were numerically larger, the American precision bombing was having a greater affect on the enemy's war industry. The Germans had destroyed an impressive number of American bombers, but in this one-year period the bomber force had increased from about 100 to almost 600. The Luftwaffe was weakening and less formidable in its efforts against the American fighters, due largely to Goering's demands to ignore them, whenever possible, and concentrate on shooting down bombers. Allied intelligence reported a build-up of enemy fighter forces that had to be destroyed in order to obtain the air superiority critical to the forthcoming European invasion.

General Arnold sent the following message to General Eaker:

Destroy the Luftwaffe wherever you find them, in the air, on the ground, and in the factories.

January 1, 1944 - March 2, 1944

On the first of January Lieutenant Colonel Blakeslee took command of the Fourth from Colonel C. Peterson, who left to serve as Combat Operation Officer of the 9th Air Force. Until this time Blakeslee had been deputy leader of the group; after becoming C.O., he didn't waste any time setting the priorities for the unit. He was going to make the Fourth the top Fighter Group in the 8th Air Force. He wanted all his pilots to fight aggressively and if they did not want to they could transfer out of the group. Either they kept up with him and his aggressive assault on the enemy or they were better off leaving the unit.

Also during January the entire American Air Force in Europe and the Mediterranean was reorganised. General Spaatz took command of the 8th and 15th Air Forces. The Eighth would now be commanded by Lt. General Jimmy Doolittle, replacing General Eaker, who was transferred to command the entire Allied Air Force in the Mediterranean. Eaker's transfer was not a demotion; it resulted from a request by General Eisenhower, who had worked well with Spaatz and Doolittle in the North African campaign.

On January 4, 1944, in one of the first operations of the year, Doolittle sent sixty-eight bombers to drop 192 tons of bombs on Munster, Germany. Gentile and wingman Flying Officer Van Wyk departed at 9:05 a.m. with Major Halsey commanding the squadron. They were joined by 430 other P-47s providing fighter escort for the bombers. For Don, it was the same old story. They rendezvoused with the Forts at the target area and protected the rear of the formation, but all of the action was at the front. By the time he got there it was all over and the enemy was gone. Not only did he and the group not get near a German fighter, they didn't even see one.

January 5, 1944. By this time the Eighth was totally committed to daily bombing raids, but the Fourth was only a small part of the entire fighter armada now available to lash out at the enemy. There were three major problems to contend with in order to obtain the air supremacy necessary for the D-Day invasion - the weather, the fighters, and flak. England's proximity to the North Sea made her weather worse than the Continent's. In fact, every year saw an average 240 days of adverse weather.

The Fourth had one other problem particular to their group: They did not like the P-47 and lacked faith in the craft. They were the first group with the 8th Air Force, ex-R.A.F.. pilots, experienced and seasoned. They had given a very impressive accounting of themselves while flying Spitfires, but not with the P-47. What else could be the problem? This lack of faith in the Thunderbolt prevented the pilots from going below 18,000 feet for combat. But other groups were doing it, going down after the enemy and destroying him. Those groups felt that if the Luftwaffe would not come up to their altitude, then they had better go down after them. The Fourth finally shifted their strategy of pursuit of the enemy.

The next day was a typical English winter day, very cold and shrouded in a thick haze that only allowed marginal visibility. The Fourth and the 352nd Fighter Group provided 149 P-47 fighters as support for seventy-eight B-17 bombers to Tours airfield in France. The bombers dropped 178 tons of bombs and only lost one aircraft.

Lieutenant Colonel Blakeslee was leading the Fourth and Major Halsey was in command of the 336th Squadron. Gentile was in charge of 'B' Flight with Lieutenant Godfrey as his wingman. As they took off at 10:30 a.m. Don had a smile on his face and a feeling of confidence swept over him. He felt an empty feeling, a sensation of suspense in the pit of his stomach and he knew. For a split second time stood still and he stared blankly at the air speed indicator in front of him on the instrument panel. He knew, yes, he knew, that this morning his luck was going to change. It was written in the stars and God was going to help him fulfil his destiny and he could feel it in every bone in his body. They raced across the Channel in formation, with the haze and fog obliterating everything but the sea barely twenty feet below them. They rendezvoused with the lead bombers at 11:29 a.m. and provided escort to the target.

Gentile was leading Shirtblue Squadron[1], Red section, in the Red 1 position, Godfrey was Red 2, First Lieutenant Messenger, Red 3, and Second Lt. Robert Hughes was in the Red 4 position. On their way home, some thirty miles from the target, Captain Goodson, leading Shirtblue Blue Section, saw FW 190s to the rear of the first box of bombers. He led his section in a dive on the enemy, frantically trying to get on their tails. Goodson called for help from Red Section when one of the 190s began firing on his Blue 4 pilot, Lieutenant Carlson.

In a dive, Gentile led Red Section to the aid of Blue Section. They would close in on the Germans and meet them head-on. Now both the American and German pilots faced physical and psychological predicaments. The physical problem was in judging the correct range; if not, they would collide. The psychological challenge was to fly on a collision course and force the opposition to break off the attack first. The one who turns away first goes on the defence, permitting the other pilot to get on his tail with the chance to destroy him.

The Gentile force was approaching in a shallow dive at a speed exceeding 500 miles per hour; the enemy was in a slight climb at 375 miles per hour. This head-on attack, starting when the aircraft were about two miles apart, allowed Gentile eleven seconds to select the target, aim, fire, and break away. At 1,000 yards he would have two seconds; at 250 yards, the optimum firing distance, he had only one-fifth of a second to break away before collision. Don fired and broke to the right; the two enemy aircraft dove for the deck.

Gentile and Godfrey followed them, and as they started to pull out of the dive Don gave the leader a one-second burst of fire. He continued to close on the 190, narrowing the distance to 250 yards, and made strikes on the engine and cockpit. A flash of flames and smoke engulfed the cockpit area.

At the same time Godfrey was firing on one of the other FW 190s and making strikes. Gentile left the plane he had hit as it plunged to earth, and swung over to assist Godfrey, giving his opponent a short burst. Lieutenant Messenger and his wingman remained above to provide top cover for Gentile and when they observed an enemy fighter ready to attack Don, Messenger dove and met him head on. His fire connected and the plane went down in smoke, but the German pilot bailed out at 3,000 feet.

After they returned to base at 1:35 p.m. Gentile and Messenger were each credited with one FW 190 destroyed and Godfrey with one FW 190 damaged.

January 7, 1944. Four hundred and twenty bombers escorted by 571 fighters including seventy-one P-38s and thirty-seven P-51s headed for Ludwigshafen in southern Germany. The American fighters were to cover the bombers at 23,000 feet and the R.A.F. Spitfires were to sweep the area at 15,000 feet. Major Jimmy Stewart, the movie star, was the air commander of the 445th Bomb Group, a B-24 unit, in this raid. More than 1,001 tons of bombs were dropped, including incendiary of 100, 250, and 500-pounds and 500- and 1000-pound high explosive bombs. Twelve bombers were lost.

Lieutenant Colonel Blakeslee was flying with the 336th Fighter Squadron, leading the 4th Fighter Group covering withdrawal support of the bombers from the target. The weather was crystal clear. In the vicinity of Hesdin, France, twenty FW 190s in finger-four formation came down from up-sun to attack the straggling bombers. A few miles from here lay Abbeville, to the east St Omer, and a short distant south, Poix. These were the home bases of the Luftwaffe's crack JG-2 unit, led by Egon Mayer. There were numerous R.A.F. Spitfire fighters in the area and when Blakeslee dove down to attack, the Spitfires cut him off from his quarry. He pushed back on the control stick and just missed a collision by passing over the Spits in a steep climbing turn to the left.

Blakeslee lost his wingman and Gentile's White Section in this manoeuvre and had to join up with Red Section, led by Captain Goodson. As he came around again, he saw some 190s below him. He dove on them, leaving Goodson's section to provide top cover for him. At 3,000 feet he pulled up under his prey, retarded his throttle, and coasted up without being noticed in a climb dead astern of the enemy. As he sprayed the craft unmercifully three FW 190s slipped on his tail and began blowing holes in his aircraft. Goodson immediately dove on the three; he picked out one and gave him short squirts of gunfire. He struck the 190 and watched it do two and a half flickrolls before plunging to the ground.

When the day was over Blakeslee had to make a force landing at an emergency field with eighty-one holes in his aircraft. The hunting was good; Goodson claimed two, and Garrison and Blakeslee each claimed one destroyed.

January 11, 1944. The Eighth sent out 663 bombers in a three-phase effort to attack and destroy aircraft parts-and-assembly complexes in Germany. The second and third forces had to abort because of the inclement weather. The first force sent 139 B-17s to the FW 190 assembly plant at Oschersleben. They bombarded the target with 456 tons of bombs and met the heaviest enemy opposition since the October 14, 1943, Schweinfurt mission. The Luftwaffe was using drop tanks which allowed them extra air time to continue their violent attacks; they decimated several formations and caused the loss of thirty-four bombers.

Led by Lieutenant Colonel Blakeslee, the Fourth was to provide withdrawal support for the Fortresses returning from Oschersleben. The overcast weather was a solid front from 14,000 to 31,000 feet. Gentile and wingman Godfrey took off at 11:10 a.m. and while they circled the field they watched Lieutenant Herter start his takeoff. As he sped down the runway his right tire blew and caused the right wing to plough into the ground, sending his aircraft spinning savagely from side to side. Gentile, watching from above, unconsciously tried to fly the stricken aeroplane himself. He could feel his muscles flexing and giving with the erratic course of the ship. It went crashing into a parked Cessna aeroplane and this mangled mass bounced into an ambulance, shearing off the engine. As if in slow motion the craft bounced twice more and at the crest of the last bounce hurtled into a crash truck.

Don felt the impact with his whole body, his tendons taut, as the ripping, tearing noises faded slowly into silence. Then the silence was shattered by a tremendous explosion which engulfed the entire area in flames. Fragments and debris arced up towards them as they circled above. Don forced himself to look a second more, and to his utter amazement he saw Lieutenant Herter emerge unhurt from the tangled smoking mass. He whispered a silent thanks for the mercy He had lust displayed.

They gained altitude and headed for the Channel. As they continued the crossing the cloud and haze forced the group to split up into sections. At the time they reached the Continent they were recalled and all aircraft returned and landed at 1:05 p.m.

January 14, 1944. Five hundred and thirty-one bombers, including 175 B-24s, were dispatched to the Pas de Calais area of France to start the 'No Ball' missions, the code name for attacks on V-weapon sites. The Germans were building V-1 launching sites all along this coastal area. The raid had been planned in early 1944 when there was adverse weather over Germany. Twenty out of twenty-one known sites were hit with 500-pound bombs, totalling 1,553 tons. The escort was made up of by ninety-eight P-38s, forty-three P-51s, and 504 P-47s from nine groups, including the Fourth.

Flying Officer Richards, wingman to Gentile, tagged on his tail as they climbed through the thick overcast. They made a climbing turn to the right and formed up with the group after topping the overcast at 26,000 feet. Coming out of the overcast in pairs, the other aircraft manoeuvred and formed up into their respective squadrons behind the group leader, Lieutenant Colonel Edner.

With three and a half destroyed, many probables and some damaged, Don still had not become an ace. This was because they had been flying close support and could not go all out. The fighters could not follow the enemy past the point at which they broke off their attack on the bombers. They had to return to protect them because there were not enough fighters to allow them to do anything else.

Now the numbers were such that some of the fighters could leave the bombers to pursue the Luftwaffe. Don was ready; in two years of combat he had learned a great deal and he was ripe for hot pursuit. The Fourth crossed the enemy occupied coast at 2:28 p.m. at 26,000 feet. When they were near Paris, Gentile reported a gaggle of fifteen to twenty Focke-Wulf 190s 4,000 feet below and flying east. Don and his wingman Richards were flying south so they turned and dove down on the enemy. He opened the throttle and built up speed, and as he headed for the Germans he yelled to his wingman. Richards responded, 'Keep going, I am right behind you.'

The Germans finally saw them coming and split, fanshaped, into two groups, turning into them. Don reached over to the left side of the cockpit below the throttle and adjusted the rheostat to the N-3A gun sight and then flipped off the safety switch to the guns. Four, five-no, eight 190s came thundering toward them from six o'clock. Don's throat tightened and he knew that in the next few seconds he would be either alive or dead. He was not afraid. He continued the dive and slowly the sight of enemy aircraft began to fill his windshield. He talked to himself, 'No nearer...no nearer, Don. Wait!' Don leaned forward into the gun sight and patiently waited for one of the aircraft to get into range. Two of them broke together, hard to the left and straight into Don's gunfire. One of the FW 190's engines began to smoke and Gentile swung around like a rearing stallion and positioned himself on his tail. He knew they were afraid of him and that he was going to kill them. The two Germans dove straight for the deck. Don was at a disadvantage here in his Thunderbolt but he thought he had the psychological edge because of the confidence he had in himself and their fear that he was going to kill them. He closed to 300 yards and gave a long burst of fire. He saw a mushroom of dense black oily smoke come out of the cockpit. The 190 rolled over very slowly and went into a vertical spiral dive and crashed into the woods.

While Don was positioning himself on the tail of another 190, Flying Officer Richards sighted a German, about 800 yards away, firing at Don. This was Richards' first combat and he was scared; he tried to speak but could not. It was no use. His heart was pounding in his throat, he could not swallow, his breath rasped. He needed air - he couldn't breathe. He ripped off his oxygen mask and sucked the delicious fresh air. He was recovering now, but he still was completely speechless and could not warn Don of the imminent danger. He immediately turned into the enemy as hard as he could, in a head-on collision course. He fired as the enemy pulled up and went over him; his gun sight went out. He turned and got on the enemy's tail, diving away and turning at the same time, and gave him a large deflection shot. By this time they were just 200 feet above ground. Richards panicked and screamed for help. He yelled and yelled but no one knew where he was.

He was so frightened he felt sick; he knew from what he had heard that the 190 could out turn a P-47. On the deck the FW 190 was in its element, while the Thunderbolt only came into its own above 20,000 feet. He realised that no one was coming to help him and the only way he would get out of this mess was by himself. Richards and the 190 went around and around in a circle, each trying to get on the other's tail; then somehow they were attacking head-on. Finally the German's engine roared and, with his guns still firing, he tried to get away by heading for the Fatherland. Richards came in on his tail, firing, and saw black smoke coming out of the German's engine. The 190 rolled over on its back and plummeted downward, crashing into the trees. Richards was jubilant - both at cheating death and at getting his first kill. He was so excited and relieved he didn't know what to do next. He could not find Captain Gentile and realised also he was out of ammunition, so he set his course at 320 degrees and headed for home.

During Richards' debouchment, Gentile was closing in a shallow dive from

Don's air battle over Paris. Note Eiffel Tower in background of photo below.

4,000 feet to 250 yards behind the second 190's tail. He commenced firing and continued to close to 150 yards. Don was scoring strikes around the German's cockpit yards. Don was scoring strikes around the German's cockpit and engine. He continued to follow him down, bounced around by the turbulence of his slipstream, but he kept following and firing and striking until the aircraft hit the woods in a flaming inferno. Don was almost sucked into the ground by the impact of the crash. He wrenched the stick, pulled it hard into the pit of his stomach, and just missed the woods. As he climbed back up towards blue sky a voice on the R/T shouted, 'Break, Gentle, Break! Break, Gentle, you damn fool!'

Gentile reefed his Thunderbolt hard to the left and watched as a holocaust of tracers tore up the sky around him. They were everywhere - above, below, ahead, astern. Don yawed, finked, sideslipped, and spun through the onslaught of bullets, but despite his twisting efforts to shake the lead 190, the enemy was sticking like glue and making a lot of hits. Don watched in disbelief as the hot metal tore into the fuselage and right wing, exploding and ripping large jagged chunks out of the skin. The aeroplane shivered like a horse with colic every time it was hit. The lead 190 was so close, he could hear the chugging of his machine guns and the thump-thump-thump of his 20mm cannons. His eyes were wide open, the pupils dilated as he stared hard into the torrential spray from the blinking 20mm cannon and machine gun fire. He heard a voice in the cockpit yelling, 'What the hell are they doing - didn't they see me shoot down those two 190s?'

Don suddenly realised he was without his wingman, without anyone to help him. He was at a disadvantage with the 190 on the deck, and evidently these two were not afraid of him, or they hadn't seen him destroy two of their compatriots. He shook his head violently but it was no use, he couldn't rid himself of this unreal and ugly scene. It was really happening. Fear gripped his heart and visions of his family and friends flashed across his mind's eye.

Now the first 190 went over him, but he stayed in the port turn because the second was still coming. Don met him head-on. He gave a short squirt and the German turned chicken and headed east for home. In the meantime the number one fighter had positioned himself for another attack, but Don broke hard to the right, leaving him with a very poor deflection shot. There are not many pilots who could out turn an FW 190 on the deck with a Thunderbolt, but Gentile was a superb pilot and he had the skill. He quickly swung to the starboard and positioned himself for a head-on attack. Don waited patiently while stroking and caressing the squeeze trigger on the control stick with his gloved right hand.

The two planes were rushing towards each other at a closing speed in excess of 3,000 yards per second. Gentile squinted as he peered through the reflector sight into the bright sun. His face was tense, slightly flushed, and his eyes were wide open as he concentrated as he had never concentrated before, waiting for the right time to fire. His intensity did not mean that he was indifferent to the danger or impervious to fear. Fear was something he was well acquainted with, but his years in combat had taught him the discipline he needed to control it. As the distance rapidly closed Don felt as if he was growing older and older; he felt as if he was reaching the end of his life. He fired - nothing happened! He fired again - nothing! Panic!

With his left hand he pressed the microphone button located on the engine throttle, screaming, 'Help! Help! I'm being clobbered!'

First Lieutenant Millikan, leading the rest of Gentile's section several miles above, in a calm, detached voice called down, 'Would the individual with the screaming voice please give us his call letters and tell us his exact position as to altitude, longitude, and latitude.'

Don did not have time to look around and find out exactly where he was because he didn't dare take his eyes off his crafty foe. He sure wasn't a new boy; he had to be one of the old pros, and a tough one at that.

'I'm down by the railroad tracks with a 190.'

He knew there was no way they could find him against the dark background of the black forest of Compiegne and even if they could they couldn't get to him in time.

For a fleeting moment he thought of giving up, of gaining altitude and going over the side, but he had too much pride for that. The thought vanished.

[[Ref]] Over the black forest of Compiegne.

The enemy opened fire and a hail of 20mm cannon shells and machine gun bullets streaked past him and veered off into his right wing. One moment the 190 was a clearly defined shape, the entire aircraft filling his gun sight, but in the next instant it became a blur covering the windshield. Then they hit!

Incredibly, it was a slight glancing blow which caused minimum damage and did not effect the flying ability of either aeroplane. The collision was a result of the German's poor judgement. It would have been worse if Gentile had been holding the control stick with both hands to steady the aircraft while getting ready to fire. He and most German pilots held the stick with their right hand while operating the throttle with the left; that was the way the Germans were trained, and Don had learned it in his civilian flying. This gave them a slight left-hand bias; they broke more often to the left because it was easier to push the control stick than to pull it to the right.

Death was something that happened to someone else, not him. But now Gentile mentally accepted the fact of death. It was simply a question of the next second or the next minute. He had always thought that He would allow him to fulfil his destiny. Like most Italian-Americans, he was brought up to believe in God, country, and family. His parents indoctrinated this creed in him throughout

Over the black forest of Compiegne.

his life. As he reflected on his stewardship he knew that God would smile approvingly. Hadn't his mother and Sister Teresa driven home the point? Yes, he had made his peace with his Maker and if this was it, well, he was ready.

Here he was, a twenty-three year old American with no ties to England, who had left a peaceful nation to join this madness in the name of freedom and adventure. He had rightly predicted the United States' entrance in the debauchery and now he was serving his own beloved country. He had always tried to do his very best-to be available always as a spare. Hadn't he only taken a two-day pass twice, so he wouldn't miss a chance to fly an extra mission? He had long passed the normal length of combat tour by signing up for extra missions.

And hadn't he always honored his father and mother by behaving responsible? Well...not always, but he hadn't hurt anybody. He did try hard-very hard-to bring honor and respect to the family. He remembered his father telling him to wear the family name as a shield, to honor it and never disgrace it. God knows he had always tried to do this, or. why was he over here? He wanted his beloved country and hometown of Piqua to be proud of him and to know he had done his best to do his duty as God had seen that duty.

His fate was sealed. There was no hope, no chance, no doubts, no possible escape. So why wasn't he terrified and frightened, instead of feeling so very calm. It finally dawned on him it was the certainty of the situation that gave him the courage to remain so calm. There was nothing he could do that could possibly change anything...but wait! Hey, wait! They didn't know what happened.

'If I don't get back, tell them I got two 190s;' Gentile transmitted on the R/T.

With these words he realised that the two kills and his previous three and a half made him an ace! Really an ace! Five and a half-that's a real All-American Yankee Doodle Ace! But his excitement and jubilation very slowly disintegrated into mild despair and finally anger. His death would cheat his family and hometown of having a live hero. He had always been confident he would become an ace and make them all proud of him. He was so sure, he had often visualised himself in a parade down Piqua's Main Street, the high school band playing, the townspeople shaking his hand and cheering. He had seen it so many times in his dreams it felt as if it had actually happened.

And now this goose-stepping animated marionette wearing an oxygen-mask was going to destroy that fantasy. Gentile was mad, madder than he had ever been, and suddenly he swerved his plane around, right into the German. He thought, if I am going to die at least I can take him with me. And besides, that would make it six and a half - that should make them all the more proud of him. The enemy seemed to sense Don's determination and honked his ship up and over Don, positioning himself for another attack. Don tried to out turn him, but each turn found his opponent inside him and firing. He had realised Gentile was out of ammunition so he began pressing the attack for the kill. His tracers slowly walked towards Don's cockpit as he continued to correct his firing.

Don had one very slim chance for survival - to get the enemy to expend all of his ammunition. This would be a duel where he would pit his flying skill against his enemy's marksmanship. If he could keep him off balance by his twisting and turning, he would only have deflection shots - and poor ones at that. As the tracers came lapping towards him like a tidal wave, he began talking to himself. 'Get a hold of yourself - don't panic! Wait!' He concentrated, watching the tracers come closer, ever closer. When they were ready to enter the cockpit, he pulled up hard in a tight turn, taking the seven-ton aircraft almost to the point of a stall.

Then it flicked over. He was hedgehopping over treetops, rooftops, rivers, and railroad tracks; he was skidding, sliding, and twisting in this inverted position. As he recovered he pushed the throttle and the control stick around to direct 'bonnie Boy's' 2,300-horsepower 18-cylinder Pratt & Whitney radial engine. He poured the water injection to his plane for the maximum emergency power. He kept turning and skidding, anxiously looking over his shoulder at his determined enemy's guns blinking and sending their corruption at him. He honked his plane again in a tight turn in the opposite direction, so tight that the German overshot and slid under him. He held this turn up until the whole plane quivered and shuddered and finally flicked. In his inverted position the entire windshield filled with the green of the forest of Compiegne. Don was so low to the ground that the trees and bushes swayed back and forth as he passed over them. The duel over the forest continued for fifteen more minutes, reverse turns and head-on attacks that pitted Gentile's exceptional flying ability against machine guns and cannons.

All of a sudden there was nothing but silence, silence! Unbelievable, safe, blessed silence! The hard-nosed German had run out of ammunition!

'I made it! I outlasted you, you gutsy, wise fox. You didn't get me, did you?' Don was so excited at first he didn't notice the German circling slowly and finally coming alongside him. The startled Gentile watched as his enemy gave him a stiff salute and flew away, wigwagging his wings as he disappeared into the blue infinity of sky.

When Don landed he was weak and trembling from fatigue, soaked to the bone with sweat. There was no way he could ever describe the terror and then the relief when the mission was over. He sat for what seemed an eternity, completely exhausted, too weary to even pull himself from the cockpit. He had been cramped into that narrow space for more than four hours, unable to move anything but his neck, hands, and feet, going through one of the toughest fights of his entire life.

The ground crew came running over to meet him, jumping up and down and waving excitedly. His crew chief leaped on the wing and said, 'Boy, are we glad to see you, Captain. We heard you were a goner.' As he talked his eyes sadly surveyed the battered aircraft. In a broken voice he said, 'Boy, Captain, you really took a beating. It's going to take a couple of weeks to get her all patched up and ready to fly again. That's if we can get her flying again.'

Gentile looked up blankly and slowly nodded. With unsteady hands he removed his helmet and parachute harness.

He walked to his quarters in a daze. But as a hot shower soothed his bone-weary body the weariness and frustration of the day's combat slowly left him. He reflected on what he had learned. He knew God had protected and spared him again. He also knew he could out fight and out fly almost any German, for didn't he prove that today. He had achieved his lifelong goal of acehood and now he could go home.

But, no. This would not be enough, he was going to stay and shoot down more Germans than anyone else in the group. No, he was going to do better than that. He was going to break Captain Eddie Rickenbacker's record of twenty-six kills, win the case of Scotch, and go home 'America's Ace of Aces.'

Later that evening, Don sat by the fire with a cigar at the Officers' Club. While he planned how he was going to shoot down the twenty-six-plus enemy planes, he heard Lieutenant Raphael of Tacoma, Washington, start to play the piano. The tune he played was 'Tramp, Tramp, Tramp. The Boys are Marching.' The words he sang went like this:

It was down upon the deck
I became a nervous wreck
As I dodged the trees just east of old Beauvai,
Jerries drove me nearly frantic
And I soon began to panic
Everyone of C-channel soon heard me say,
Help, help I'm being clobbered
Down here by the railroad track.
Two 190s chase me 'round
And we're damn near to the ground,
Tell them I got two if I don't make it back!
Went down with my Number 2
Just to see what we could do.
And I soon found out that I was left alone.
How I shuddered as I turned,
All my ammunition burned
And I cried out in a very anguished tone:
Help, help I'm being clobbered...

This became the 4th Fighter Group theme song.

January 21, 1944. The bombers flew to the V-1 missile launching sites in the

Pas de Calais area of France. These raids once were milk runs because they were short missions. But lately, the enemy had reinforced substantially the antiaircraft defences and on this particular sortie the Luftwaffe was out in force. Seven hundred and ninety-five bombers were dispatched, but only 394 bombed twenty-four of the thirty-six sites, dropping 1,200 tons of bombs. They were escorted by 628 fighters from the Fourth and twelve other Fighter Groups.

During takeoff at one of the B-24 bases, a truck transporting personnel pulled off the taxi-way to allow a bomber to pass. But it did not pull over far enough, and when the plane passed, its propellers ploughed through the canvas top of the truck and decapitated two aircraft mechanics riding in the rear.

Other accidents plagued this hapless B-24 group on their way over the Channel. A target marker malfunctioned and went off in a bomb bay and smoke and flames engulfed the mid and rear sections of the aircraft. Thinking the plane was about to blow up, four airmen parachuted to their death into the bitterly cold Channel. Too late, the bombardier realised what had happened and jettisoned the bomb load. During the confusion this B-24 collided with another aircraft. The other bomber sustained little damage but the one that had the fire barely made it back to England with a badly sheared tail.

One of the B-17s developed a fire in its top turret during takeoff and the pilot, Lt. Marco Demara, ordered the crew to bail out. Demara decided to try a belly landing rather than let the Fort crash in a heavily populated residential area. His navigator, bombardier, and co-pilot elected to stay with him, and all four were killed in the crash.

One of the B-17's parachuting gunners, Sergeant Webb, was coming down in a field where a horse was munching grass. He manipulated his chute to clear some electrical high tension wires, only to realise he was coming down on top of the horse. He yelled frantically but the horse paid no attention and kept on munching. The sergeant landed astride the horse, it reared up in alarm, bucked off Webb, and bolted off across the field.

Despite these mishaps the bomber force continued on to the target, but the overcast conditions made target identification very difficult. Some ten runs were required before it was finally attacked. These extra runs ran the escort fighters low on fuel so they had to leave the bombers as enemy fighters attacked. Five bombers were lost.

Gentile was flying as Purple 1[2] in Shirtblue Squadron at 20,000 feet. When he sighted two FW 190s at 15,000 feet, he ordered Lieutenants Garrison and Herter to attack with him, but they lost them in the clouds. Don came out of the clouds alone and turned sharply to starboard to make sure no one was on his tail. He saw four FW 190s at eight o'clock and made a steep climb to 600 yards, shooting at the 'tail end Charlie.' He began to close in on this aircraft when a heavy barrage of flak opened up on him and he had to duck for cover in the clouds.

Lieutenants Richards and Peterson each claimed an FW 190.

Don's next fourteen missions were frustrating ones, with no opportunity for combat. He developed radio trouble on the February 3 bomber escort mission to Emden, Germany, and had to return to base. Some of the pilots scored kills on this raid, but others experienced all sorts of mechanical and radio problems with the P-47, and were bombarded by flak.

Before each mission Don always had the same things on his mind. Where are we going today? Will my aircraft operate all right? Will I get a kill? How many kills have the other pilots got? It was the same old stuff after a couple of hundred missions. Yet still the same old questions occupied his mind and the same butterflies fluttered in the pit of his stomach. But once he entered the cockpit of his aircraft they vanished.

Since the end of November they had waged a co-ordinated attack against the airframe and final assembly plants of the German aircraft industry. These joint attacks by the 8th Air Force, the 15th Air Force, and the R.A.F. were code-named 'Argument.' However, the effective completion of the operation was adversely effected by the inclement winter weather.

Rumours circulated that soon they were to receive a new offensive weapon, the P-51. All the pilots were excited about the change because the P-51 had two internal tanks in the

wings and one behind the pilot, plus two external belly tanks. These additional fuel tanks would extend their range so the fighters could go all the way to the target with the bomber formations.

On February 24, another three-prong attack was initiated. Eight hundred and eight bombers from the Third Bomb Division went unescorted to targets at the German/Polish border, at Posen, Tutow, and Kreising. They flew over the North Sea, then east over the Baltic, and lastly Northeast of Berlin toward the targets. Each site was heavily covered with clouds, so they went on to the secondary target at Rostock. They met light opposition and did an effective bombing job.

Two other divisions went to central Germany. The First Bomb Division attacked Schweinfurt from a crystal clear blue sky; their 238 B-17s caused heavy damage to Schweinfurt's anti-friction bearing factories, but the heavy smoke caused the rear wing to drop their bombs instead on a jam and gelatine factory, which was deemed to have limited value in ending the war.

Two hundred and thirteen B-24s from the Second made it to the Me 110 factories in Gotha. Just before the IP the lead wing bombardier suffered anoxia caused by a malfunctioning oxygen mask. He collapsed over the bomb sight, tripping the release switch prematurely and causing the rest of the wing to bomb off course. The following wings realised the error, made corrections, and had good bombing results on the Me 110 assembly plant but the key machine shops were missed, resulting in only a month's loss of production.

The 4th Fighter Group, led by Lieutenant Colonel Edner, provided escort to the Forts going to Schweinfurt. The enemy usually concentrated their attacks on the bombers just prior to the target, when wing formations had to be broken for bombing. But this time they engaged early, during penetration, when the fighter force was the weakest. The bombers signalled for help by shooting up green flares calling for friendly fighter assistance and the Fourth came in to intercept.

Gentile was flying Blue 1 in Shirtblue Squadron at 25,000 feet, when four FW 190s made a head-on attack on the lead box of bombers at 21,000 feet. Don led the Blue Section down in a hard starboard turn, coming out at six o'clock between the enemy fighters and the bombers. The Germans attacked in phalanxes of four, coming in close with their wings lit up like Christmas trees as they fired at Gentile. Just before collision with the American fighters, they broke and rolled down through the bomber formations, firing as they went.

Gentile followed one of the 190s through the bomber formation. The Forts were spraying hot lead at the enemy and as Don followed he felt like he was flying through a garden sprinkler. It would be a miracle if he didn't get shot down or collide with his own bombers. They weaved, twisted, and yawed out of the path of one bomber into a procession of others. Don could feel a shaking as they went past, either from their propeller wash or from the air compression caused by their proximity. As soon as Don slipped by one another would come hurtling at him. Gentile kept following the 190 through the formations, closing the distance to 500 yards as they broke clear of the bombers. He gave the enemy a one-minute squirt and then a couple of short bursts. He saw smoke and the 190 rolled over on its back and plunged straight down. Don continued firing. He broke off the attack at 8,000 feet and turned and watched his foe continue his fall to earth. He turned and started the climb back to the bombers.

It was a costly day; forty-nine bombers and ten fighters were lost. Captain Gentile destroyed an FW 190 and Lieutenant Millikan claimed one FW 190 probably destroyed and one damaged.

Lt. Joseph W. Sullivan of New York City, New York, did not return.

On February 25, 'Argument' reached its climax as the Eighth undertook its fifth major attack in six days using 685 bombers. This time it was a four-prong attack. Two hundred sixty-seven B-17s from the Third Bomb Division went to the Regensburg Messerschmitt factories. This factory was also to be bombed by the 15th Air Force an hour before the arrival of the Eighth. Thirty-three bombers were lost in the 15th's raid, but they drew more than 200 enemy fighters in the course of the attack. The B-17s of the Eighth only encountered fifty fighters, and with clear skies and excellent visibility, they waged such destruction that aircraft production was retarded for more than four months.

The First Bomb Division split its force by sending fifty B17s to the VFK ball bearing works at Stuttgart and 196 to the Me 110 assembly plant at Augsburg. The Second Bomb Division sent 172 B-24s to the Me 110 component factory and finished aircraft park at Furth. They both enjoyed good bombing results with a combined loss of thirty-one bombers for all raids. Lieutenant Colonel Edner led the Fourth and Major Halsey commanded the 336th Squadron in providing penetration support to the fifty bombers bound for Stuttgart. They rendezvoused near the target and saw five FW 190s start a frontal attack on a B-17. The fighters came at the bomber from twelve o'clock high, straight out of the sun, barrel-rolling through the formation. The Fortress' number three engine began smoking and soon a tongue of flame like a giant blowtorch spewed from the engine, extending practically to the tail of the aircraft. A large hole gaped in the right side of the fuselage, just opposite the waist gunner position, and almost big enough to walk through. The pilot peeled out of the formation, fearing they might damage the other bombers if the flames ignited the incendiary bombs still on board. As the plane fell to the left out of formation its number three engine came off and flew past the German fighter. Seven chutes were counted as the bomber went into a spiralling dive.

At 25,000 feet, Gentile was flying Red 1 in Shirtblue Squadron with Lieutenant Guest as his wingman. He saw the attack on the bomber at three o'clock, 15,000 feet below him. Don led his Section down in a diving attack. He and Lieutenant Herter picked out two of the enemy, Don bouncing the one on the starboard and Herter taking the one on the port. Gentile closed to 400 yards and gave him his first burst. He fired again at 300 yards, and when he closed to seventy-five yards he could see numerous strikes and chunks of plane falling downward. Wingman Guest pulled up sharply to avoid the fragments, but in spite of all the manoeuvres his engine cowling and propeller were pierced.

Don's plane was covered with oil and the flying fragments bounced off like hailstones, their resonating pings making chills go up and down his spine. Just as he pulled away from the enemy he saw the smoking fighter's wheels fall off. The last Don saw of him he was very near the ground, headed straight down. He thought, 'Well, he definitely had it.'

Gentile, Herter, and Garrison each were credited with an FW 190.

Lieutenant Colonel Blakeslee begged Major General Kepner, the commanding officer of the 8th Fighter Command, to give the 4th Fighter Group the P-51 Mustang Fighter. He knew its capabilities because he had led the 354th on its first P-51 fighter sweep to France. He was aware of its unique performance abilities as an offensive weapon and that it could escort the bombers all the way to the target and back. General Kepner had just finished the 'Big Week' and was readying operations for 'Big B,' the biggest air offensive to date. He did not want to stop the offensive to allow the Fourth time to familiarise itself with this new aircraft. Blakeslee promised they would fly their normal missions and get the pilots checked out in the Mustang in between them. When he returned to Debden he told his pilots, 'You can learn to fly them on the way to the target if need be.'

On February 14, 1944, three P-51B Mustangs arrived at Debden, one for each squadron's training. Gentile took the Mustang up five times for a total of four hours before he would fly it in combat. Normally it would take a pilot weeks to master a new fighter aircraft and much longer for the mechanics to learn how to repair it.

From the beginning the Mustang was plagued with all sorts of motor, gas, and radio problems. Particularly troublesome were the cockpit windows[3] and the icing up of the machine guns. Throughout 'Big B' they flew the P-51, bugs and all, correcting them as they went.

Cockpit windows/P-51B. One of the greatest problems with this early Mustang was the limited visibility aft of the cockpit. The razorback cockpit canopy arrangement was standard with all single-engine fighters. The problem was solved after a method for forming a Plexiglas canopy was devised. The improved model with the Plexiglas bubble canopy, which eliminated the razorback area aft of the cockpit, was designated the P-51D.

On February 28, one hundred and thirty-two B-17s were sent to bomb the 'No Ball' complex in France. This was the Fourth's first escort mission in the Mustangs. Major Clark led the group to Boulogne-Compiegne, France. Lieutenant Millikan had to return early because of a glycol leak , and Lieutenant Dunn had carburettor trouble. Gentile and Lieutenant Hughes had trouble with their seventy-five gallon wing tanks; the firewall-mounted electric booster pump that drew the fuel from the wing tanks was malfunctioning.

Lieutenant Garrison shared a JU 88 destroyed with Captain Beeson and Lieutenants Megura and Bill Smith.

February 29 saw 218 B-17s raid Brunswick, Germany, from above a solid undercast. The escort of 554 fighters included the 336th Squadron, led by Lieutenant Colonel Blakeslee. Multiple problems developed with the Mustang fighter. Lieutenant Richards' gun sight went out; Lieutenant Simon's belly tank fell off; Lieutenant Millikan's canopy came off in flight; Lieutenant Godfrey's oxygen supply was used up prematurely; Mills' prop began throwing oil and his wing tanks would not feed; Biel's cooling system and R/T went out; Rafalovich could not get enough manifold pressure and his R/T quit. Some of the disgruntled pilots and mechanics were now leery of the P-51, but most of them had less than one hour to master this new mount. The mechanics were taxed to the limit trying to maintain the P-47s for 'Big Week' in addition to familiarizing and solving the myriad mechanical problems with this new bird.

The war had passed a turning point. The British, emerging from the fourth winter of war, realised the crisis years had passed. It was clear that D-Day was fast approaching. The Russians had pushed the Germans back and would soon enter Czechoslovakia. The Americans, in the Pacific, invaded the Marshall Islands while in Italy they were at Cassino.

In March the American fighters were allotted additional tasks. After the decisive blow against the German aircraft industry during 'Big Week,' the fighters received orders to abandon their defensive role of only protecting the bombers. They were to go on the offensive and destroy the Luftwaffe fighters. Now the Americans could initiate hot pursuit of the enemy rather than being glued to the slow-moving bombers.

The second of March, 375 bombers flew to Frankfurt, Germany. The bad weather continued as the Fourth escorted the heavies to the target, so the target was bombed by radar through the undercast. Lieutenant Herter destroyed an FW 190. Lieutenant Van Wyk's starboard wing was badly damaged by some extremely accurate flak. Gentile and his wingman, Lieutenant Hughes, returned without engaging the enemy.

March 3, 1944 - March 29, 1944

March 3, 1944. The Target was 'Big B' - Berlin. It was inevitable that the 8th Air Force would eventually turn its attention to the huge capital of the Reich. Before the war, Berlin had a population of more than 4,300,000. It was the greatest industrial and commercial city in Europe and the sixth largest city in the world. In addition to its function as the seat of German government, half of the German electrical industry was situated there. The Heinkel works turned out twenty-six Heinkel 177 four-engine bombers every month. It was also an important production and transportation centre for the ball bearing industry. Today the Allies would attempt to knock out the Erkner bearing plant sixteen miles Southeast of the city.

Seven hundred and forty-eight bombers were dispatched on this first scheduled raid to Berlin. There were known to be more than 450 antiaircraft guns protecting the city. The bomber flight to Berlin and back to base was more than ten hours and cost the American taxpayers half a billion dollars. The heavies were to be escorted by eighty-nine P-38s, 484 P-47s, and 130 P-51s from twenty Fighter Groups, including the Fourth, which had only been flying the Mustang for four days and still was experiencing problems. Particularly bad weather conditions caused some of the bombers to abandon the mission, while others used up too much fuel during the difficult assembly and also aborted. However, seventy-nine of the heavies did reach and bomb the target of opportunity through 10/10 cloud.

At the 8th Fighter Command, located in a quiet English country hotel, W.A.C. plotters moved small metal markers across a large map of England and the Continent, following the progress of the bombers and fighters on their mission to Berlin. They kept track of their movement by monitoring the R/T conversations of the fighters and bombers, and through reports the pilots called to their headquarters.

At Debden, all pilot leaves were cancelled. They were alerted that Saturday, March 3, was to be an important mission and most guessed what it might be. The blower[1] announced, 'All pilots report to the briefing room at 0900 hours.' The pilots filed into the room and quickly filled the benches. A hush fell over the room as they noticed on the wall map a red line extending from Debden to the target - Berlin! There were whistles, smiles, and finally cheers as they realised where they were being sent. The briefing ended with a time-tick, as watches were synchronised.

The first squadron of the group took off at 9:30 a.m. with Lieutenant Colonel Blakeslee leading; led by Major Halsey the 336th departed at 9:45 a.m. This was to be Don Gentile's roughest mission so far and later he prayed it would be the last of that kind.

The weather was the worst he had seen; he could not even see down the runway. He ran into a mountainous frontal formation of cloud. At 15,000 feet the outside temperature was 40 degrees below zero; as he continued to climb to break through the overcast the outside temperature was 60 degrees below at 22,000 feet. And still he was in the soup flying on instruments. Throughout the flight and as they neared the target Don could hear various members of the group on the R/T saying they were returning either because of problems with their aircraft or the worsening weather. Of sixteen planes from the 336th, only thirteen aircraft made it airborne and four of those had to abort.

Don finally broke through the overcast at 33,000 feet after flying on instruments for more than an hour. He thought of quitting and returning to base but he kept on course. Still no one joined him for a couple of hours and he continued on alone. Unbeknown to Don, there were eight others like him, continuing their flight to Berlin, split from the rest of the group, and unable to hear Horseback[2] telling all planes to return to base, that the raid had been aborted. When Don was 100 miles from Berlin, between Hamburg and Berlin, the weather cleared as cleanly as if it had been cut by a knife. As he entered the clearing he could see fifty Do 217s[3] in the distance climbing for altitude in formation. Above them were another 100 FW 190s preparing to attack the bombers head-on. He searched the skies, looking in vain for an American aeroplane. There was none in sight; it was just him against the 150-plus.

It seemed as if Don had run smack into the entire Luftwaffe. It looked like there were millions of enemy aircraft, Me 110s[4], Me 410s[5] JU 88s, FW 190s-you name it, all looking sinister and menacing, above, below, and all around him. Don rolled to the starboard and dove down on the fifty Do 217s, hoping to break them up, so the bombers could bomb before the Germans fighters could organise for another attack, and also before the 100 190s could reach him. He flashed head-on down the middle of their formation, causing them to break off in all directions. He created a great deal of confusion, allowing the bombers to get over the target.

The enemy could not believe they were being attacked by a sole aircraft and some began to run for cover. Gentile skidded in a port turn and began firing at the 'tail end Charlie,' giving him a short burst which got the aircraft smoking, but then his canopy was so badly frosted he couldn't see anything. Scared he might ram him, he pulled up until it defrosted and as his canopy started to clear there was an Me 110, right beside him and firing. He broke away and was immediately bounced by three FW 190s. He turned into them and met them head-on and they just kept going. Don made a port turn and bounced the Do 217 again, managing another short burst, when his gun sight went out. The two 190s flashed past, one on each side, so he pulled away.

Gentile, Red 1 in Shirtblue Squadron, now saw Lieutenant Millikan, Red 3, the only other member of his section. White Section was still intact: Major Halsey, Lieutenants Dunn, Herter, and Godfrey, White 4. Blue section had two men, Lieutenants Garrison and Carlson, and also a Greenbelt,[6] Lt. George Barnes, who had joined up with them. The sky began to fill, like filaments from a spider's web, with the vapour trails of enemy aircraft converging on them. The nine assembled as best they could and made a gentle starboard turn. They were at 23,000 feet when out of the sun from two o'clock at 30,000 feet there were sixty to eighty FW 190s diving down on them, with 100 more above and at twelve o'clock getting ready to dive. They turned and met them head-on and Don thought, 'This is it, like Ouster's last stand.' As he fondled the small silver statuette of the Infant Jesus, he said a silent prayer, knowing there was no way he could survive this time.

His thoughts were interrupted by Major Halsey on the R/T saying, 'Jesus Christ! Look at all those goddamned Jerries! Let's get the hell out of here!'

Immediately the Americans jettisoned their belly tanks and so did the enemy. The Luftwaffe came in such numbers they seemed to pour on the Americans, who were tremendously outnumbered. It was a case of every man for himself. The nine Americans were caught in a trap and diving and screaming planes were everywhere. None of the Americans dared to fire a shot because that would mean they would have to fly straight and level for a time to ensure accuracy. Instead they were all twisting and turning, climbing and banking, trying to avoid the fire of the Germans. A gaggle of enemy fighters approached head-on, firing as they came. At the last moment they did a Split-S[7] and some of the Americans broke and pursued them. But it was a trap, the enemy had lured them with a decoy and now attacked with forty 190s.

Millikan, trying to fly on Gentile's wing, looked up and realised Don was gone. He had escaped the jaws of the trap and was diving on two 190s on the tail of Herter, who was chasing two other FW 190s. Ten or more enemy fighters were preparing to go after Don so Millikan flew out in front of them. These 190s were black and long-nosed, with white or grey bands around their noses.[8] They looked remarkably heavy and fierce, and a lot like the P-47s.

Most of the enemy fighters, who were in a dive, left Gentile and turned and attacked Millikan with heavy fire from their 20mm cannons, but two continued to dive on Don, firing as they closed the distance. He saw tracers, like glowing balls of fire, go past his cockpit. He jerked back on the throttle, gave his prop full fine pitch, jammed the flaps down, and violently skidded his plane down and out of the gunfire. By dumping the flaps and changing his prop pitch he greatly decreased his speed, causing the German to overshoot him. Now Don was on his tail firing two-second bursts with armour-piercing incendiary bullets that hit the enemy fighter in the right wing, fuselage, and engine. Black smoke billowed from the 190 and a tiny stream of glycol began seeping out of the engine, slowly increasing in size and volume until it poured out. This white liquid lubricant keeps the engine from overheating; once you lose it you are done for, because you only have a couple of minutes left before the engine blows up or catches on fire.

Gentile called on the R/T, 'Are you with me, Millie?'

'Hell, I'm fighting ten FWs,' Millikan shouted back.

Don immediately called for help from the odd Mustangs in the vicinity and told them to join up. He led his small band of two in a vertical climb to untangle 'Millie' from the pursuing enemy. Don hurled himself at his foes and found he was all alone again in the midst of twelve or fourteen 190s. He twisted and turned until he broke so hard that his aeroplane started doing snap rolls. When he got it back under control he managed to get on the tail of another 190, brightly decorated in the style of the top aces. This Luftwaffe pilot really knew his business. Don could always recognise an experienced German because he flew like a drunk. The Germans called them alter hase, or 'old hare.' He dove for the deck with Don on his tail, dropping down just above the treetops, twisting and weaving, making it impossible for him to get a good shot. Every once in a while Don's bullets would knock a piece off his aircraft, until after fifteen minutes or more of fighting the damage gradually grew. Don wondered how much longer he could keep this up; he was running low on fuel and ammunition and he wasn't making much progress. His nerves were frayed and he had a knot in the pit of his stomach. Still he desperately hung on, fighting the fatigue and tension.

Apparently the German was feeling the same strain; every second seemed like an eternity. But suddenly something happened to the crafty veteran. Don could see it, he was coming unravelled under the enormous pressure and fear. He froze at the stick and flew straight away. Don eased the throttle forward and slowly closed the range to 100 yards, thinking, 'This should do it.' He squeezed the trigger and the 190 burst into flames, small fingers of fire streaming back from the engine like long red snakes' tongues. They multiplied and eventually engulfed the fuselage beyond the cockpit. The smoke began to drift through the firewall and into the cockpit until it filled with smoke, big black billows of it rolling out.

The German writhed in his seat, moving his head erratically from side to side. Fire burst out in the cockpit and a burning gloved hand clawed at the cockpit release latch, fists banging in an attempt to dislodge it. The canopy blew off, the aircraft inverted, and a figure shrouded in flames stood up, the fire slowly eating away at his clothing and the flesh underneath. Now the burning thing was trying to clamber out of the cockpit but the slipstream kept him pinned. He seemed to turn toward Don, extending an outreached hand and trying to speak. Don was only fifty yards away, viewing this agonising scene from the security of his own cockpit.

It took a long time for the Luftwaffe pilot to die, and Don prayed he would die soon. With tears streaking down his cheeks, he started to position his craft to help end the agony of his opponent, when the burning mass slumped in his seat, followed by an enormous explosion. The sky was filled with swirling bits of metal, dismembered limbs, and pieces of flesh. Don's visceral juices churned and his oxygen mask filled with half-digested food, the stench of it assaulting his nostrils.

He was shocked back to reality by voices in his earphones. The frantic calls for help penetrated his grey matter and caused his adrenaline to pump. He was low on ammunition and fuel and had earned the right to head home. Without hesitation he pulled up in a starboard climb and flew back into the tempest. Now Gentile was all over the sky, twisting and turning, climbing and breaking up attacks, calling out warnings of the enemy approaches to his fellow Mustang pilots. He was everywhere in the battle.

Four 190s came roaring out of the sun towards Don. He met them head-on, but as he fired his right bank of guns jammed. In the ensuing dogfight Don was afraid to fire because the erratic movements might affect the feed of the ammunition to the only guns he had operating, causing them to jam too. He was also running low on fuel and ammunition and had to conserve his fire power. He broke away from them and into the path of two diving FW 190s. He broke away again and saw three 190s on the tail of a Mustang that was pouring smoke. He yelled for the Mustang pilot to break; he did a quick snap roll, then went straight down.

Don dove down to get the 190s off his tail but could not catch them, so he pulled up again. Later he saw two more Mustangs and discovered they were piloted by Major Halsey and Lieutenant Dunn. He asked them to join up with him and at the same time noticed two 190s closing very fast on the major. Don looked up and saw eight more getting ready to attack him. He yelled to Halsey to break. The major did three snap rolls and Don met the two 190s in a frontal quarter attack. Neither of them fired; the 190s flicked and went down. Don checked to see if the major was all right and then pulled up sharply to meet the eight diving 190s. They passed him as he was on his back and kept on going.

Don told Major Halsey and Lieutenant Dunn to join up with him and steered 250 degrees for home. They were flying in the clouds on instruments. Lieutenant Dunn was having engine trouble.

'Hey, Don,' said Dunn in a sad voice, 'I guess I won't make it back.'

'You can make it. We will do a slow port turn so that you can catch up.' In the turn Don fell behind and that was the last he saw of Dunn.

When Don let down he did not know where he was because he had lost his maps during the fight. He hit the coast, but it did not look familiar. He finally recognised the Jersey Islands, which meant he was some 200 miles south of the Dutch coast where they were supposed to have come out. He had only twenty gallons of fuel left and he would never make it home. He throttled back to near nothing and barely stayed in the air; he was going to have to 'ride in on the fumes.' As Don made his approach on Ford emergency field, he ran out of gas and had to make a dead stick landing.

Of the nine, five Mustang pilots from the Fourth, including Lt. Glenn A. Herter, did not return.

That night Don kicked and writhed in his sleep as he refought the battle with the Luftwaffe. The following day Don made this entry in his lo

I was just notified that the brightly coloured FW . 190 I got a couple of days ago was a German ace who had 150 Allied victories to his credit, Kurt Von Meyer. Thank God I didn't know it was him or I'd probably have bailed out.

On March 5, 164 B-24s were sent to bomb the airfields in the Bordeaux area. The route would take them across the Channel and then in a south-easterly direction to the Pyrenees Mountains, located between Spain and France.

The Fourth and seven other groups were to provide 307 fighters as target support to the bombers. Blakeslee leading the group and Major Goodson commanding the 336th Squadron met the bombers at 23,000 feet and west of Cognac. As they flew their escort Gentile thought to himself, 'Boy are the Forts majestic with their gracious curved lines. But these B-24s look like a herd of pregnant cows.' Their awkward appearance was caused by two large vertical stabilisers and a deep slab-sided fuselage. They flew faster, twenty miles per hour faster, than a Fort carrying the same load. They could go farther and with a much heavier bomb load, but their controls were cumbersome, making it difficult to fly in tight formation. 'Now the Forts, they have dignity. Give me them anytime,' Don concluded.

Later, Gentile and Blakeslee were forced to abort due to a rough engine.

Steve Pisanos shot down two 109s and damaged two more but was forced to bail out. He tried to get out of the aircraft before it crashed but was only half out when it hit the ground.

When the Fourth returned to base, Captain Duane W. Beeson approached Gentile. His eyes were downcast and he hesitated before saying, 'Don, I thought you should know, Steve was shot down and they think he bought it. He was last seen somewhere near the Channel. I am sorry, he was a great guy.'

Don was thunderstruck, he couldn't believe it, not Steve. They were roommates...they had planned what they were going to do after the war. They were close, closer than brothers...not Steve, no! Not Steve!

Several pilots gathered around and lion looked quizzically at the faces about him. No one spoke. They wanted to, but no one knew quite what to say. They knew Don was closer to the Greek than the other pilots. Without responding to Beeson, Don walked over to closest plane and climbed into the cockpit. The mechanics connected the battery cart up and started her up. Don taxied out on the flight line, weaving left to right in order to see ahead. The aircraft moved forward and when its speed reached 100 miles per hour it became airborne. Don flew back and forth along the Channel, near the coast of the Continent, looking for Steve. But he never found him.

Exhausted from the search, Don threw himself on his bed and stared at the ceiling. Even with death all around, it was difficult for him to believe that death could come to Steve. He had escaped so many times, it was difficult to believe. Steve's fate had shaken Don and his grief was profound. He was glad he had always encouraged Steve to go to the chapel with him to pray. If Steve was dead, Don knew he was with the Lord. The sight of Steve's bed depressed him and he got on his knees and began to pray for his friend. In the end, Steve's death hardened Don and his fighting became even more aggressive.

A few days later Lt. Peter G. Lehman, son of a former governor of New York, moved in with Gentile. Pete was a big, likeable, good natured sort of guy who gave up a promising career in his father's famous investment banking firm and left a wife and two children to join the Royal Canadian Air Force and later the 4th Fighter Group. His brother also joined the service and became a captain in the Tank Corps, and his father had declined a second term as governor to become director of the United Nations Rehabilitation Relief Administration at age seventy.

As a light snow blew across the darkened airfields of the bomber bases in

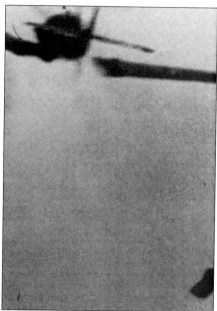

Gentile's twenty-seventh kill, Major Kurt Von Meyer.

England, 672 bombers took off on March 6 for another try on Berlin. They were escorted by 801 fighters from seventeen groups, including the 4th Fighter Group. The Luftwaffe was ready for them and deployed their forces; the mission had to run the gamut of some 590 enemy aircraft. It was the costliest mission the Eighth would ever fly.

Sixty-nine bombers did not return, and of the ones which made it back 102 had major damage, 245 lesser damage, and three were totalled. They also lost eleven fighters, with the Fourth losing four aircraft in the process of shooting down seventeen of the enemy. Major Halsey's and Captain Gentile's engines repeatedly cut out; Lieutenant Lehman had R/T and oxygen problems; Lieutenant Braley's problems were electrical, and Lieutenant Bond's were with his wing tank and R/T, causing them to abort the mission.

The next day, new spark plugs were placed in all the Mustang kites to see if this would improve the engine problems.

March 8, 1944. Bad weather caused a day's layoff, but today the Eighth returned to Berlin with 539 bombers (188 B-24s and 351 B-17s) to bomb the Ekner ball bearing plant sixteen miles Southeast of Berlin. Because of the tremendous scale and ferocity of the fighter attacks on the last mission to Berlin, Bomber Command planned a large fighter umbrella over the heavies. Eight hundred and ninety-one fighters provided escort from seventeen groups of both the 8th and the 9th Air Force.

The target was blanketed with 10/10 cloud, but they were able to drop 928 .tons of bombs on the city using radar. The bombing put the factories out of action for quite some time and it was considered a very successful day.

At 3:30 a.m., the bomber crews awakened to a breakfast of ham and eggs. At 5:30 a.m. they attended the briefing while the cooks packed candy, oranges, coffee, and food for the bomber crews. By then everyone was up and the entire base was bustling with activity.

After the general briefing the gunners were dismissed and sent to a briefing on the type of enemy aircraft they might encounter. The navigators went to a special briefing where they were given maps and charts and information on locating the target. The armourers gave instruction on the type of bomb they would drop this day and how it was fused. The co-pilots picked up the crews' escape kits.

When the bombers were ready to depart, the flying control officer in the tower shot off a green flare. As it arced across the sky and slowly descended, the bombers' engines came to life. The lead aircraft's idling engines sprung into a thunderous roar and the pilot pushed his throttle to full power, watching the manifold pressure needles climb to peak power. He released his brakes and the big bird started its takeoff. As they rolled down the runway their speed gradually increased to 115 miles per hour and then they became airborne. The pilot hit the brakes to stop the wheels from spinning as he activated the wheels-up lever. Soon the skies over England were filled with hundreds of deep throated bombers laden with thousands of pounds of fuel, bombs, ammunition, and men on their way to Germany.

Once the bombers reached 15,000 feet they broke through the overcast and presented a bomber stream more than sixty miles long. A new formation had been introduced in January, 1944, which had a group of thirty-six bombers spread out at four-mile intervals. These four-mile wide gaps between the groups were necessary for a tight formation without flying into the turbulence of the preceding group, and prevented congestion when they lined up for the bombing run.

They knew the enemy's radar was plotting their course and trying to determine where their large force was heading. The Germans had a new weapon to meet the challenge of the Mustang - the all new high altitude Messerschmitt 109. This kite was specially fitted with a Daimler-Benz high altitude engine. It could outperform any opponent - especially on climbing. It could reach altitudes of 37,000 feet while most American planes topped out at about 30,000 feet. It did not carry any belly tanks or any outboard machine guns. The lack of an auxiliary tank limited its endurance, so the guns were removed to lighten the weight and further aid in obtaining higher altitudes.

New tactics were employed which had the special Me 109s waiting high in the sky and swooping down out of the sun on the American escort fighters. The dogfights would draw the American fighters away from the bombers, so heavily fortified and armed German fighters could attack and destroy the bombers.

Back at Debden it is 5:00 a.m. and the batmen are waking up the pilots for the day's mission. It was going to be a difficult and long one, with a 100-mile sea crossing to Holland and a straight shot across hostile enemy-held Europe the 500 miles to Berlin. And then the long haul back over the 600-plus miles to home base.

At 10:55 a.m. everything was covered with wet snow and Gentile trundled across the field. Little did he know that this day would not only be the start of the Gentile-Godfrey team, but also the most publicised fighter escort mission in the annals of air warfare.

Gentile wrote the following in his flight log:

Wednesday was another day of excitement for me - because I stuck out my neck as usual - and of course having the Good Lord on my side paid off. I know my prayers are being answered. It was a stinking day for a flight to Berlin but the weather cleared off in the Berlin area.

The 4th Fighter Group took off with Lieutenant Colonel Blakeslee in command. On the way to the target the clouds were unbroken and extended to 17,000 feet with occasional pillars reaching heights of more than 28,000 feet.

During the flight Don could hear on the R/T, one by one, aircraft from the various sections of the 336th abort for myriad mechanical and navigational problems. There were now only four left: Gentile, Red 1, the only one from the Red Section; Godfrey, Green 3, and the only one left from his Green Section; Second Lt. Robert S. Tussey, from White section as White 4, and First Lt. Woodrow F. Sooman, Blue 3, the only one left from the Blue section.

As they arrived at the outskirts of Berlin, Don felt the warmth of the sun through the canopy as he broke through the clouds into the clear. He could now see the bombers below at 27,000 feet and saw that a gaggle of forty Me 109s were making a shallow head-on attack from 30,000 feet on the lead box of Forts. He looked around and saw fifty-odd enemy planes in the area. Looking up sun he could see more tiny specks flashing in the sun far ahead. Twelve to fifteen bombers were going down in flames, some blowing up.

He could only find one friendly aeroplane in the area; it was Godfrey. He wondered if he should get into the same fix he did a few days ago. He knew the bombers were depending on them and they wanted to go home in one piece. He depressed the throat microphone switch on the end of the throttle and said, 'Johnny, shall we break them up?' Don knew they were badly outnumbered and there were no other friendly planes to help them protect the Forts.

'You're the boss, Don.'

Gentile smiled and thought, 'Good old Johnny, he would never let me down.'

He depressed the button again and said, 'Come on, Johnny, let's go get them. They're getting ready to make a pass on the bombers.'

When Godfrey got into position on Don's tail they dove to attack and met five Me 109s head-on. Don had an aggressive spirit in the air, a fierce determination and ruthlessness. They broke and Don singled out two who turned to the port. The 109s twisted and turned, making six or seven turns, with Gentile closing the distance and sticking like glue.

The turns were so violent that Don was having a hard time turning without flaps. Godfrey, acting as his wingman, managed to keep up with him, but with difficulty. He closed to seventy-five yards and delivered a one-second squirt. The enemy rolled over and Don gave him a deadly burst. The 109 spiralled out of control and white smoke streamed out, almost obscuring it. Finally they saw the pilot bail out just before the aircraft went crashing to the ground. Godfrey locked on the tail of another 109 and Don said, 'Okay, I'll cover you,' and with that he acted as John's wingman, who clobbered the enemy. Gentile, the maestro, pressed the microphone button and said, 'Give him more Johnny, more.' The enemy aircraft caught on fire and exploded and went spinning towards earth.

They joined up and had climbed back to 20,000 feet when john noticed a formation of Me 109s 2,000 feet below. They had the advantage of height over the

Briefing before a mission by Colonel Blakeslee.

Pin-ups girls decorate the ready room of the 336th Squadron. Even 'Carlo,' the pet mastiff, registers indifference to their charms.

109s diving in and out of the formations of bombers. Don was fearless as he hurled himself at the enemy. The sheer fury of his assault instilled fear and confusion, separating the shaken German pilots. When they approached two of the enemy, Don said, 'Johnny, you take the one on the right while I get the one on the left.'

When Don was in the R.A.F. some of the older pilots had talked about when they got their 'shooting eye.' They said they could almost pinpoint that particular moment. Don never believed them; he thought they were pulling his leg and was always amused by the stories. But today he felt he knew what they were talking about. He felt he had arrived: He could see a sudden and dramatic improvement in his aerial marksmanship.

First Lt. Raymond P. Clotfelter appeared on the scene and tried to hook up with Gentile and Godfrey but found it harder and harder to keep up with them in their violent aerobatics. Don was twisting and turning and aiming and firing as if his guns were under the control of a computer. The precision of his firing, even at almost incredible angles, was only exceeded by the damage he inflicted. He put strikes right into a cockpit, hitting the pilot, who slumped in his seat. The plane rolled over and went down in flames.

Godfrey yelled excitedly, 'You got him, Don.' Don could see the pilot make a desperate attempt to free himself from the aircraft before he was covered in flames. Gentile felt sick with revulsion.

Shortly after this, Godfrey fired at another German who still had his belly tank and it burst into a white flash of flames. Its burning and smoking remnants went crashing to the ground.

Gentile could see planes falling everywhere, some American and some German, leaving smoke trails which floated lazily up from the crashed aircraft. It was a sight Don would never forget.

The bomber formation looked like a piece of Swiss cheese, with wide holes left by the bombers which had been shot down. The pilots were working frantically to close up the gaps and tighten up the formation. This called for complete concentration and was extremely tiring. It required a sliding movement rather than a wing over or banking manoeuvre because the close proximity to other bombers could cause a collision.

Don switched his radio to C, the bomber channel, and his earphones filled with the chatter of so many excited voices he could not understand what was being said. He flipped back to the fighter channel but before he could speak Godfrey's voice came screaming forth, 'Sixty to eighty enemy fighters getting ready to attack the bombers at twelve o'clock.' Now Don knew why the bomber crews were talking so excitedly.

Gentile took his force of two into the swarm of enemy planes like a winged missile and suddenly it seemed to him like the world had come to an end. As usual, Don asked the Good Lord not to forget him. They were all mixed up, a real circus, everything going around in circles and the enemy trying to get on their tails. They had saved the bombers again by breaking up the Luftwaffe's attack.

Don got on the tail of an FW 190 and gave it a burst. His left bank of guns jammed, causing the Mustang to pull violently to the right and making flying while firing very difficult. Few pilots had the ability to overcome such a problem but Don made the proper corrections; by holding the stick firmly in both hands, braced on the side of the cockpit, he fired again and again and watched as the 190 caught on fire. Its canopy flew off and the pilot jumped out with a plume of fire behind him. His parachute opened but it was on fire, and the flames spread until they had enveloped the chute and its rider. In an instant all that remained was a black residue. Small dark particles floated slowly to the ground like leaves from a tree in autumn.

Don's face tensed and flushed as he watched, his eyes wide open and staring in pain. He thought to himself, 'Oh, how I wish he would not have died. Why did his parachute have to catch on fire?' He swallowed hard against a dry throat. He felt cold, almost freezing, but sweat ran down his forehead and over his oxygen mask.

The silence was penetrated by an excited voice yelling, on the R/T, 'You got him, Don!' But Godfrey too witnessed the tragic drama and his voice trailed off as he said, barely audibly, 'Poor devil, too bad he couldn't...have...made it....'

They had lost altitude and now were flying parallel to the bomber stream. There were no more enemy aircraft attacking the formations but it had not been accomplished without losses - Lieutenant Colonel Edner, the commanding officer of the 336th Squadron, went down to become a prisoner of war.

The bombers unloaded their bombs through heavy flakit was everywhere. The sky was full of death for miles around but the bombers kept lumbering along. Gentile was marvelling at the raw courage of the bomber crews when he saw an Me 109 at six o'clock high, diving down on Godfrey.

'At six o'clock high there's a single bandit diving on you; break into him, Johnny.'

Godfrey turned and saw the 109. Neither he nor Gentile could believe this, either the pilot was stupid or exceptionally brave. Later they realised he was brave and fearless.

'When I say break, Johnny, you break to the right and I will go to the left.' The seconds seemed to crawl by as they waited, then Don yelled, 'Break!' They both broke and the 109 followed Godfrey around to the right. He got on his tail but John tightened his turns and only gave him deflection shots. They went through three tight turns, slowly losing altitude, and met Don as they came around on the last turn. He met them head-on and tried to give the enemy a short burst, but the

German was an experienced combatant who anticipated the move and broke into a Split-S for the deck.

They both followed and Don got to him first; he fired and scored strikes on the wings, fuselage, and engine but then overshot and barely pulled out of his dive above the treetops. He swung to the port, near John, and Don yelled, 'He's coming your way, Johnny...nail him!' Godfrey got on his tail and fired, making strikes on the aircraft while Don climbed to gain altitude. The German twisted and turned with John on his tail and firing away. They gradually were losing altitude when John ran out of ammunition.

He yelled, 'Finish him, Don, I'm out of ammunition.'

'Cover me, I'll finish him.' Don's strikes connected on the 109's belly tank and it caught on fire; the plane climbed to 1,000 feet before the pilot bailed out. His chute opened at 500 feet and he landed safely, while his aircraft went crashing into the woods.

It was time to head home. They both were low on fuel and out of ammunition, so they climbed and headed west. On the way, they noticed a small speck in the sky at nine o'clock at 15,000 feet. At first they thought it was an enemy aircraft but as they got closer they realised if was a crippled B17 trying to make its way home. They approached with caution; bomber crews were known to shoot first and identify later.

They circled the bomber and surveyed her damage. The bomber was barely staying aloft and looked shot to pieces. A large hole under the pilot's compartment trailed torn electrical and control cables. A two-foot square section of the nose was torn out. Part of the right wing had been shattered and the number three engine was out. At just fifty miles west of Berlin, they had a long way to go.

Don switched the R/T to Channel C and spoke. 'Hello, big friend, this is Shirtblue Red 1, need company? Are you all right?'

'Boy, are we glad to see you guys. We were really worried, but we'll be all right now. There are reports of bandits in the area. Don't leave us, we have wounded aboard.'

'We looked you over, you'll make it. We'll stay as long as our gas holds out,' replied Don. He thought, 'Boy, are they in terrible shape, I hope they can make it. I wonder what they would think if they knew we were out of ammunition.'

'Little friend, bandits at eight o'clock, don't leave us.'

'Don't worry, we won't leave, we'll take care of them. Johnny, lets go.' They climbed to attack head-on with no ammunition and very little fuel. These manoeuvres ate up even more of their precious fuel and made their situation critical. They were sore from sitting in the cramped cockpit; they had been at it for more than five hours. They would have liked to highball it home at top speed, but they couldn't. leave this Fort at the mercy of the Luftwaffe. They would stick with them.

The Germans met them head-on, then broke and did a Split-S and headed home. They broke up several similar attacks and each time they returned alongside the bomber, the crew threw kisses at them. At the same time they were dumping everything they could to lighten their load and cut down on fuel consumption.

The B-17 pilot came back on the R/T. 'Thanks, little friend. We couldn't make it without your help. Stay with us, don't leave us. How is your fuel holding out?'

Don bit his lip when he said, 'We are in good shape, fuel wise. You are drifting off course; make corrections to 280 degrees. You are doing fine, hang on. I contacted Air-Sea Rescue and they have our bearings. We will keep them apprised of your situation and position.'

'Roger, Shirtblue. God bless you, we couldn't make it without you, don't leave.' They were barely crawling through the sky. The fighters had throttled back to near nothing, just barely keeping in the air and with them. The B17 pilot kept smiling at them, making the thumbs-up sign, while the crew continued to throw kisses and make deep bows in their direction.

When they reached the North Sea, Don said, 'Rescue launch below you.' He could see the crew jumping and cheering. They were lucky to have made it this far.

The English coast showed as a faint line in the distance and the Mustang's fuel was almost gone. Don switched to Channel C and depressed the button on the R/T. 'Big friend, can you make it from here? We will be over England in a minute or so. We have enjoyed the company.'

'Little friend, thanks, very, very much, we couldn't have made it without you.

'Our pleasure. Lets go home, Johnny.'

When they reached Debden, the ground crews, cooks, and other ground pounders[9] rushed outside to see who had returned. The planes flashed by and did several victory rolls before they realised it was Gentile and Godfrey.

One of the cooks yelled out, 'Oh my God, Gentile got three and a half and Godfrey got two and a half. What a day they had. That ties Gentile with Beeson at fourteen each. And they're only three behind Johnson of the 56th, who has seventeen kills and is the Eighth's top American ace.'

Later that evening Don wrote in his flight log the following, at the end of his report of the days activities:
Another mission like my last couple and I'll be ready for a pencil-pushing job (that is, if I can still hold a pencil).

The next day, March 9, they were off to Berlin again. The squadron was led by Major Goodson and the group by the newly promoted Colonel Blakeslee. The bombers were fifty minutes late at the rendezvous, but otherwise the trip was uneventful. Not a single German rose to challenge them.

March 16, 1944. From the first mission with the P-51 until now, it had been a nightmare for the mechanics who tried to correct the mechanical problems they were having with the new aircraft, the Mustang. Rough engines, props throwing oil, glycol leaks, and auxiliary tank feed problems were just a few of the difficulties causing aborts on every mission. To get a full squadron up was a minor miracle.

Today the squadron was led to Munich by Major Goodson on a target support for 675 bombers. The group was led by Colonel Blakeslee. They shot down thirteen of the enemy with the loss of one pilot. There were many aborts due to mechanical problems, including the Mustangs flown by Lieutenants Sooman, Lehman, Van Wyk, Millikan, Norley, Raphael, and Captain Gentile.

The strain of the gruelling missions could be detected among the pilots and the ground crews. The pilots had mixed feelings about the Mustang because of the problems, but no one refused to fly. They were glad to go and so they did, defects and all, despite the fact that the problems were responsible for at least seven pilots lost and had robbed them of many successes.

Yet there was a bright note during this period, and a buoyant, exultant spirit which stemmed from the pilots' performance with their new mounts. They were having their finest hour. After flying the Mustang, even with all its problems, the pilots concluded it was the finest fighter aircraft in the world.

On days the missions were cancelled because of inclement weather, many of the Fourth pilots, including Don Gentile, would fly up to the 56th Fighter Group's base at Halesworth, for simulated dogfights with Colonel Zemke's Wolfpack[10]. The combat pilots were pitted against each other, Thunderbolt against the Mustang. The P-47s had been greatly improved with paddle-bladed propellers and a water injection fuel system, and after combat the Fourth's pilots were favourably impressed with the 56th, even on the deck.

There was enormous competition between these two top scoring Fighter Groups, but in the end the Fourth held the highest score for enemy aircraft destroyed. The leading American ace at the time was Captain Robert Johnson, of the 56th, who had twenty-one air victories. The 56th also boasted 300 planes destroyed to the Fourth's 212 1/2 kills. Though intense, their rivalry was a sport rather than a bitter conflict.

At Fourth headquarters there was keen competition between the pilots for top spot in the group as well as the race to break Captain Eddie Rickenbacker's World War I score of twenty-six kills. The champion of the Fourth's 334th Squadron was Captain Duane Beeson, who was an expert in deflection shooting. Captain Don S. Gentile, who was a born natural pilot and an excellent shot, led the 336th Squadron. The two were locked in a rivalry to become the Ace of Aces.

March 18, 1944. The 8th Air Force sent 480 B-17s and 198 B24s with 925 escort fighters to attack eight airfields and aircraft component and assembly plants in the Munich and Friedrichshafen areas of south central Germany.

Aces High. Left to right: Capt. Duane 'Bee' Beeson, Capt. Don 'Gentle' Gentile, Major James 'Goody' Goodson.

Col. Donald Blakeslee, Commander, 4th Fighter Group.

Josephina and Patsy Gentile listening to news about Don over the BBC

Colonel Blakeslee led the 336th Squadron to Munich as target withdrawal support for the bombers; Captain Gentile was his wingman. They left Debden at 11:40 a.m. and rendezvoused with the B-17s east of Augsburg at 2:45 p.m. at 25,000 feet. They became separated from the rest of the group and found themselves all alone with the bombers. They were flying at 27,000 feet when six FW 190s made a head-on pass at the bombers. As the enemy turned to go down for a pass at another box, Don and the colonel dove to engage them. The 109s saw them coming and began to dive away. Blakeslee directed Don to the one on the left while he took the other straggler. Don's FW flicked and separated from the other. He let the colonel know he was behind him, covering him, on Blakeslee's starboard side, and went streaking toward another enemy plane.

Don flew his Mustang with silent elegance, coldly and clinically approaching the enemy with his death. Everything the German did was wrong. He kicked the starboard rudder instead of the port, dove when he should have rolled, pulled back when he should have poled forward. Meanwhile, Don was everywhere, yawing, rolling, spinning, and firing all the while. A hammering torrent hit the 190 and it lost sections of its starboard wing and elevator. Don continued his dance of death with six muzzles blazing away at his terrified foe. The German aircraft shuddered and shook as tracers snaked around it like whiplashes. He was flying in a no man's land between life and death and his engine began spitting oil, coating the windshield.

The Luftwaffe pilot inverted his aircraft, raised himself in his seat, and slid the canopy back; it flew off and he rolled out. Like a gymnastic tumbler he went pitching forward, rolling and somersaulting, just missing Don's kite, and heading toward the earth. Don could not watch any longer to see if his chute opened because he had to keep an eye on Blakeslee.

Gentile banked to the port and told the colonel he was still covering his tail. Blakeslee was chasing two 190s, firing, when three others did a climbing turn to the port. Don watched the three, then came around and bounced them. He charged with every gun blazing, but he was having difficulty concentrating on his firing and the colonel at the same time. The three flicked and dove away so he went back to Blakeslee in time to see him clobber an FW 190.

'Okay, Don, pull in tight and let's get home!'

Just then two yellow, long-nosed FW 190s got on Gentile's tail and hit his aircraft in the engine. He yelled 'Break!' made a violent tight turn to the starboard, and kept turning. Self-destroying and tracer ammunition burst through the sky and whipped past him. Panic-stricken, he poled hard to the right and out turned them.

Over the R/T the colonel said, 'Keep turning, I'll try to get behind them.' But as Blakeslee moved in they left Don and bounced him. Gentile reversed his turn quickly, rammed the throttle forward, poured on the emergency power, and gently eased the stick back and fell in behind them. They flicked on their back and went down. Don got on Blakeslee's wing and they headed home at full bore, landing five hours after they had started.

Gentile and Blakeslee were each credited with destroying a FW 190, bringing the Fourth's total to twelve destroyed.

Sooman and Freeburger did not return.

March 20, 1944. The target was Frankfurt but high clouds caused most of the 147 bombers to abandon the mission. Escort was provided by 594 fighters. The Fourth, led by Major Carpenter, remained on the course until 11:30 a.m. but saw no bombers. Don Gentile and his wingman Lieutenant Johnson were flying with the 336th, led by Major Goodson. They finally located thirty-one Forts near Linburg at 11:45 a.m. and escorted them to the target and back. When Goodson developed mechanical problems, Don and his wingman escorted him home. Lieutenant Godfrey flew with the 334th Squadron on this show.

Goodson, Gentile, and Johnson all landed at 1:00 p.m.

The next day found some of the squadron working on low level mock dog fighting. One of the participants was Lt. Peter G. Lehman, Don's roommate. During these low level manoeuvres Lehman flicked over and spun into the ground and was killed. One of the problems of the early P-51s was the tank in the fuselage behind the cockpit, and it was believed to be the cause of this crash. The increased torque caused by the tank changed the centre of gravity.

Gentile grieved the loss of his second roommate and after this did not have another.

March 22, 1944. The 8th Air Force sent 657 bombers back to bomb Berlin. They were escorted by 817 fighters, including the Fourth. Colonel Blakeslee commanded the group from the 336th and also acted as squadron commander. Gentile and wingman Johnson took off with Lieutenant Van Wyk and his wingman Godfrey on this 'ho hum' mission which saw no enemies or action. The pilots wondered why no enemy came up to fight.

The 8th Air Force resolved that if Germany would not send their aircraft up then the Allies would have to go down, seeking them out and annihilating them on the ground.

To encourage ground strafing the 8th Fighter Command decided to give equal credit for planes destroyed on the ground as for those destroyed in the air. It was possibly the most dangerous job for a combat pilot. He had to fly hundreds of miles across enemy territory, running the gauntlet of guns set to cross-fire in the path of the Strafer, as he zoomed down the airfield. There was no hiding from the ground gunners; they knew where the Strafer would be coming across the field and they had their guns pre-set and waiting for him. He would have to fly a mere ten feet off the ground, travelling at 450 miles per hour, and avoiding any obstructions - including aircraft.

As he came in at low altitude they would throw everything at him, and he was very vulnerable and presented an easy target. As he came in for a strafing, following other aircraft, he lacked the advantage of surprise; the enemy would be set and waiting for him. He had to fly through the smoke, fire, and dust from the damage caused by the preceding aeroplanes. If he had to gain altitude to miss high structures or to head home he became terribly vulnerable to being shot down. All the pilots dreaded these missions and more aces were brought down on strafing missions than in air battles. Survival was considered pure luck.

The Germans invented strafing during World War I; the word means 'to punish.'

March 23, 1944. Colonel Blakeslee led a target support escort for 707 bombers to Brunswick, Germany. The Fourth was part of a fighter escort of 841 aircraft. The 336th Squadron took off at 9:05 a.m. with Major Goodson in command. They were supposed to rendezvous with the bombers over Brunswick, but the bombers were thirty minutes early and had left the target area when the fighters arrived. They finally caught up to them over Munster at 11:20 a.m. at 24,000 feet. The last box of bombers was under heavy attack on all sides by more than forty members of the Luftwaffe.

Goodson led them down to attack and suddenly there was a mass of nearly seventy fighters fighting savagely in a wild, screaming battle. The sky appeared a twisting and churning nightmare. Tracers flashed through the maelstrom, interwoven with white flashes from the cannons of the FWs and the American planes. It was a duel to the death. Don's feet kicked the rudder pedals, his hands pulled and poled the control stick and throttle, his eyes and head turned constantly as he twisted, dove, and skidded his aircraft. Many times he missed collisions by just a fraction of an inch.

Gentile provided cover while Goodson flamed two Me 109s, then he and Godfrey broke to the starboard. He pulled up on the tail of an Me 109 and they both dove at full speed. The German started to pull up but Don was going so very fast he had to shoot soon or he would overshoot him. He opened fire at 350 yards and kept firing until he flew through his slipstream, which almost put him on his back. After he passed the enemy, he looked back and saw the 109 was on fire and the pilot had bailed out. Don pulled up and around in a starboard turn and bounced another 109. He closed to eighty yards, got good strikes, and the 109 rolled over on its back and went straight down to crash.

'Johnny, it's your turn, take a crack at the one at six o'clock. I'll cover.'

John dove on the 109 at 10,000 feet but instead of the enemy turning into him he dove, trying to reach the relative safety of the clouds. Godfrey followed and rapidly closed the distance. The enemy must have panicked, for when John fired he flicked over on his back and went straight down in a half roll to the ground.

They climbed to 4,000 feet and set a course for home.

Gentile was credited with two Me 109 kills and Godfrey with one.

Duane Beeson was small in stature, built like a youth, with big hands and wrists, but he and Gentile were two of the deadliest pilots in the United States Air Force. He was a master at deflection shooting and was locked in a friendly rivalry with Don to be number one in the Fourth and also to be the first to break Captain Eddie Rickenbacker's record. He was an aggressive and determined combatant.

Gentile and Godfrey were gulping a steaming cup of coffee in the Fourth's briefing room, when Beeson walked in and went over to the blackboard listing the enemy kills. Annoyed, he stared at the board as the sergeant added today's mission to the pilots' kill totals. Don had passed Bee's score of sixteen kills by one and assumed the lead for the 4th Fighter Group.

Beeson turned to Gentile and with a boyish grin said, 'Damn you, Don!'

Don was grinning from ear to ear.

March 24, 1944. On this morning, 403 bombers returned to Schweinfurt. They were to be escorted by 540 fighters from ten groups. Major Clark led a penetration target withdrawal support for the Fourth; Don Gentile and wingman Lieutenant Patchen led the 336th Squadron. The target name had fearful associations to the bomber crews, but all of the fighter pilots were looking forward to hot combat. Unfortunately for the eager Fourth fighter pilots, the Luftwaffe presence was not in evidence this day. One Ju 52 was seen but escaped into the clouds.

On March 27, 701 bombers dropped 960 tons of bombs on GAF. installations in France, concentrating on Bordeaux and the air bases used by the German long-range aircraft to bomb ships in the eastern Atlantic.

Major Clark led the target support and 'free lance' to PauPont Long airdrome, Bordeaux, France. The 336th Squadron, including Captain Gentile and his wingman Lieutenant Johnson, was led by Major Goodson who got them airborne at 12:00 noon. They rendezvoused with the bombers at 2:47 p.m. over the Bay of Biscayne at 22,000 feet. After the airfield was bombed with 583 tons of bombs, and the relieving P-38 fighter escort took over, Major Clark ordered one section to attack the aircraft on the field. Captain Gentile, Shirtblue Blue leader, and his number two, Lieutenant Johnson, all that remained of the Blue section, and Green leader Lieutenant Millikan and his number two, Lieutenant Norley (the only remaining members of the Green Section), went down to strafe the airfield.

Gentile throttled back and rolled into a steep dive, commencing the attack from 14,000 feet the moment the last box of bombers passed. As they rapidly closed on the airfield, they noticed the accuracy of the bombing had been exceptionally good; practically every building had been hit and was burning, particularly on the west side of the airfield. Tremendous billows of black smoke and flames covered the drome, excepting the Northeast corner which had not received much damage. Lieutenants Millikan, Johnson, and Norley overshot Don and started the attack across the airfield. They were flying at more than 500 miles per hour and firing wildly at the parked aircraft.

Gentile eased his stick back ever so gently to break out of the dive. He skimmed over the treetops and onto the airfield, only a few feet above the ground. He was all alone now, following the others by quite a distance, and he could see the gunners were in position to release their deadly flak. All at once the sky was alive with bright balls of fire that sailed slowly towards him and then suddenly went whizzing by. Tracers and white puffs of exploding 20-millimeter shells travelled towards him. The field was covered with a concentration of criss-cross fire from a hundred guns, assaulting from every angle, even from gunners who were on the hangar roofs and firing down on him as he streaked by. He had never seen the like of this barrage. He fought an impulse to turn back from this madness to the woods flanking the field.

Someone in the cockpit was yelling, 'Don't. lose your nerve, Squirt, not now. Take it easy, boy, you will be all right.'

Automatically, with sweat-soaked hands, he began weaving and finking, stomping one rudder and then the other, skidding and sideslipping but never taking his eyes from his target, two black-crossed Me 110s parked under some trees. He began to calculate the range, his right thumb ready to press the firing button. He was ready to fire. He pressed the trigger and walked his bullets across the field into the cockpit and engine of the first 110, then continued the spray into the second aircraft.

The first plane raised up in the air, then fell on its left wing, causing it to careen in a counter-clockwise motion before bursting into a sheet of flames. The other plane buckled and pieces of it went flying every which way as his shells riddled the length of the fuselage. It too burst into flames. As he passed the molten mass its ammunition exploded, sending particles flying towards him. He flew through the smoke and debris of the former aircraft. The smoke from his guns curled back over his wings, and somehow that gave him a sense of security.

In his intense concentration he had forgotten about the flak gunners who were firing madly away at him. He sped across the field and all their shells fell behind him. Some instinct made him focus on the end of the airfield. His only path for a getaway was blocked by hangars with high tension wires and trees over and around them. He was boxed in and felt trapped. He was always conscious of the mixed odours of oil, sweat, and fuel in his aeroplane, but now a new smell penetrated his nostrils - fear! He was petrified with fear, but he knew the meaning of fear and fought to control it. His years in combat and his temperament kept him

First Lt. John Godfrey and friend Lucky.

Capt. Duane Beeson congratulating Don Gentile on taking the lead in

from panicking, for if he panicked he would indeed be dead.

As he approached the obstacles he was flying about ten inches above the airfield. He noticed one hangar had a narrow gap between it and the other buildings. If he could, at the last minute, bank his aeroplane on its wing and sandwich it between the buildings, he would be clear. That would narrow his problems to two - the high tension wires and the trees. He determined that if he could make a very tight banking turn to the port and then the same to the starboard and go under the wires, he just might make it. It would have to be executed with precision and accuracy and timed perfectly, but it was his only hope.

His heart beat wildly in his throat as he hurtled through the gap. He was followed by the ever present tracers bursting all around him as he came out over a curved cobblestone road lined with tall trees. He held down the Mustang so it was only a few feet above the road, hoping to be soon out of range of the enemy flak guns. In the distance he saw a group of cyclists coming down the road towards him. He realised they were Frenchmen and as he zoomed past, he gained altitude and wigwagged his wings. At first they were startled and began jumping off their bikes and heading for the ditch, but once they recognised the U.S. insignia and the silhouette of the Mustang, they took off their hats and excitedly waved them at Don until he disappeared into the setting sun.

Gentile was credited with two Me 110 kills.

From this mission Captain Archie W. Chatterley did not return.

On the 28th of March the group, consisting of 453 fighters, provided escort for 364 bombers to the airfields of Chateaudun. Gentile and his wingman Lieutenant Hughes flew with the 336th Squadron, led by Major Goodson. At 1:23 p.m. and 24,000 feet they sighted the bombers at 18,000 feet and escorted them to the target. The bombers destroyed the hangars and the ammunition dumps with the loss of only one Fort to the flak. Enemy fighters were reported in the area but were not located. They returned at 3:50 p.m.

March 29, 1944. Two hundred and thirty-three B-17 bombers made their way to Brunswick, Germany, with 428 fighters, including the Fourth, as escort. The group was led by newly promoted Lieutenant Colonel Clark and the 336th Squadron was led by Major Goodson. Captain Gentile led Blue Section with his wingman Second Lt. Oscar P. Lajeunesse. They met the bombers at 1:30 p.m. south of Nienburg, where their section of bombers was attacked by a gaggle of thirty or more German fighters coming towards them from the Northeast at 18,000 feet. The rear box of bombers was simultaneously attacked by twenty-odd enemy fighters coming from the south.

The group, flying at 26,000 feet, bounced both formations of the enemy who split and half-rolled down and away from them. Gentile led Blue Section down on a bounce of seven or eight 190s underneath the bombers at 17,000 feet. It was too late for complete surprise and when the enemy saw them they went down in a spiral dive. Don pulled up to the last one and when he was 300 yards astern, he opened fire. His first burst was wide of the mark because the aircraft was bucking from the speed and coarse skidding manoeuvres. He corrected his fire and saw strikes around the cockpit. The enemy slowly rolled over in a port turn and went vertically down. Now Don was at 5,000 feet and in a slight dive, doing 500 miles per hour.

Godfrey, flying Blue 3, followed the section down in the dive but was getting farther behind because his engine kept cutting out. He saw two FW 190s trying to position themselves behind Gentile. Don started to level out below the clouds when Godfrey yelled on the R/T, 'Break! Don, Break!' One of the enemy was already firing when Don made a tight port orbit, causing him to black out. When he recovered he found a 190 in front of him so he closed the distance to 200 yards and fired. The aircraft began to smoke and pieces of the wing and fuselage broke off. The pilot inverted the aircraft and bailed out at 1,500 feet.

Looking around and finding himself all alone, Don made a tight port climbing spiral to 10,000 feet through a hole in the cloud, where he found another Mustang that he asked to join him. They were climbing back toward the bombers when the other Mustang was attacked by two Me 109s. Gentile yelled to break but apparently the other pilot did not hear him because he continued to fly straight and level. Don broke into the 109, which half-rolled into the clouds. Don could not see what had happened to the other Mustang but later found out he was not hit and got home safely.

Suddenly he saw tracers streak in front of the cockpit. He wildly searched the sky but he could not find the foe. He yawed the tail of the Mustang to cover the blind spot, kicked a rudder, dropped each wing, and searched the area below and there he was...a 109 getting ready to fire again. He banked to the port and broke into the enemy, then reversed his turn to the starboard and fell below and astern of him. Don climbed and the underbelly of the aircraft, where there was no armour plate, only oil and hydraulic lines and the engine and fuel tanks, filled the bull's eye of his gun sight. Don took one more look behind to make sure his tail was clear, then his guns came alive, spewing corruption into the thin fuselage. A stream of glycol poured out, followed by the pilot bailing out.

He climbed back alone to the bombers from 7,000 feet and located other members of the Fourth with whom he came home.

Gentile made three victory rolls over Debden and was officially credited with two FW 190s and one Me 109.

From this mission Captain Kenneth D. Peterson and Lt. William E. Newell did not return.

Unfit for flying

April 1, 1944. The first of April was April Fool's Day, and to prove it dawn went forward an hour, forming the British Double Summer Time. Moving the clocks forward an extra hour gave them more daylight in their summer workdays. The unsettled weather during April also reduced the bomber operations.

Four hundred and forty bombers headed for Ludwigshafen, Germany, but the inclement weather caused all but 165 to return. They were escorted by 475 fighters; the Fourth was led by Colonel Blakeslee. Gentile was flying as White 3 to Blakeslee with John Godfrey as his wingman. The sweep netted nothing, but when they were south of Stuttgart, Germany, they observed in the distance two boxes of Liberators under attack by a gaggle of 109s at 19,000 feet. One B-24 had lost two engines and the crew was bailing out. They were at 23,000 feet when they started their dive but when the Germans saw them coming they too went into a steep spiral dive. As Don began to close the distance on the last one, he flattened out and began a violent skidding evasive action. At 10,000 feet he had come within 350 yards of his foe. He was aware of the fantastic visibility above the layer of haze, an ever enthralling sight if only he had time to enjoy it.

Automatically, he kicked the rudder to the left to bring the 109 to right angles, turned off the safety, and let go with a two -second burst. He saw the tracers from his guns thud home. He continued twisting and turning, firing short bursts at every opportunity, scoring many good strikes around the engine and cockpit. For a second the German seemed to hang motionless then, trailing black smoke, he steepened his dive. Now Gentile was at the top of the clouds and he began to pull out of the dive through a hole in the clouds. The pilot of the 109 tried to pull out but his speed was so great he crashed, a blazing inferno in a ploughed field.

Don started his pull-out at 6,000 feet and just barely cleared the woods north of the wreckage of the 109. If he had started it a second closer to the ground he would also have crashed because his speed and angle of dive had made his controls almost rigid.

As he taxied to his parking place, his aircraft spewed thick white smoke from the right side of the engine. A crowd of supporters awaited Gentile and Beeson. They were anxious to hear the score of victories and to learn who now was in the lead.

As the smoke increased in volume someone asked, 'What happened?'

'It overheated,' replied a weary Gentile.

Dozens of pairs of eyes swung to Gentile. They could scarcely believe the casualness of the remark. They all understood what was happening. Too many hours of sitting in that cockpit fighting fatigue and fear. Don's face was ashen; sweat poured copiously down his face, his shoulder blades, and the backs of his legs.

His crew chief, Sgt. John Ferra, removed the panel from the right side of the engine and pried loose part of a cannon shell, saying as he handed it to Don, 'Sir, another inch lower and your engine would have blown up.'

The crowd saw the strain in Don's face break into a faint smile as he weakly nodded. He strode slowly to his quarters. They all knew they were looking at a young man walking precariously on the edge of his grave and how difficult it was to survive against the airborne firing squads of the Luftwaffe.

Gentile was credited with an Me 109 kill. This made 300 destroyed for the 4th Fighter Group, second to the 56th Fighter Group which had 400 and was well in the lead in the kill column. By the end of the war in Europe, the Fourth would be credited with 1,016 victories - 550 in the air and 566 on the ground. The 56th would end up with 1,006 1/2 - 680 of them in the air. Beeson also scored a kill, putting him in second place with twenty-one to Gentile's twenty-two. There were forty eager members of the Fourth out looking for a kill this day but only three were shot down. Bee and Gentile beat them with their two victories.

The following 8th Air Force communication was received by Colonel Blakeslee From Major General William Kepner, Commander, Eighth Fighter Command.

Restricted SFC P1090E.

To: Colonel Blakeslee, all officers and enlisted men of Fourth Fighter Group. My congratulations to you for your remarkable record of enemy aircraft destroyed this month. As far as I know, this is the largest number of enemy aircraft destroyed by one fighter group in one month in the history of aerial warfare. But more important is your outstanding contribution to our Allied objective of winning this war. To enable our forces to carry out their mission, we must destroy the German Air Force. You are a scourge to the Hun in the air and on the ground. He can ill afford the loss rate you have imposed upon him.

Major General William Kepner

Commander, VIII Fighter Command

The noses of the Fourth's Mustangs were painted a bright red. It may have been be symbolic, because in the month of March they had tasted blood and went wild, destroying 156 enemy aeroplanes. More than 100 were destroyed in less than fifteen days during this period, as bad weather had allowed them to fly but seven missions.

But it was not always so. It took the Fourth almost sixteen months to bag their first 100 aeroplanes. Gentile's track record was similar. He entered March, 1944, with seven victories, including the two he shot down during the Dieppe raid on August 17, 1942. But during March he doubled the score of the previous year and a half to fourteen. The kill he got on the first of April brought his total to twenty-two. A fighter pilot becomes an ace with five victories. Of the twenty aces in the Fourth, fourteen had become so during the month of March.

To date the group had many firsts:

It was the first Fighter Group over Berlin.

It was the first group to engage the enemy over Berlin.

It fought the first aerial battle over Paris.

It was the first Fighter Group in the European Theater of Operation.It was one of the few American Fighter Groups to fly Spitfires

In today's list of high-scoring pilots for the entire E.T.O., the 4th Fighter Group has seven among the first fifteen.

April 5, 1944. Four hundred and fifty-six fighters went on a Jackpot Operation[1] to several airdromes in Germany. The Fourth, led by Colonel Blakeslee, descended through the clouds near Berlin at 2:00 p.m. to attack Friedersdorf, Stendal, Plaue, Brandenburg, and Pottsdam. Major Goodson was in command of the 336th and Gentile led Blue section with his wingman Second Lt. Warren E. Johnson. The 336th was ordered to beat up[2] the Stendal airfield.

At 3:15 p.m. Goodson led the squadron down on a field containing more than sixty-five enemy aircraft. On the first pass Major Goodson and Lieutenants Emerson, Carlson, and Tussey (White Section) picked out the planes on the east side of the field, while Captain Hobart, Lieutenant Patchen, and Flying Officer Glover (Red Section) selected targets on the south end. The Blue Section, composed of Captain Gentile and Lieutenants Johnson, Godfrey, and Hughes, also attacked planes on the southernmost end of the field.

On the first pass Lieutenant Carlson destroyed a Ju 88 but inadvertently passed in front of his wingman's line of fire and was forced to return to base escorted by Lieutenant Hughes.

Gentile, following Goodson down the airfield with his section, picked a Ju 88 out of many parked on the Southwest end of the field. He made a head-on attack and immediately turned the German plane into a flaming and total wreck. He turned quickly to the starboard and then the port and picked out another aircraft, attacking it from the rear quarter and getting many strikes on the front part of the plane. He continued across the field to the Northeast corner and attacked the third aircraft from the beam, scoring strikes from the engines back to a point behind the wings. As he pulled up he looked back and could see both aircraft in flames.

Now he turned to the port and dove on a Ju 88 at the Northwest corner of the airfield that had been attacked by Goodson. It was not on fire when he got to it, but as he pulled up again he saw the aircraft ablaze.

Don approached a fifth enemy aeroplane on the Southwest end of the field from the south. As he riddled the aircraft with 50-caliber machine gun bullets, Lieutenant Godfrey came along and fired on and hit the same plane. It also was left burning. Don noticed a biplane sitting in back of a hangar on the north end of the field but because he was out of ammunition he could do nothing about it.

Lt. Franklin Bunte, a Ray Bolger look-alike, was speeding across the field at about 425 miles per hour when he felt heat. As he pulled off the smoking airfield he looked down to see flames coming back from his plane's motor along the left side. He thought he had been hit by flak; it wasn't until after the war that he learned the damage had been caused by his aircraft hitting a high-tension wire. His boots and pants were on fire. He looked over the side and saw he was too low to bail out. Then he noticed a lake off to the left. He jammed the stick forward and dove into the lake.

Gentile saw his plane plunge into the water. As the aircraft rapidly settled toward its final plunge, Don could see the water rise around Bunte in the cockpit, covering him. He circled the area and prayed that the clownish Floridian would come up, but all that was left were concentric waves on the surface.

Bunte had been knocked out by the force of the crash but the shock of the cold water revived him. He was still buckled to the seat when his plane settled on the bottom of the lake.

He did not drown because, luckily, he still had on his oxygen mask. He panicked, trying to release the parachute harness instead of the safety belt, and passed out again. When he came to again he had somehow made it to the surface. He tried frantically to pull on his Mae West but could only manage one side; he did not have enough strength to pull on the other. After what seemed an eternity of passing in and out of consciousness he found himself on the shore. He laid there until he was captured by a farmer who turned him over to the Luftwaffe.

Meanwhile, Captain Beeson of the 334th Squadron and Lieutenants Carr and Biel bore down on the field and each clobbered and set on fire a Ju 88 while the enemy flak gunners put up an effective barrage. Captain Beeson's aircraft was hit and started streaming glycol, and his wingman, Carr, took a direct hit in the engine and also began losing glycol. Lieutenant Biel suffered extensive damage to his aircraft's fuselage and tail unit.

'Got to bail out...tell Bud his good luck charm didn't work so well,' Beeson uttered over the R/T, and with that he went over the side.

On the reform Captain Hobert complained of being hit, so his wingman F/O Fred W. Glover and Second Lt. Donald Patchen checked over his plane and observed a coolant leak. His cockpit began to frost up and he could only fly with his left window open. He throttled back to a very low RPM and manifold pressure. Flying Officer Glover stayed with him until they were over the North Sea, with only ninety miles to go to base. He lost Hobert in the clouds but heard

Gentile and wingman John Godfrey

Major Goodson and Don Gentile

Lt. Spiro 'Steve' Pisanos of Athens, Greece, and Plainfield, New Jersey, with roommate Gentile.

The 'Blakesleewaffe.' Pilots of the 4th Fighter Group relax before a mission.

Ground crew sweating out first Berlin mission. Darrell L. Frolke, Bradford, Ohio, third from right.

The 334th armourers line up with the 50 - calibre ammunition carried by one of the new Mustang P-51 fighters. Second from left, Leroy Nitschke.

Armorer loads half-inch armour-piercing incendiaries in Mustang guns.

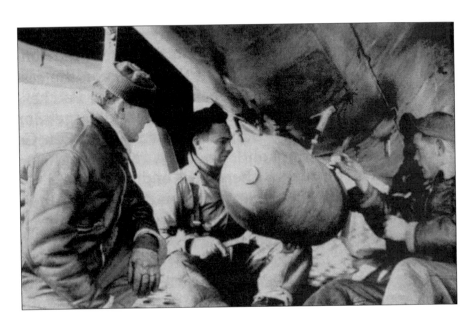

Slinging a bomb to the belly of P-47 Thunderbolt.

him say his engine was seizing up and he was getting ready to bail out. Glover circled the area for some time but due to the poor visibility he could not find him and had to return to base.

When they landed, some pilots were so exhausted their ground crews had to lift them out of the cockpit, place them on the grass field, and massage them before they were able to walk back to the mess hall for their combat ration of alcohol and a debriefing.

Major Goodson mustered three pilots who had enough fuel left to go back and look for Captain Hobert, who was down in the cold North Sea. The whole squadron would have gone if they had sufficient fuel; the code called for it. Hobert was located and they guided the Air-Sea Rescue launch to pick him up. He had suffered so badly from exposure that he died that night.

Don was credited with five Ju 88 victories. The 8th Fighter Command directed the 4th Fighter Group to abstain from announcing that Gentile had broken the record until Gentile's claims had been assessed by the Claims Board and officially confirmed.

The group had a field day, with fifty planes destroyed on the ground and thirty-eight more damaged. But it was a bittersweet accomplishment for the group because four did not return: Carr, Bunte, Hobert, and Beeson. The loss of Bee in particular put a damper on the celebration and had an especially depressing affect on Gentile.

Don walked through the next few days in a fog of shocked disbelief. 'Bee got shot down...he didn't beat the game. He was a good friend, a great competitor, and a fantastic shot but he didn't beat it. Anyhow, no German pilot got Beeson. Flak got the Boise Bee. No flyer can avoid flak. It doesn't matter how good you are, with flak. How long can I keep this up? The odds are against me...my luck might be running out. But I can't turn back,' he kept telling himself, 'even though the strain is almost unbearable. I got to make sure I broke Rickenbacker's record.'

Don became what is known as 'news' and war correspondents approached him everywhere he went, wanting to know: 'When are you going to break the record?' He tried to explain that it wasn't like going down to the corner grocery store and picking out some fruit. Yet they still hounded him. Everywhere he turned there was a reporter waiting for him, asking the same old question.

Don was no longer smiling as usual. His face had become lean and bony. He always looked tired and nervous, and he was getting really jumpy. He had driven himself incessantly toward his goal. He just couldn't turn back. He had to make sure he broke the record and was the first to do it.

Three days later, 140 B-24s were sent to bomb Brunswick, Germany. The Fourth, led by Major Carpenter, had Captain Gentile leading the 336th Squadron with Lieutenant Frederick as his wingman. As they walked towards the briefing room Nicholas 'Cowboy' Megura, one of the group's best fighter pilots, said, 'Don, you're taking too damn many chances. Don't run after things without looking around. My God, look around. You're trying too hard. You know the old story, he who runs today comes back to fight another day.... Be a coward once in a while - remember, discretion before valour. You're getting tired. Hell Don, when we strafe an airfield we are walking on the damn shrapnel. You know they got a thousand guns firing at you at the same time. It's just a matter of luck getting out of there. Quit Don, and go home. You have had too many extensions... take a leave, you have more than earned it...no one would blame you.'

Another pilot, 'Swede' Carlson, noticed the tired look in Don's eyes and came up and put his arms around him, saying, 'Hey Gentle, don't worry, the whole damn squadron will be your wingman today.'

Half an hour after crossing the German border they arrived at the rendezvous, five minutes late, and heard the bombers calling for help. They swung south as they dropped their auxiliary tanks and came up on the starboard side of the Liberator bombers. Don saw more than a hundred 190s and 109s coming towards the bombers from the Northeast at 21,000 feet. The group was still four miles from the B-24s but they could see the Germans easily because there were so many of them. They attacked like a tremendous swarm of insects, their cannon shells bursting all around the Liberators. The whole bomber formation lit up as they fired back at the attacking enemy. The first Luftwaffe attack caused six B-24s to plummet out of formation and go crashing into the countryside. Some of the enemy were knocked down by the bomber gunners.

Gentile led his squadron of thirteen Mustangs down in a dive on more than seventy single-engine enemy fighters. The German force was composed of 190s and 109s, coming in from beneath the bombers and making a climbing port turn. This was to become one of the fiercest aerial battles of the war. The Mustangs attacked head-on and broke up the villainous but excellently commanded force. Some went for the deck while others stayed for the dogfighting.

Don picked a target and as he turned he started to close in, but six 190s bounced him and he had to break away. He closed in fast on another 190 until he was within 300 yards and then opened fire. The 190 started to smoke and immediately broke to the left in a spiral dive. Don followed him down and around, delivering deflection strikes on the port wing, engine, and cockpit, sending him out of control and crashing into the forest below. The 190 came to rest near an exploding B-24.

Don pulled around in a port climbing turn and saw a 190 firing at a Mustang. He tried desperately to get close enough to aid the stricken pilot, but he was too late and watched him crash.

Gentile engaged the victorious 190 in an extended dogfight ranging from

22,000 to 6,000 feet. Don was mad, he always got mad when 'one of our boys bought it.' The enemy started to pull up to out climb him, but Don got him with deflection strikes and forced him to bail out. He was still angry at the German for killing another American and followed him down in a power dive, but abstained from firing when his chute opened. No matter how mad he was he just couldn't kill another person if he could avoid it.

He climbed again, at full bore, and attacked another 190. The enemy turned into him and made several passes, firing all the while. They went down to the deck and around and around for a full ten minutes. The 190 finally went into a very tight climbing turn to the starboard and Don dropped his flaps twenty degrees and out turned him. They completed the turn and he followed the 190 as it rolled and again dove for the deck. He closed from 300 to fifty yards, releasing some very effective bursts. The 190 splattered to the ground in a flaming pile. When Don pulled up he had to fly through smoke and debris, the burning wreckage scorching his windscreen[3] and wings.

Now Gentile had more than broken the record. He was the first to have exceeded the victories of fellow Buckeye Eddie Rickenbacker of World War I fame.

At the base the ground pounders listened with strained ears for the distant roar of the planes' engines, as if it held some whispered message. Who would make it back? How many did they get? Did Gentile become the first to break the record? Godfrey had been forced to return right after they crossed over into the Continent, but he'd had nothing to report because he had left before the start of any action.

Tired and apprehensive, they waited on the grassy hillside and listened for sounds in the sky. Suddenly an unheard vibration caused a pilot's dog to sit up and bark. Excitement mounted at the first sound heard through the infinite afternoon radiance, alien but familiar. The faint hum became louder and louder until a speck appeared in the distance and slowly grew into the shape of an aeroplane. They immediately recognised it as Gentile's by the red and white checkerboard painted cowling.

He dove to 100 feet above the 336th dispersal, so low the windowpanes rattled. Then he pulled up and went into three victory rolls over the hangars and turned into the landing strip so short his starboard wing almost touched the ground.

Don had never felt so tired and elated as he did at this moment. He said, as he held up three fingers, 'I got three.' He had a total of thirty, eighteen of those victories in one month. With his score now at thirty, news of his victory could not be suppressed. The Air Force threw up its hands, and newspapers all over the world proclaimed Gentile the Ace of Aces. He became the focus of a huge part of the world. Newspapers, wire services, broadcasting networks, all heralded his exploits. He was a national hero. He was big news now and on the receiving end of numerous requests for personal accounts, all accompanied by cash offers impossible to pass up.

Ira Wolfert, author turned correspondent, got to him first with a promise of $2,500 for the rights to his life story. Wolfert moved into his room and settled down to pump his subject between missions, the results being a thin fifty-page magazine story titled, 'One Man Air Force.'

Four did not return. Lt. Howard N. Moulton, Jr., from Sheffield, Massachusetts, who got one before bailing out; Lt. Robert Hughes, Houston, Texas; Captain Frank R. Boyles, Denver, Colorado, and Second Lt. Robert P. Claus, Bronx, New York.

April 11, 1944. Supreme Allied Commander General Dwight Eisenhower visited the base with Generals Doolittle, Spaatz, Auton, and Kepner to decorate two flyers with the Distinguished Service Cross. Colonel Blakeslee met the generals at the main gate and let Eisenhower inspect an honor guard of MPs and listen to a staged mock briefing and the narration of several combat films. The films showed combat scenes in which Gentile shot down some of the enemy.

Without mentioning the Invasion, General Eisenhower told the Fourth fighter pilots, 'The time is coming when you will be flying from dawn to dusk and missing much sleep and food...I am going to drive you very hard.... Fighter pilots are doing their part in the land, sea, and air trinity which finally is going to crush the Germans.... For the moment it is entirely the airmen's show.'

Later he pinned the D.S.C. decoration, America's second highest award, on Gentile, and called him a 'one man air force,' saying his citation read like one of the great deeds of heroism in the war.

Don was cited for 'extraordinary courage' in shooting down three Focke-Wulf 190s on April 8, although he was outnumbered by more than three to one and his supplies of gasoline and ammunition were critically low.

Gentile appeared a little nervous and blushed slightly when the citation was read. He said, 'I feel very proud.'

Ike also pinned the D.S.C. on Colonel Blakeslee, commander of Gentile's squadron.

The next day Gentile was sent to London for a broadcast. He thought it would be all right to take a day off because he was so far ahead of everyone else. Back in Piqua his parents and thousands of Piquads were disappointed when atmospheric conditions scrambled reception of the short-wave broadcast. However, later a copy of Don's answers to questions posed by a BBC commentator were read over the air to highlight the program for the residents of Piqua and Miami County.

Don's family was quietly proud but showing the strain of the excitement and acclaim. For a few days rest they went to visit Mr and Mrs Frank Cipriano in

Columbus, Ohio. Mr Cipriano, an attorney, was a brother of Mrs Gentile and a former Italian consular agent. They were not successful in getting the needed rest because friends and the press gathered at the Cipriano home before they arrived and hounded them during their entire stay.

The Piqua City Commissioners telegraphed a request to President Roosevelt and General H. H. Arnold of the War Department which said:

It has been suggested that the city of Piqua use its influence to bring about the return of Captain Gentile to this country for a much deserved rest.

We, the official representatives of the city of Piqua, do not know if this is in accord with the War Department regulations or orders, but sincerely hope and concur in the wish that he can be returned home in the very near future as a deserving tribute to an outstanding flyer.

Gentile had completed his tour of duty a long time prior and had received three time-extensions at his request. But now the War Department wanted him to leave the combat zone and go home. They were planning a series of war bond rallies across the country and they wanted Don for these personal appearances. They also wanted a live hero to impress the youth of the nation that one can survive the evil of war and return to a grateful nation as a hero. The country needed a live hero at this time, and that plus the pressure from the state of Ohio, Piqua, and Don's family and friends convinced them of the desirability of his return.

The War Department also wanted to emphasise the importance of teamwork in combat. While they were going over Don's record they found many comments on teamwork and references to his 'you-hold-him-and-I'll-hit him' system against the Luftwaffe with his wingman Lt. John Godfrey on March 8, 1944. Don had emphasised the importance of a good wingman with the comment, 'Without a good wingman you are likely to be much more cautious and much less effective.' In describing the action over Berlin on the eighth, he said:

'During the combat many 109s were in the area and we were able to pick the best bounces. It was the way that Lieutenant Godfrey stayed with me in every manoeuvre that made our success possible.'

It was decided that the next mission would be Gentile's last and he would be sent home with Godfrey on an extensive bond rally as soon as possible.

April 13, 1944. Five hundred and sixty-six bombers were to hit Schweinfurt and the twin-engine fighter centres at Oberpfaffenhofen, Lechfeld, and Augsburg in Germany. They were to be escorted by 871 fighters from fifteen fighter groups. Colonel Blakeslee led the Fourth and Gentile was in command of the 336th Squadron.

While Gentile was sitting in his aircraft awaiting the signal for takeoff, some army newsreel men were setting up their cameras. One yelled over to Don,

'Captain, on the way back come in real low and let us have some good shots of you buzzing the field.' A tired Don gave a faint smile, nodded his head, and said, 'Okay, when I get back....'

Silence settled over the field, with not a movement anywhere. The pilots had their eyes glued to Don as he consulted his watch. The engines of the 336th were turning and the thirteen Mustangs began lining up on either side and behind Don in combat formation. The squadron was ready, engines purring, wings glinting in the sun, and the pilots adjusting their goggles and tightening their harnesses. Blakeslee raised his arm and the group started forward. In his turn Don raised his gloved hand and slowly opened the throttle. The Mustang's wheels bounced clumsily on the field and then left the ground - they were airborne.

Gentile raised the wheels and locked them, throttled back, and adjusted the airscrew pitch. It was a typical English flying day - a bagful of visibility and a couple of yards of altitude - that demanded careful flying from Don as he led the squadron in tight formation across the English countryside past villages and fields indistinguishable from one another.

Don had led the squadron in a starboard turn over the target to await the arrival of the bombers when he heard reports coming in on the R/T that the bombers were being attacked. They were a half-hour from the rendezvous and could do nothing about it. He turned the squadron to the south looking for the bombers.

Over the radio Gentile heard shouts and calls from the other squadrons of the group saying a big formation of enemy aircraft was in the area and flying east at a higher altitude. He saw them silhouetted against the sun and ordered his squadron to follow him in the climb while dropping their belly tanks. The enemy made a wide port orbit and Don met them almost head-on after they made the turn. Everyone flew in a mad circle trying to get on each other's tail. Don manoeuvred onto the tails of three FW 190s flying in line abreast. They were piloted by new, raw, inexperienced men who would not give him any trouble.

The sky, which had been filled with hurtling Mustangs and FW 190s, seemed suddenly empty and his wingman had disappeared. As he tightened up his circle, trying to get a proper lead on the last one, he studied the beautiful features of the 190s - the short wings, the radial engines, the long transparent hoods, and the lively colouring. They had pale yellow bodies and grey-green backs, and the big black crosses were outlined in white.

He fired a two-second burst at the first, getting some good strikes around the cockpit and engine. They were duck soup, easy kills. All he had to do was go down the line taking one at a time and these beginners would not know what hit them. The eternal micro-seconds of mortal combat dragged by, as the enemy slowly floated into the circle of his gun sight, expanding and filling it as his aircraft was

April, 1944. Capt. Don S. Gentile and his VF-T 43-6913 'Shangri-la' at the time he broke Capt. Eddie Rickenbacker's record of 26 kills.

Note: Rickenbacker's official tally was 25, not 26, and of those four were balloons, two of which were destroyed on the ground. He also shared three of his victories with fellow pilots of his squadron. Thus it appears that Don Gentile, with 23 kills in the air and seven on the ground, at this time had already surpassed the great World War I ace's record by 23 to 22 and seven to three. However, Rickenbacker received the Medal of Honor, while Gentile did not.

Top Brass Visit Debden Left to right: General Eisenhower; General Carl 'Tooey' Spaatz, Commander of USAAFE; General James Doolittle, Commander, 8th Air Force; Major General William Kepner, Commander, 8th Fighter Command.

The 4th Fighter Group turns out for General of the Army Eisenhower's April 11, 1944, presentation of D.S.C. to Gentile and Blakeslee

Lieutenant Colonel Cohen (left, facing camera), Major General Kepner, Lieutenant Colonel Clark, Mr Banks (standing), General Eisenhower, Colonel Blakeslee, Lieutenant General Spaatz, Captain Gentile, Brigadier General Auton, Lieutenant Lang.

Colonel Fallows (left, nearest camera), Brigadier General Curbs, Major Goodson, Lieutenant General Doolittle, Capt. Bob Johnson, Lt. Commander Harry Butcher, U.S.N., Captain Markel, Lieutenant Rowles.

General Dwight D. Eisenhower presents the Distinguished Service Cross to Captain Don S. Gentile of Piqua, Ohio, and his group commander, Colonel Donald Blakeslee, of Fairport Harbor, Connecticut.

buffeted by the 190's slipstream. Suddenly out of the corner of his eye he glimpsed something else. A Mustang from the group was firing away at a 190 but at the same time two 190s were screaming down on the American plane, attacking with machine guns and cannons.

Instinctively his reflexes put Don into a quick half-roll on his back while his finger curled around the firing button and pressed against the spring-loaded tension of the trigger.

There was no way he would let any of his countrymen die without trying to prevent it. It was his code, his sense of duty, to prevent it. All of his faculties, all of his being, were focused on one single thought: Get those FWs off that Mustang's tail. He gained on them and as he closed the distance, he pressed his mike button and yelled, 'Break, Mustang. Break hard to the left.'

The American broke and Don fired from 600 yards, scoring light hits around the wings of the last 190. He continued to close and fire, but they went down under the 10/10 cloud and he lost them. He stooged around for a while but he never saw them again.

The sky had emptied as if by magic. Not one plane left. He was absolutely alone and low on fuel and ammunition so he set his course for England.

He crossed the Channel, its dirty waves edged with foam, and as a hazy blue line appeared on the horizon he knew it was England. The white cliffs of Dover emerged from the mist and as he lost altitude he saw a British coast guard vessel rocking with the swells and surrounded by a swarm of seagulls.

Gentile gave the 336th's dispersal its customary buzz job and as he pulled up from the dive, he noticed the reporters and their newsreel cameras set up on the far edge of the field. He remembered they wanted him to come in low, as if he were flying into their lenses. He was extremely tired after more than seven hours of combat flying, but this was his last mission and he had promised them he would do it, so he thought, 'Well, why not. Let's do a good job of it and really make them happy.'

Don pushed the stick forward, went into an almost vertical dive, and then levelled out just a few feet above the ground. The airfield at Debden was slightly higher in the centre and he had not circled enough on the deck to get re-acclimated and re-orient his depth perception.

He came in low but failed to pull up when he got to the knoll. The three-bladed propeller dug deep into the turf just in front of the cameramen and spectators. With cat-like reflexes, Don pulled back on the stick and gunned his engine; the bent blades of the propeller began to windmill but he gained altitude and sailed over the horrified onlookers, who scattered in every direction. When he gunned the engine the roar brought men running from dugouts, quarters, and other buildings to see what had happened.

The plane went straight up, almost standing on its tail, when Don pulled it over the flagpole atop the operational but at what seemed to be an eighty-degree angle. He cleared the treetops but stalled and the aircraft flicked over onto its back. He began to rapidly lose altitude while with superhuman strength in his legs and arms he fought to right the craft. At the last possible moment he managed to turn the Mustang over and crashed in a ploughed field some two and a half miles away, missing by inches a ditch and some high tension wires.

In the fifty seconds from the time he gunned his motor until he crashed, Gentile performed a score of operations with instinctive reactions born of his long training and experience.

He levelled the plane, tried his chute - he found one buckle loose and in any case was too low to use it - nursed the engine, gauged the propeller revolutions, righted the aircraft, picked his landing spot, cut the engine to avert fire, and then brought 'Shangri-la' down.

The crash truck, rescue team, and base personnel who got to the crash scene first were sure he would be dead because he had been coming in at more than 350 miles per hour. But when they arrived they found him sitting on the wing with his legs crossed, looking dejectedly at his kite with its broken back. His only wounds were a possible slight concussion, a bruised shoulder, and a sprained finger.

Word that Gentile was a charmed man spread around the Debden base when they learned he had walked away from the wreck. His unerring co-ordination saved his life and probably the lives of the twenty others who were gathered in front of the operations hut when his plane crashed.

Blakeslee was sitting at his desk and saw Gentile prang his plane. He said, 'I saw him buzzing the field!' He stood up and glared at the reporters in the room. A glint of fire flashed into his eyes and his face hardened when he said, 'You people have just ruined my best pilot.'

Back in Piqua, Don's mother was in the kitchen, cooking. Lately she almost always had the radio on, day and night, to listen for news about her son. She constantly worried about him, praying for his immediate return to her. During the midday news, the announcer came on with a news bulletin that Captain Don Gentile had crashed in England. Josephina passed out. At Patsy's bar he heard the same news bulletin. Without saying a word he ran from the bar and down the sidewalk towards home.

Patsy caught up with a car stopped at the traffic light at the corner. He yelled, 'Hey! Hey! Please...take me down to South Street... drop me off there. I got trouble home...I've got to get home!' He jumped on the running board of the car and when they got to the corner of his street, he jumped off and ran into the house.

He found his wife unconscious on the floor. He shook her forcefully, trying to revive her, but she did not respond. He placed a chair under her hips, picked it up, and carried her in the chair to the living room. He called the doctor, who revived her with spirits of ammonia but had to give her sedative shots because she was weeping uncontrollably, wailing, 'Mio bambino, mio piccolo bambino.'

The Gentiles did not sleep well that night. In the morning they got up early, and since no one had contacted them yet they rushed to the news-stand to see if anything was in the latest edition of the Dayton newspaper. On the front page was a picture of Don smiling from a hospital bed.

'Look at that, Josephina, your son only broke his little finger. Not a single scratch. Boy, is he tough. He got that way from playing football,' said Patsy excitedly.

'Oh, my poor boy. When will they let him come home? Hasn't he done enough for them? I want my...son.'

Later that day they received a telegram from the War Department saying Don was fine and would soon leave the combat area to come home on a leave.

In his three years of constant combat, Don had rarely left the base because he gave up his 48-hour leave each week to other pilots, in order to be available to fly on missions in their places. Being available for flying made another victory possible, bringing closer the realisation of his lifelong dream. When he flew in a fellow pilot's place it often imposed a sort of demotion; instead of leading an element, a section or the squadron, he was frequently relegated to the less favoured position of wingman or 'tail end Charlie.' But he did not care as long as he could participate in the sortie.

While on base he kept busy attending Mass daily, writing letters home, perfecting his skills of flying and gunnery. His schedule left little spare time to fraternise with members of the opposite sex. From time to time his mind would drift back to a young lady he knew in Columbus. He had first met her when they were children. They had played together with other children when Don came to Columbus, Ohio, with his family to visit his uncle, Frank Cipriano. Mr Cipriano was a lawyer in Columbus who was married to the sister of the mother of the young lady in question, Isabella Masdea. Don had often written his sister asking about Isabella.

'Josephina, who is this Isabella your son always writes about?' asked Patsy. 'Isabella, Isabella... 'How is Isabella getting along?' What Isabella is he talking about? What Isabella you know from Columbus? What's going on? Is something happening?'

May 4, 1944 - February 2, 1951

On May 4, 1944, John Godfrey was promoted to captain and he and Gentile left

England for the United States. When the news reached Piqua, it touched off plans for a big celebration and sent a ripple of excitement through the campus of a girls' school, Western College at Oxford, Ohio. Piqua's city commissioners began making plans for 'Don Gentile Day.' Governor John W. Bricker, the state's senators and congressmen, members of the War Department, ranking officers from Wright-Patterson Air Force Base, and Captain Eddie Rickenbacker were invited to the festivities.

Gentile and Godfrey left from Greenock, Scotland, aboard the Ile de France. The boat was not crowded because most of the traffic was coming to England rather than going to the United States. The majority of the passengers were American airmen, wounded or finished with their tour of duty. They had an uneventful seven-day cruise with nothing to do but eat and sleep.

After docking in New York harbour they were spirited off to a waiting C-47 at Newark Airport for a briefing at the Pentagon in Washington, D.C., by the Air Force Public Relations Officers. They were not to mention single combat but to stress teamwork. They were presented to the press as 'America's Greatest Combat Team in Air Force History.'

Both thought it a lark but went along with it and laid it on heavy. The actual truth of the matter was that of the thirty-two-odd planes Gentile had shot down, Godfrey had helped in less than ten of them.

The next day they met General Hap Arnold, commanding general of the U.S. Air Force. They spent a memorable half-hour during which he questioned them about combat over Germany. He was very interested in how the German fighter pilots and their aircraft compared to the Americans. He was cordial and knowledgeable and they felt they did not tell him anything he did not already know.

They were feted at the Senate Building with members of Congress, including their respective senators, Taft from Ohio and Green from Rhode Island. During the Washington visit they were doggedly followed everywhere by members of the press who insistently flashed their bulbs at them.

They went to see Senator Lehman of New York, whose son had been Don's roommate but was killed in a mock combat practice session in the new P-51. They gave him his son's log book and explained the circumstances of his death. It was probably one of the most difficult tasks Don ever had to do.

Patsy Gentile was told by Don's uncle, Frank Cipriano, who was also Isabella's uncle, that the government would not allow both parents to meet their son in Washington. Only the mother could visit him there. Patsy did not understand the why of this but he reluctantly accepted the condition. Josephina took the train to D.C.; her brother Frank got on at Columbus and accompanied her to Washington.

They arrived in the afternoon and met Don and John Godfrey and his parents.

Captain Don S. Gentile, fighter ace credited with 23 enemy planes destroyed in the air and seven on the ground, walked away from his wrecked Mustang 'Shangri-La' after returning from an escort mission to Schweinfurt. Narrowly missing a building at the base, he lifted the ship at low altitude and crashed-landed in a field. He had hoped to bring the plane back to America.

The reunion was recorded by the ever-present press. They had dinner together and afterwards Don flew his family back home in General Arnold's aeroplane.

When they took off from Washington there was no hint of weather; the storm was miles away and silent. But later they found the weather was down solid. From Pennsylvania to Columbus, the rain was heavy and unrelenting. The cloud ceiling was above 30,000 feet and right down to the ground. Lightning bolts struck with a crackling electrical explosion that seemed to singe the air and shake the sky, violently rocking General Arnold's personally-furnished Army transport plane.

As overpowering as the rainstorm was, it was the lightning and the thunder that worried Don the most. Outside was total darkness, broken only by splashes of lightning. Don flew on instruments, chatting about flying and remarking on the English weather to his co-pilot. The storm reminded him of England, where for days in a row it would often be a matter of outwitting the weather and your own basic fears and getting where you wanted to go in spite of things.

Don tightened his shoulder harness and lap belt and said a silent prayer, then tensely settled back to fight it out. It was a strange feeling to face such a storm in this transport plane rather than a single-engine aircraft. The plane vibrated and danced at every bolt of lighting that spit out across the canopy. Don held the heading as best he could, while the aeroplane bounced along and the radio crackled with static. Don prayed even more fervently.

He was brawling with the elements when, like a miracle, they broke out of the storm directly into a calm and clear sky over Columbus.

It was Saturday and Isabella usually worked until noon as a bookkeeper at Commercial Motors Freight, Inc. She and the other women employees performed a ritual every Saturday of having lunch together and doing a little shopping before going home. But this particular day Isabella had an irresistible urge to go straight home.

When she arrived her house was in complete bedlam since Don's uncle had called her father from Washington and asked him to provide transportation to Piqua for some of the passengers on the plane. His uncle did not know that the city officials had already arranged the necessary transportation for the party.

Since Don had entered the service Isabella had heard tales of his military exploits and secretly thought about him. When she heard he was coming to Columbus she too wanted to meet the hero the nation was toasting as the Ace of Aces. Her father, who was a very proud and honorable man and did not want anyone to think he was promoting his daughter's interests, at first refused permission. But after being subjected to a most persuasive argument by both his wife and daughter he finally consented.

Don began his descent toward Columbus, and as he made his turn onto the final approach he looked over at the gathering crowd and noticed a beautiful young

Josephina, Patsy, and Edith Gentile admire the latest photos of ace Don Gentile and the last model plane he built before leaving for the service.

Don's sister, Edith, writes to him in England.

woman he recognised from his sister Edith's description as Isabella. He thought, 'She hasn't changed much. I would have recognised her anyway...yes, she is more beautiful than I remembered.'

Isabella was thrilled with all the commotion, the dignitaries, the fuss made over the arrival of the HERO. Being rather shy, she just stood in the background, taking in all the proceedings as the occupants of the plane walked toward the crowd. As the waiting dignitaries watched Gentile and his entourage approach, the press rushed up, bulbs flashing. Out of the crowd a handsome young man with an irresistible smile and piercing deep-set eyes walked directly towards Isabella, ignoring the others.

He paused and smiled down at her, and she was struck almost physically by his charismatic beauty. To her it seemed as if each detail of his features had been wrought with infinite care by a supreme artist. The total effect was almost unreal. His eyes possessed such depth and fire. For a moment they stared at each other until Isabella, feeling an electric prickle on the skin of her forearms as she looked up at him, jerked away and dropped her gaze.

'Hi, I am Don Gentile. Are you going to the 'Gentile Day Parade?''

'No, I don't think so,' Isabella stammered in reply. Don went to her father and invited the whole family.

'Please,' he protested quickly, 'I don't want to intrude into your plans for the day but I would like your whole family to come to Piqua for the celebration.' He was a very charming and persuasive man and when he said he would not continue on to Piqua until her father agreed, he capitulated.

A procession of vehicles flanked by motorcycle police transported the Ohio governor, military and city officials, and the rest of the party to Piqua. As they came down the main street with their sirens blaring, they saw huge crowds of people standing in the rain. They wondered what could possibly be going on - was there an accident? A celebration? When they turned into the residential area of the city they saw thousands jamming the sidewalks as they approached the little white cottage where Don's father and sister were waiting. When the escorted motorcade pulled into view the crowd let out a roar and rushed forward, blocking the path of the vehicles.

The little family group tried to move toward the house, but the crowd closed in, picking up the flyer and carrying him right into the house. They tore off parts of his uniform, his captain's bars, and his hat as souvenirs, and the young ladies showered him with kisses.

His parents beamed with delight while Edith cried.

'I want that every mother and father should be as happy as Patsy Gentile is today,' Don's father said proudly.

Early the next morning, less than twenty-four hours after his return home,

Don slipped unnoticed into the hush of the church of Our Lady of Consolation at Carey, Ohio, in the company of his parents, his sister Edith, and his cousin Joe Burnetto, to attend High Mass. At the conclusion of the Mass - while hundreds waited outside to greet their hero - the entire family approached the shrine altar to render thanks in childlike simplicity at the feet of Our Lady of Consolation. As Don knelt he thought of the many narrow escapes from death that were due to the watchful care of Our Lady. How often she had protected him during his many dangerous flights he could not say. Of this, however, he was certain - he owed her a debt of gratitude.

As they knelt and prayed before the little shrine they once again fulfilled the vow his mother had made when her son was saved from death as an infant. Yearly, the Gentiles had faithfully carried out their pledge, even continuing it during Don's three years overseas.

Just before he went overseas, he and his family had agreed that on the first day of his return they would all go to the shrine. And so it was that today they came back.

'I knelt before this shrine when he, just a baby, was saved,' Mrs Gentile said. 'I am kneeling before it again as a mother whose boy has been saved for her all over again.'

His pledge accomplished, Gentile and his family left the church to mingle with the many admirers. All found Don to be a very congenial and loveable person - a typical American Catholic boy who wondered why people should single him out as a hero simply because he had done his duty. Were not countless others doing a great job on the many battlefields of the world?

Father Ambrose Finnegan, pastor of the church, took the family to a sister's home for dinner and gave Don a picture of the shrine, mounted in a silver frame, and a silver medal of Our Lady of Consolation.

'You have plenty of medals already,' Father Finnegan told Don, 'but you have none like this.'

The priest attached it to a chain on which Gentile also wore the medals of St Christopher and the Blessed Mother.

Don took off his wings and presented them to Reverend Finnegan. They in turn were blessed and placed on a plaque with the wings left at the shrine altar by other airmen.

On May 25, the city of Piqua, joined by thousands of western Ohioans, paid tribute to Don with a special war bond sales rally called 'Don Gentile Day.' The event had a threefold purpose: to sell war bonds, to welcome home Gentile, and to honor all from Miami County in the armed services.

Representatives from the War Department and ranking officers of Wright and Patterson airfields as well as officers from Lockbourne Air Base in Columbus came with thousands of enlisted men and women and other civilian officials to pay homage to the heroes.

The highlight of the day was a gigantic parade through the downtown streets of Piqua, with Don sitting on the back of an open car as ten thousand Piquads cheered and waved along the route to Roosevelt Park, where official tribute was paid to the famed fighter pilot.

On the platform with him for that occasion were three other Piquads home from the war. They were Martin Minnich, bomber pilot, who escaped from the enemy through the European underground; Gilbert Steinke, a Marine injured at Guadalcanal; and Sgt. Kenneth Hart, home on furlough from the Anzio beachhead in Italy.

When it was Gentile's turn to speak, he said, 'I do not consider this magnificent demonstration a personal honor. Rather it belongs to all the boys fighting on all the warfronts for the cause of democracy. I thank God for the day my parents came to the United States. This is the happiest day of my life.

'Returning from a combat zone, may I tell you that your sons, and brothers, and husbands, and my fellow fighting men, have the highest morale and are confident of victory. With the help of God we will win.'

It was apparent to all, Don Gentile was a bloody hero.

The next few days were hectic, with newspapermen following Don around and friends parading in and out of his house wanting to say hello. The telephone rang off the hook. Don found little time to rest.

He received an offer for $500 plus expenses to appear with John Godfrey on the NBC radio program 'The Wide Horizons Show' in New York City. He agreed. Later that evening the flyers got a taste of the city's night life.

The day Don left to start a war bond tour, his mother passed out.

'Wake up, Josephina. Your son is calling from Washington, D.C.,' insisted Patsy.

'Naw, my son went back to the war in England.'

'No, he is in Washington, he's calling on the phone and wants to talk to you. Pick up the phone and talk to him.'

'No, Mama,' Don assured her, 'I am not back in England but in the States. I am calling from Washington and will be home in a couple of days. Will you be all right?'

His mother finally was convinced he was not returning to combat but would be away for these series of war bond tours. After the tour, Don was assigned to Wright-Patterson Air Force Base in Dayton, Ohio, as a test pilot, testing conventional-type fighters and the all new P-80 jet fighter.

One night Edith was abruptly awakened by loud yelling voices. She sat up in bed, listening intently, but there was nothing but the soft ticking of her bedroom

A hero's welcome. Edith Gentile and admiring neighbours and friends greet her brother Don Gentile, top American fighter pilot in the European Theater, upon his return home to Piqua, Ohio

Captain Don Gentile and his mother pray before the shrine of Our Lady of Consolation in Carey, Ohio

clock. She heard the sounds again and they sent a cold shiver down her spine.

She wanted to call out but her voice caught in her constricted throat. The sounds were coming from Don's bedroom. At last Edith found her voice, and frightened, asked timidly, 'Who is it?'

Instantly the sounds ceased. She waited motionless, listening, and heard a faint humming drone, not unlike a distant swarm of bees, break through the stillness. She made her way through the darkness to Don's bedroom. As her hand shook the door handle, jerking and straining at it, she sensed her father and mother rushing up behind her towards his room. Finally she forced the door open.

Through the darkness they saw a figure sitting up in bed, making noises simulating the sounds of an aeroplane. They switched on the lights.

'Don!' cried out Edith, 'What are you doing?'

They stopped, motionless, frozen by the sight. They saw a strange thing. Don was sitting up in the middle of the bed in the position he assumed when he was in the cockpit of a fighter plane. His face was contorted and grey, his eyes were wide open, stricken and full of despair. He struggled like a man trying to fight some unknown satanic force. He moved his arms as if he were shoving the throttle and control column, his legs worked the invisible rudders. His mouth made loud sounds imitating an aeroplane's engine and machine gun fire.

In a flash they knew what was happening. In his subconscious he was somewhere over Germany at 30,000 feet, fighting the Luftwaffe. Now they could clearly perceive what he had been through these past three years of intensive combat. It was very hard for them to accept that the Don they knew before the war was the man before them now. They knew that fighter pilots had to be aggressive and determined, but this picture of him... It just wasn't the loving, happy-go-lucky, gentle person that he was.

He had had too many missions, too many close calls, too much flak, seen the death of too many comrades, and had experienced too much emotional stress caused by pushing himself beyond the call of duty. He had been a walking time bomb waiting to explode, to let out all the feelings. Don's problem was not a lack of control but too much control; he never let anything out. Now they were witnessing the release of the escape valve[1].

They stood before him, hugging each other, crying and watching in horror.

'Oh God, oh, sweet Mary,' wailed Josephina. 'What have they done to you, my beautiful young son.' At first she drew back, awed and horrified, then she kneeled next to him, gently hugging and kissing him. Stroking his black wavy hair, she said, 'You go ahead Don, have all the bad dreams you want, I am here to protect you, and I am just happy you are home.' With that she closed his eyes and laid him down gently on the bed as she hummed an old lullaby she used to sing to him when he was a child.

Captain Don Gentile and his mother pray before the shrine of Our Lady of Consolation in Carey, Ohio

Don Gentile Day, Piqua, Ohio, May 25, 1944.

Don began to date Isabella. He would go to Columbus almost every day, stay with his uncle, and take Isabella out on a date. If he could not visit he would spend endless hours talking to her on the telephone. They seemed to be made for each other.

One night he stayed home, and every time Patsy looked at him he was smiling and laughing.

'What are you laughing at, Don? You won the lottery or something?' asked his father.

'No, I didn't win the lottery.'

'Why are you laughing then?'

'Oh, I just feel that way,' Don replied. 'Hey, Daddy, can you take a day off this week?'

'I suppose I could, why?'

'I would like you to go with me to Dayton.'

'What do you figure on doing with me in Dayton?'

'Hard to tell, but you get the day off and I will tell you on the way.'

'You aren't figuring on buying some property in Dayton, are you?' demanded Patsy.

'No, no, nothing like that. I just want to spend the day with you in Dayton. Let me know what day you can get off from your job and I will leave the field to go with you.'

When they got into the car to drive Dayton, Patsy said, 'Now what is this trip today about? I have got to know. When you cross a river you have to know how deep the water is, so tell me what I am in for.'

'Dad, I got a girl friend in Columbus I want to marry.'

'Well, I am glad to hear that, son.'

As they walked into a jewellery store in Dayton, the owner, George Worth, said, 'Hello, Don. Do you want to look at some engagement rings today?'

'Yes, I brought along my daddy,' replied Don. Patsy thought to himself, 'Now I know why he wants me along. He wants me to pay for the ring. When did he find time to meet this guy? He must have been here before.'

'Oh, that's nice. How much do you want to spend?'

'I would like to look at the rings first and then see if I can afford them. I am in the service and don't have a lot of money.'

As Mr Worth took out a tray of rings he said, 'Take my word that this ring right here, this diamond, if I would put it in the window and sell it, they would pay more than one thousand dollars, and that's for the diamond only, without the setting. Since I like you, I am going to work for nothing and give you this ring with the mounting for only five hundred dollars. It's over one carat, a genuine pure blue white diamond. Take it to any jewellery store and have them check and appraise it and you will find that it is worth with the mounting at least one thousand and fifty dollars.' As he said this he looked intently in Patsy's eyes.

'All right, George, I will take your word for it. I will write you a check for five hundred dollars. When can we expect the ring?'

'It will be ready for you on Friday.'

Don picked up the ring on Friday and on Saturday, June 6, in the presence of his mother, Isabella's parents, and some close friends, he said to her father, 'Mr Masdea, I would like to marry Isabella.'

All eyes turned to Isabella, who blushed and turned bright red. When Don put the ring on her finger she stared into his eyes, and he into hers. Slowly her smiling eyes filled with tears of happiness until they brimmed over, spilling down her cheeks. She cupped her head in her hands and alternately cried and laughed. She was happy beyond description.

Some months earlier, in an interview by Lee Carson of the King Features Syndicate, Inc., it was stated that Don was a friendly, amiable young man but had not formed any close friendships since his roommate, Steve Pisanos, 'got his' on a mission. The colourful eloquent little Greek boy and the quiet thoughtful Italian-American kid from Ohio had been inseparable.

'Steve was just the opposite from me,' Don said. 'He was full of vinegar, always talking, laughing, and stirring up something around here. I guess one of the things that made us so close in spite of the differences between us was that we both had Old Country backgrounds and thought America the finest place on earth. Also, we both put flying above everything else.'

For more than eleven months Don had thought that Steve Pisanos was dead, but in October, 1944, he called his uncle, Frank J. Cipriano, 'shouting like a little boy.'

'Steve's back,' he exulted. He explained that he had received a cablegram saying that Steve was alive and well. He had been forced to parachute into enemy territory and hid out for months with the aid of friendly French. He finally made it back to the American lines in Europe on August 28.

Steve was the best man at Don's wedding and he at his.

Don and Isabella were married in St John the Baptist Church on November 29, 1944. They had a beautiful Italian wedding. They honeymooned in New York City and moved to Piqua when Don was stationed at Wright-Patterson Air Force Base in Dayton.

On September 23, 1945, Don Gentile, the 'Messerschmitt Killer' was sweating out his most recent victory, the arrival of his firstborn, Dominic Salatore Gentile, Jr., his seven-pound namesake, born at Piqua Memorial hospital at 12:20 p.m. Two years later, on January 30, 1948, a second son, Joseph, was born to the Gentiles in Columbus, Ohio. Their third son, Pasquale, was born at Walter Reed Army

Hospital in Washington, D.C., on January 14, 1950.

Don Gentile and John Godfrey were offered positions as Division Directors in Sales and Services for the Globe Aircraft Corporation. Don left the service and was discharged at Wright-Patterson AFB on April 27, 1946. While working with Globe he was offered a regular Air Force commission, which he accepted on December 6, 1947. He was happy to get back into the service and fly fighters.

After attending the Air Tactical School, 3839th Squadron, Tyndall Field AFB, Florida, he was assigned to headquarters in Washington, D.C., in February, 1949.

On June 27, 1949, he started summer classes at the University of Maryland, College Park, Maryland. He was majoring in Military Science with a minor in Psychology.

On Sunday, January 28, 1951, Don went to Mass early and as he reached home his sister and her husband, Anthony Barbato, arrived from their home in Philadelphia, Pennsylvania. They had come to visit because the Gentiles were getting ready to move to Selfridge AFB, in Mt. Clemens, Michigan.

As Don stepped from his car in the parking lot he grabbed his sister, kissing her and swinging her around and throwing her up into the air, as he always did when he saw her.

'You had better stop that or the neighbours are going to talk about you having a new girl friend,' pleaded Edith.

'Oh, Edith,' Don said grinning. His teeth were particularly white and symmetrical and his smile was irresistible. 'You're my little sister and only God knows when I'll get to see you again.'

Isabella went off to church while Don watched the children. When she returned he was suited up in his flying gear.

He left for the field a little after noon with Tony, who went along to keep him company, and they promised to be back by 3:30 p.m. While Tony waited in the car reading a book, Don prepared for takeoff. He wasn't scheduled to fly today, but being in love with flying, he wanted to get one more flight in before they moved to their new base.

Don settled into the cockpit of the T-33 jet trainer[2] and as he adjusted his helmet, Sergeant Gregory D. Kirsch climbed quickly up beside his canopy and said, 'Captain, you promised me some time I could fly with you. I hear you will be leaving tomorrow for Michigan and I wonder when you would take me for a ride?'

'Well, how about now? This is as good a time as any.'

Don heard a click in his earphone followed by the voice of the senior controller on duty at the flight tower, Staff Sgt. Alan C. Steinhauer, who gave the takeoff instructions. Don eased back on the stick and the jet aircraft, serial 49-905A, lifted off the ground. As he retracted the landing gear and flaps, he looked at his watch. It was 3:05 p.m. He eased back on the throttle from full takeoff power, waiting until they reached the proper air speed, and then put her into a climb.

While he continued his ascent the sun's rays blazed across the skin of the aircraft. Don loved to fly jets: the absence of noise and vibration; the feeling of power; the rapid climb away from the earth, they all added up to one of the most pleasant sensations he had ever experienced.

As he concentrated on this enjoyment, the spell was broken.

'Your transmitter is cutting out on 126.18 mcs. Would you switch and use frequency 121.50 mcs as a secondary measure?'

'Roger, over and out.'

He pushed the throttle to the gate, putting her into a battle climb, and as the jet's nose penetrated the hazy blue sky, the increased power and gravity pressed him back into the seat. For the sake of his young passenger he put her through all of the aerobatics, using every manoeuvre in the book and some he had perfected on his own. He buzzed his apartment around 3:10 p.m. to let Isabella know that he would be home shortly. Don always buzzed their home whenever he was flying; in fact, he had done it when she was working or at her parents' home before they were married. She got a particular thrill out of it.

The tower personnel observed Don flying in their vicinity at an altitude of 2,500 feet and shortly thereafter he called for a radio check and they informed him his reception was loud and clear.

The horizon revolved across the nose of the jet as the wing came over and he put the plane into a power dive. Suddenly the aeroplane became uncontrollable. Don frantically pulled back on the control column, his arms and shoulders aching as he fought to control the aircraft. He slowly brought the craft out of the dive and into a soaring roll. He called frantically on the intercom for the sergeant to eject, but the young soldier froze. Don yelled again and again but he did not respond. In a micro-second he had to decide whether to save himself or try to land the craft and hopefully save both of them.

At 3:18 p.m. Staff Sergeant Steinhauer, in the control tower, observed a large cloud of smoke Northeast of the station. The Crash Station and Base Operations were notified to check the source of the smoke. The pilot of Navy 178 was requested to fly over the area and make a visual check. He reported he could not determine the source. The pilot of another aircraft in the area, Navy 1742, was then requested to make a check. He informed the tower the fire was caused by an aircraft crash. All facilities concerned were notified and crash equipment was dispatched. Navy 119 advised that he was over the scene and would keep the tower advised. At 3:40 p.m. Navy 119 advised them that the crash equipment had reached the scene of the accident. The aircraft was determined to be Captain

Gentile's and was destroyed on ground impact 4.5 miles Northeast of Andrews Air Force base. There were no survivors.

Back at the airfield Tony was reading a book while waiting for Don in the car when he overheard two Air Force flyers talking. One of them said, 'Oh, what a shame something like that had to happen to Don Gentile after all his close calls in combat.'

Tony rushed from the car and asked, 'What did you say happened to Don Gentile?' Before he could get an answer, he was asked to go to the field security office accompanied by one of the officers.

They entered the office of the adjutant. 'Have a chair,' a major said casually, sitting on a corner of the desk. 'Might I ask who you are? Do you have any identification?'

'I am Tony Barbato. I have a driver's license, would that be all right?'

'Yes, that will suffice. Tony Barbato, huh.' He looked at the other officer and smiled grimly. 'What do you know about Captain Gentile?'

'I don't know anything. I came on the base with him and I heard one of the officers here say something happened. I wanted to know what that meant.'

The major returned Tony's driver's license and asked, 'How do you know the Captain? Why are you on our base?'

'Gentile is my brother-in-law and I drove him here to do some flying. I was waiting to drive him home. What happened? What was the officer talking about?'

'Mr Barbato, the Captain has had a fatal accident. He crashed...about half an hour ago. We are still investigating the cause of the crash. That's why we were curious about your inquiries. You can understand our concern, can't you?'

'Yes, of course.' His voice was heavy, stricken. As he stared intently at the floor he gulped and slowly collected himself.

'We are all very sorry, we'll miss him.'

His voice broke the silence. Tony walked over to him, shook his hand, and said, 'Thank you. I had better go now and notify the family.'

When Don did not arrive home at the time he was expected, they became concerned because he never was late. Isabella had dinner ready and the table set, and she continued to wait with Edith. She called Operations to check on when he landed but was put off and given no definite answer. This was very unusual. Later she called the base again but got the run-around.

As the hours slipped by, they became more nervous but tried not to show it. Five-year-old Don, Jr., who was sitting next to his mother on the sofa said, 'Oh, I bet something's happened to Daddy.'

'Look Isabella, if you want to drive to the field, go ahead, I can stay with the children,' said Edith.

Isabella, her face fixed to the window, had to speak over her shoulder.

Don Gentile and Major Bong, test pilots at Wright-Patterson Air Force Base, Dayton, Ohio.

'Maybe I should go, he probably ran into an old friend or something.'

She went into another room to get her coat and purse. Edith got up from the sofa and went to the window. When she saw her husband getting out of his car she yelled out, 'Oh, Isabella, here they are.' It was then she noticed that the other man was not Don.

As they came up the walk, she knew something was wrong, Tony's face was white as a sheet and the other man was a priest. They rushed out to meet them and as they met on the stairs, Edith said, 'Well, how's Don?'

'He's fine, don't worry about him;' replied Tony.

Edith, thinking him hurt and in the hospital replied, 'Well, let's go to him.'

Tony grabbed her hand gently and said, 'No...no...that's not what I mean. I mean he is fine with God. They found him with his rosary in his hand.'

Edith, hoarse with sorrow, said, 'No, not Don, oh, no, please God, not Don.'

Isabella went into shock and collapsed, unconscious. They carried her to the apartment and summoned a doctor, who placed her under heavy sedation.

'Edith,' said Tony, 'we had better call home and tell them what has happen. We don't want them to hear it on the television.'

'Yes Tony, you had better call them. I don't want them to hear it on the news, especially Mama.'

Within hours the news of Don's death had circulated through news agencies around the world.

Mrs Josephina Gentile turned on the television and heard Ed Sullivan say, 'One lovely April night in Chester, Pennsylvania, none of us dreamed that the big lean nice-looking kid was racing against a clock that was running out on him. So all the youngsters who heard him at that St James Catholic High School team banquet must have experienced the same dreadful sensation that belted me in the pit of the stomach when we heard of the death of Captain Don Gentile, killed in a routine jet flight.'

He went on to say, 'When a Don Gentile is killed, the country loses a giant, far and above the common mould of clay.'

And lastly he concluded with, 'On my desk is this thin book, penned by Ira Wolfert, and on the flyleaf is this scrawled dedication: 'To Ed, with great appreciation. Don Gentile, 26 June '50'. I am going to ask the padres of St James Catholic High School if they'd like this prized book for their school library as a record of Don's visit.'

Tony Barbato called the Reverend A. C. Monter, of Piqua's St Boniface Church, and asked him to notify the relatives but when Patsy got home he found Josephina unconscious on the floor.

It became a nightmare for the family. If it had not been for their strong religious faith, it would have been unbearable.

The Gentile family went to Washington to make the arrangements for Don's burial. They returned the next day and Captain Spiros (Steve) N. Pisanos accompanied the coffin alone to Columbus for the funeral.

General Hoyt S. Vandenberg, chief of staff of the U.S. Air Force, paid tribute to Don in a telegram to his wife which said: 'On behalf of the men and women of the United States Air Force, I extend deepest sympathy to you and your family on the untimely death of your husband, Major Don Gentile. As one of World War II's most noted aces, Major Gentile made an outstanding combat record.

'His loss will be keenly felt, not only by those who knew him personally, but throughout a country that knew him as a courageous fighter for freedom.'

Both houses of the Ohio General Assembly adopted a resolution in tribute to Don.

In Piqua, plans were being formulated for an official representation of local citizens, city officials, and friends at the full military services which were held Friday, February 2, 1951, in St John the Baptist Church in Columbus. The city had to send extra police to handle the huge crowd that came to pay final respects to Don.

Celebrant of the Solemn Requiem High Mass was the Reverend Father Charles Sala, administrator of St John the Baptist Church. The Reverend Father Angelo Castera of Cincinnati, a cousin of Don's, was deacon. The Reverend Casto Marrapesce, assistant at St John the Baptist, was subdeacon. Two chaplains from Wright-Patterson AFB, Col. Paul J. Giergerich and Captain C. J. Lewandowski, handled the graveside services. Father Lewandowski also spoke after the Mass and extended the sympathies of the Air Force. He praised Gentile as 'one of the greatest heroes of the European skies,' as a 'true Christian and Catholic worthy of the name, who was ever loyal to God and his Church,' and as 'a soldier of his God and his country.'

More than 300 people braved temperatures of twenty degrees below zero and ice and snow-covered streets to attend the funeral.

After the funeral service a mile-long procession moved from the church through the downtown area to St Joseph's Cemetery, where Don was laid to rest with full military honors.

After the traditional three volleys over his grave and the last bugle note had faded away, Don's mother led the procession of family members to kiss the coffin. As she bent over her lips formed the same words she had sobbed with joy seven years before when she was informed her son had shot down three enemy aeroplanes.

'God bless my boy.' But these were not yesteryear's sobs of joy.

After the family had withdrawn, Captain Steve Pisanos stepped back, turned, and stiffly saluted the grave. He said simply:

'I'll miss you, Don.'

Thus, Ohio and the nation buried a hero, the captain buried a friend, Isabella buried a husband and the father of her three children, and Patsy and Josephina lost a loving son.

Mr Alberto Tarchiani, Italian Ambassador to the United States, presents the Italian 'Croce Al Merito di Guerra' and 'Medaglia D'Argento - La Valour Militare' to Capt. Don S. Gentile, U.S Air Force, April 20, 1948. (U.S Air Force photo, Wash., D.C.)

Maj. John Godfrey, Illinois Governor Dwight Green, and Maj. Don S. Gentile. Godfrey and Gentile were the greatest fighter pilot team in the history of the U.S. Air Force. As you can see by the displays over their hearts, both received some recognition.photo, Wash., D.C.)

Major Don S. Gentile

539 South Wayne Street, Piqua, Ohio, where Don grew up and the home he returned to after his years in combat.

Don's grave at St Joseph's Cemetery, Columbus, Ohio.

Epilogue

With Don's death Josephina too became a casualty. She had always been overly protective of Don, particularly since his childhood brush with death. Her love for him was profound. She suffered a paroxysm of grief, and as time passed she was drawn into a web of despair and lost her will to live.

For the family who cared for her and everyone who knew her, it was agony to watch her health slowly ebb away. Nobody quite knew what to do. She was in and out of the hospitals. She became bitter at life itself; she constantly talked of death. She could not understand why God had left her and had taken her beloved Don.

Patsy could no longer take his wife downtown because she would rush up to any soldier in uniform, thinking he was her Don. She would say to passers-by, 'Oh, no. I had a son like that, but you see I lost him.' Sometimes Patsy would awaken in the middle of the night to check on his wife and find her in Don's room, clutching a small picture of him to her breast and moaning, 'Oh Don, oh Don.' She carried this picture with her always, even to bed. Don had given it to her, and Josephina constantly reminded the family that when she died she wanted to be buried with it.

Patsy tried to reason with her, pointing out that many parents were not even lucky enough to get back the bodies of their dead sons. In reply she would only jump up, truculent, and wave her arms towards the door, saying, 'Get out! Leave me alone!'

Josephina never accepted her son's death. This was probably due to the closed coffin policy which prevented her from seeing him dead. Patsy had placed a call to President Truman at the White House in an effort to reverse the policy.

The president tried to side-step the issue by saying, 'Mr Gentile, I am afraid we can't do this. The law would not allow it, it would take a special act of Congress and I feel politically it would not be feasible. I am sorry.'

During Josephine's final lap of life, she developed leukaemia. For the last three months, Edith lived with her in the hospital. They would hold hands and reminisce about old times. How after school she would have baked goods waiting for Don and Edith and their friends. How Don would refer to himself even in adult life as 'her little boy.' How he would talk and tease her in such a cute and funny way.

On September 28, 1973, at 6:00 p.m., Josephina called to Edith to shut the hospital room door. Edith got up, turned to the door and said bewilderedly, 'Mama, the door is already closed.' She turned back to her mother and watched her face break into a faint smile. Her eyes swung from her mother to the area of the door where she directed her smile. Her mother's dark eyes, full of energy and life, completely dominated her face. Edith had the feeling her mother was seeing something in her mind; she too felt its presence and it was strange. Her mother sat up, put her head back on the pillow, and with a widening smile she extended her arms in an embrace, caressing something that only she could see.

When Josephina was buried they placed the picture of Don she always carried with her in the casket next to her heart.

Notes to Text

1925-1935

1 Sopwith Camel. British World War I fighter biplane introduced into combat in June, 1917. It became the superlative combat aircraft of the Great War, with a claimed victory tally of 2,790 enemy planes by the time of the Armistice in November, 1918.

2 Lafayette Escadrille. Early in 1916, a year before the United States entered World War I, a handful of valiant Americans banded together as the Lafayette Escadrille and flew combat for France.

3 Jenny. The Jenny, officially the JN - 4D, was America's first mass produced commercially successful aeroplane. It became the standard military trainer throughout World War I, but gained immortality from the 'gypsy pilots' who used her for barnstorming across America.

4 0X5. The Jenny was propelled by the treacherous OX5 engine. Although the Jennies were being used up, this was not the case with the war surplus OX5s. They were plentiful and cheap ($50 each) and there was almost no other engine available.

1936-1938

1 Beat-up. A thorough job of flying low over a ground object.

1939-1941

1 Pilot Officer. The equivalent of a U.S. second lieutenant. In the R.A.F., the

pilot training system designated the highest rated one - third of each class as Pilot Officers, while the remaining two-thirds became Sergeant Pilots.

2 Rotte. Two Rotte made a Schwarm, four aircraft; three Schwarms made up a Stoffel, twelve aircraft; three Stoffels made up a Gruppe, or thirty-six aircraft; three Gruppes made up a Geschwader or 'wing.'

June 22, 1942 - September 16, 1942

1 Boston bomber. Known also as A-20 Douglas Havoc, this was a light bomber and tactical support aircraft that could fly at 350 miles per hour, carry a 1,000-pound bomb load, a crew of three, and eight machine guns, six of them in the nose of the plane.

2 Ramrod. Combined fighter and bomber operation.

3 Jinking. Sharp manoeuvre, sudden evasive action by aircraft.

4 Flak. 'Flieger Abwebr Kanonen,' flying defence cannon; in Allies' terms, anti-aircraft.

5 R/T. Radio telephone for receiving and sending in each aircraft.

6 FW 190 A-3. This Focke-wulf aircraft was designed in late 1937 as a fighter but did not see combat until September 1, 1941. Conceived as an advance over the Messerschmitt BF 109, which was gradually losing ground to the superior Allied fighters, the FW 190 was the first serious challenge to the Spitfire. It was responsive and light on the controls; it had quick acceleration and a small turning radius, considered vital to combat operation. It was loved by the German pilots but feared by the English, Americans, and Russians.

7 Petrol Dump. Fuel storage area.

8 Starboard. The right side of the aircraft. Port is the left.

9 Gaggle. A cluster or pack of planes ranging from ten up to fifty or more in number.

10 Down on the deck. Flying just above the ground.

11 Douhet Theory. Douhet was an Italian general whose writings immediately after World War I had a remarkable influence on the doctrine of air power. He believed future wars would be determined by air power alone. He suggested that the decisive campaign would be the long range bomber offensive, which would destroy the enemy's cities, drive its people to despair, and force its government to capitulate.

12 Twelve O'clock High. In the movie Savage, played by Gregory Peck, arrived to take command and security on the base was so lax, everyone was gone except a squadron commander. In reality, this major was Tibbets, who was promptly appointed executive officer.

13 Light flak. Refers not to the intensity of the flak, but to the calibre of the

guns. There were two types of flak, light and heavy. Light flak was seen below 8,000 feet and became increasing inaccurate above that height. It was fired by fully automatic 37mm Bofors, either fixed or mobile units. As long as the firing pedal was depressed and four-round clips fed into the breech, the Bofor would fire armour-piercing, incendiary, or explosive shells which would detonate on contact or by fuse, emitting a deadly red or green fireball. Heavy flak is fired by guns three or more inches in diameter. One of the most famous was the '88,' which could slam its twenty -two pound shell through heavy armour at a distance of over one mile. These projectiles are thrown up blindly in a barrage in the area of the aircraft, and upon exploding form a dark circle of smoke up to twenty-five feet in diameter, with a dull red glowing centre which is destructive within 200 feet. The closer the contact the more intense the damage they inflict.

14 Clock code. Direction method. Twelve o'clock is vertical above the cockpit; three o'clock is straight ahead, in front of nose of plane; nine o'clock is directly astern.

15 Overcast. Overcast is rated in tenths. For example, if the sky is completely overcast, then it is described as ten-tenths cloud, while half-overcast is called five-tenths cloud.

16 Rhubarb. A small number of aeroplanes doing a strafing sweep of ground targets at low level, usually during poor weather conditions.

17 Batman. English WWI retired soldiers who the officers hired to do mundane duties such as dean their quarters, polish brass, and so on.

18 Tit. A red button in the Spitfire that when pushed gives extra speed in an emergency.

19 Junker 88. German medium bomber with a crew of four (pilot, observer/bomb aimer, radio operator/gunner, engineer/gunner). Its maximum speed was 292 miles per hour at 17,390 feet, and it had seven 7.9mm MG 81 machine guns, three firing forward on fixed or flexible mounts, two firing aft from the rear of the cockpit, and two firing aft below the fuselage from the gondola. Bomb capacity, 7,935 pounds.

20 LCT. Landing craft with tanks.

21 BOQ. Bachelor Officers' Quarters.

September 16, 1942 - December 20, 1942

1 Bubble and Squeak. A dish made of collards and potatoes served to most British troops for breakfast. It was cheap, plentiful, and nutritious, but not very tasty by American standards.

2 Mayday. The international sign of distress. It comes from the French 'm'aidez,' help me, but it has been Americanised to Mayday.

January 13, 1943 - July 29, 1943

1 Element. Two aircraft. Two elements made up a flight; four flights made a squadron.

2 Probable. Term for enemy aircraft that are believed to have been destroyed, yet the actual destruction is not seen. A score is called 'Destroyed' when the enemy aircraft is dearly seen to hit the ground or sea, is seen to break up in the air or descend in flames, or the pilot is seen bailing out. 'Damaged' refers to enemy aircraft observed to have considerable damage or when parts of the plane are shot away.

3 Bounced. R.A.F. term for an attack.

4 1340 hours. Military time is based on a day being 2400 hours, starting at 1:00 a.m.; e.g., 0100 hours is 1:00 a.m.; 1200 hours is noon 2000 hours is 8:00 p.m.; 2400 hours is midnight, and so on. Therefore, 1340 hours would be 1:40 p.m.

5 Big friends. Bombers; fighters were called 'little friends.'

July 31, 1943 - August 17, 1943

1 Matthews bailed out, managed to evade his captors, and made it back to Debden in October to confirm his kill.

2 IP. Point at which the pilot turns over the controls of the bomber to the bombardier to begin the bombing run.

3 Gruppe. German 'group'; individual unit of the Luftwaffe. A group usually consisted of three squadrons of thirty-six aircraft.

October 10, 1943 - December 31, 1943

1 10/10. The portion of the sky covered with clouds is assessed in tenths. For example, if half the sky is clouded over, it is described as 5/10 cloud while complete overcast would be 10/10.

2 FW 200. This was a reconnaissance bomber carrying a bomb load of 4,626 pounds and a crew of seven (pilot, co-pilot, observer, radio-operator, engineer, and two gunners). They carried out anti-shipping strikes and were a danger to convoys. There were only a few (263) in service but they were occasionally utilised in other roles, such as the unsuccessful bombing of Allied bomber formations. By 1944 they had practically disappeared from operational use.

January 1, 1944 - March 2, 1944

1 Shirtblue Squadron. Code name for the 336th.

2 Purple 1. The flight commander's slot in the section of eight aircraft commanded by Gentile.

3 Cockpit windows/P-51B. One of the greatest problems with the early Mustang was the limited visibility aft of the cockpit. Te razorback cockpit canopy arrangement was standard with all single-engine fighters. The problem was solved after a method for forming a plexiglas canopy was devised. The improved model with the plexiglas bubble canopy, which elimiated the razorback area aft of the cockpit, was designated the P-51D.

March 3, 1944 - March 29, 1944

1 Blower. The base public address system.

2 Horseback. Coded call letters for Lieutenant Colonel Blakeslee.

3 Do 217. The Dornier 217 was a German heavy bomber. It had a crew of four: pilot, observer, radio operator/gunner, engineer/gunner. Its maximum speed was 348 miles per hour and it could carry 5,550 pounds of bombs. It was armed with four 7.9mm MG 81 machine guns, two each in the nose and lateral positions, two 13mm MG 131s in the ventral position, and an electrically operated dorsal turret.

4 Me 110. Long range, heavy, all weather, and night fighter with a crew of three: pilot, observer, gunner or radar operator/ gunner. Its twin engines could produce 352 miles per hour at 20,000 feet. Armament: two 30mm MK 108 cannon and two 20mm MG 151 cannon firing forward; one 7.19mm MG S1Z twin machine gun on a flexible mount at the rear of cockpit.

5 Me 410. A heavy fighter, reconnaissance plane, and light bomber with a crew of two, pilot and observer. It had two 1,850 horsepower engines which gave a maximum speed of 315 miles per hour. It carried four 20mm MG 151 cannons, two 7.9mm MG 17 machine guns which fired to the rear, and two 13mm MG 131s which fired aft in remote controlled barbettes.

6 Greenbelt. Code name for the 335th Squadron of the Fourth.

7 Split-S. A break-away manoeuvre known as a half-roll by the British, a Split-S by the Americans, and die Abschwung by the Germans. It is a hard break down and inverted roll.

8 190s. This was an improved series of the FW 190D-9. It had a longer length to house the larger Jumo 213A-1 12-cylinder, liquid cooled engine. Its armament included two 13mm MG 131 cannons which fired through the spinner, and two 20mm MG 151 cannons in the wing roots. It had an increased service ceiling and flexibility in the medium to high-altitude range of operation and was superior as a high altitude fighter.

9 Ground pounded. Slang for a non-flying member of an air force.

10 Wolfpack. The nickname wen to Zemke's aggressive 56th fighter Group.

April 1, 1944 - April 13, 1944

1 Jackpot Operation. The strafing of an airfield in a predetermined area.

2 Beat up. A thorough buzz or strafing job.

3 Windscreen. British term for windshield.

May 4, 1944 - February 2, 1951

1 Escape valve. In World War I they called it shell-shock, in World War II, combat fatigue, and in the Vietnam War, PTSD or post-traumatic-stress disorder. To those veterans afflicted, the fires of battle and the deaths of comrades are realities they relive over and over in flashbacks and nightmares; the characteristic symptoms involve re-experiencing the traumatic event. Members of the Air Force seemed to recover more readily, while ground troops suffered from the effects for a good long time. The longer they last the more vivid. are the nightmares. It was felt that air combat was not as close and personal as it was for the ground troops, who could see the effects of their actions.

2 T-33 Jet Trainer. Lockheed stretched the P-80C Shooting Star jet 39 inches to make it a two-seated trainer, with the back seat higher for better visibility for the instructor.

Bibliography

Arnold, H.H., *Global Mission*, Harper & Brothers, New York, 1949

Arps, Lt Col. Leslie H. and Quigley, Frank V., '*The Origin, development and Organization of the Luftwaffe.*' October 1945

Baldwin, Hanson W., *Battles Lost and Won*, Harper & Row, New York, 1966

Baumbach. Werner, *The Life and Death of the Luftwaffe*, Coward-McMann, New York, 1960

Bekker, Cajus, *The Luftwaffe War Diaries*, Doubleday & Co., New York, 1968

Bewley, Charles, *Hermann Goering and the Third Reich*, Devin-Adair Co., New York, 1962

Brereton, Lewis H., *The Brereton Diaries*, William Morrow & Co., New York, 1946

British Air Ministry, '*Notes on the German Air Force.*' U.S. Army reprint, April 1943

Carlisle, Norman, *The Air Force Reader*, Bobbs-Merrill Co., Indianapolis, 1944

Churchill, Winston, *The Second World War* (six volumes), Houghton Mifflin Co., Cambridge, Mass., 1948-53

Davis, Kenneth S., *Experience of War*, Doubleday & Co., New York, 1965

Emme, Eugene M., *The Impact of Air Power*, Van Nostrand & Co., Princeton, NJ, 1959

Galland, Adolf, *The First and the Last*, Henry Holt & Co., New York, 1954 (also reprinted by Cerberus Publishing, Bristol, U.K., 2001)

Goerlitz, Walter, *History of the German General Staff*, Fred. A. Praeger, New York, 1953

Goldberg, Alfred, (ed.) *A History of the United States Air Force*, Van Nostrand Co., Princeton, NJ, 1957

Green, William, *Famous Bombers of the Second World War* (two volumes), Doubleday & Co., New York, 1959

Greenfield, Kent Roberts, (ed.) *Command Decisions*, Office of the Chief of Military History, Department of the Army, Washington, D.C., 1960

Gurney, Major Gene, *The War in the Air*, Crown Publishers, Inc., New York, 1962

Hall, Grover C., *1000 Destroyed*, Morgan Aviation Books, Dallas, Tx, 1961

Harris, Air Chief Marshal Sir Arthur, *Bomber Offensive*, Collins, London, 1947

Hinton, Harold B., *Air Victory*, Harper & Brother, New York, 1948

Johnson, Robert S. and Caidin, Martin, *Thunderbolt*, Rinehart & co., New York, 1958

Killen, John, *The Luftwaffe: A History*, Duckworth, London, 1946

Lee, Asher, *The German Air Force*, Duckworth, London, 1946

LeMay, General Curtis E., with Kantor, MacKinley, *Mission with LeMay*, Doubleday & Co., New York, 1965

Loesbrock, J.D., and Skinner, R.M., (eds) The Wild Blue, G.P. Putnam's, New York, 1961

Maurer, Maurer, *Air Force Combat Units of World War II*, Franklin Watts, Inc., New York, 1963

Nowarra, Heinz J., *The Messerschmitt 109 – A Famous German Fighter*, Harleyford Publications, Letchworth, Herts., U.K., 1962

Richards, Denis, and Sauders, Hiliary St George, *Royal Air Force* (three volumes), H.M.S.O., London, 1953

Shores, Christopher, and Williams, Clive, *Aces High*, Neville Spearman, London, 1966 (also reprinted by Grub Street, London, 1994)

Staubel, James H., *Air Force Diary*, Simon & Schuster, New York, 1947